Antoine Le Pautre

A French Architect of the Era of Louis XIV

The publication of this monograph has been aided by a grant from the Samuel H. Kress Foundation

Monographs on Archaeology and the Fine Arts sponsored by

THE ARCHAEOLOGICAL INSTITUTE OF AMERICA *and*

THE COLLEGE ART ASSOCIATION OF AMERICA

XVIII

Editor: ANNE COFFIN HANSON

Robert W. Berger

Brandeis University

Antoine Le Pautre

A French Architect of the Era of Louis XIV

Published by NEW YORK UNIVERSITY PRESS

for THE COLLEGE ART ASSOCIATION OF AMERICA

New York | *1969*

Copy editor: Harriet Schoenholz
Designer: Adrianne Onderdonk Dudden
Typesetter: Quinn & Boden Company, Inc.
Printer: The Meriden Gravure Company
Binder: J. F. Tapley, Inc.

PHOTOGRAPH CREDITS

Archives Nationales: 92
Archives Photographiques: 43, 91
Bibliothèque Nationale: 14, 15, 42, 58, 59, 65, 66, 76, 77, 82, 89, 94
Musées Nationaux: 68, 79
Nationalmuseum, Stockholm: 41, 51, 95, 97, 98, 99, 100
Vasari: 67
J. C. Vaysse: 6, 7, 8, 9, 10, 44, 45, 52, 53, 54, 55, 56, 57, 60, 61, 62, 63, 64, 69, 70, 71, 72, 73, 101, 103

To the memory of my father

Contents

All the monuments are in Paris unless otherwise indicated.

Acknowledgments

This study was initially written as a doctoral dissertation under the guidance of Professors James Ackerman and John Coolidge of Harvard University. I wish to express my deep gratitude for their advice and encouragement during all stages of the work.

It is not possible to thank all of the individuals who have aided me in my research, but several must be mentioned here. I had valuable discussions with the following scholars: Sir Anthony Blunt of the Courtauld Institute of Art, Professor Louis Hautecoeur of the Institut de France, Dr. Wolfgang Herrmann, Dr. Bates Lowry of the Museum of Modern Art, and Professor Henry Millon of the Massachusetts Institute of Technology. A good deal of the research was made less thorny through the assistance of Dr. Per Bjurström of the Nationalmuseum, Stockholm, M. Félix Brunau, Conservateur du Domaine de Saint-Cloud, and M. Jacques Dupont, Inspecteur Général des Monuments Historiques. I owe a special debt to M. E. Raoul-Duval of Le Vaudreuil, who graciously granted me access to his private archive. In addition, I wish to thank the Fulbright Scholarship Committee and, in particular, to record my gratitude to Professor Marcel Brion of the Académie Française, who served as adviser to Fulbright grantees while I was in Paris during 1963–64.

The manuscript benefited from the expert editorial advice of Dr. Lowry and Dr. Anne Coffin Hanson of the Museum of Modern Art. Miss Harriet Schoenholz served as a most attentive copy editor.

R. W. B.

Abbreviations

AB	*The Art Bulletin*
AN	Archives Nationales, Paris
Blunt, 1957	Anthony Blunt, *Art and Architecture in France, 1500 to 1700*, 2nd rearranged impression, Harmondsworth, 1957
BMon	*Bulletin monumental*
BSHAF	*Bulletin de la société de l'histoire de l'art français*
BurlM	*Burlington Magazine*
Estampes	Cabinet des Estampes, Bibliothèque Nationale, Paris
GBA	*Gazette des beaux-arts*
Guiffrey	Jules Guiffrey (ed.), *Comptes des bâtiments du roi sous le règne de Louis XIV*, Paris, 1881–1901, 5 vols.
Hautecoeur	Louis Hautecoeur, *Histoire de l'architecture classique en France*, Paris, 1943–57, 7 vols.
JSAH	*Journal of the Society of Architectural Historians*
JWarb	*Journal of the Warburg and Courtauld Institutes*
Laborde	Fichier Laborde, Département des Manuscrits, Bibliothèque Nationale, Paris
Lemonnier	Henry Lemonnier (ed.), *Procès-verbaux de l'Académie royale d'architecture, 1671–1793*, Paris, 1911ff., 10 vols.
Minutier	Minutier Central, Archives Nationales, Paris

List of Illustrations

Antoine Le Pautre

A French Architect of the Era of Louis XIV

Introduction

... un de nos Architectes, encore trop peu connu parmi nous, & qui mérite
néanmoins de l'être de la postérité.

J. F. Blondel, *Cours d'architecture* (1772)

Antoine Le Pautre [1] was baptized at the church of Saint-Nicolas des Champs in Paris
on January 15, 1621. [2] He was the third son of Adrien Le Pautre, a master joiner, and
Jeanne Fessart, his wife. [3] Adrien's brother Jean was also a master joiner, [4] and of
Adrien's other sons, Jean (1618–82) [5] became a famous and influential designer and
print-maker. [6] This Jean Le Pautre was in turn the father of two Pierre Le Pautres,
one (ca. 1648–1716) a brilliant draftsman and engraver, whom Fiske Kimball has
recognized as the true initiator of the Rococo style of decoration, [7] the second (1660–
1744) a sculptor of renown. [8] Antoine also begot artists: his son Jean (1648–1735) was
a sculptor; Claude (b. 1649) was the first architect-pensioner of the French Academy
in Rome (1667–69). [9] Hence, Antoine was a member of a most distinguished dynasty
of French artists.

Jean Le Pautre, the celebrated print-maker and elder brother of Antoine, was

---

1. The architect himself spelled his name
"Anthoine le Paultre" in his *Desseins de plusieurs
palais,* but I have adopted the form usually encountered in the literature, and have used "Le Pautre" as
the form of the family name of his relatives. Variants
include Lepautre, Le Potre, Le Postre, etc.

2. A. Jal, *Dictionnaire critique de biographie
et d'histoire,* 2d ed. (Paris, 1872), p. 773.

3. The only specific activity of which we have
knowledge concerning Adrien is furnished by a contract of August 7, 1646, in which he was called upon
to make wood carvings for the sacristy of the Church
of the Sorbonne, based on those in Saint-Paul-Saint-
Louis, both in Paris (R. A. Weigert, *L'église de la
Sorbonne* [Paris, 1947], p. 6).

4. He carved choir stalls for Saint-Germain

des Prés, Paris, in 1655 (Minutier, CX 97 [February
17, 1655]).

5. Jean's year of birth is sometimes erroneously given as 1617. The error was first made in the
"Avertissement" of 1751 (see n. 10).

6. Adrien had another son Jean (b. 1622), a
mason, who died prematurely on June 14, 1648
(Laborde, nouv. acq. franç. 12141, no. 42.356).

7. F. Kimball, *The Creation of the Rococo*
(Philadelphia, 1943), pp. 63ff.

8. It is frequently stated that Pierre Le Pautre
sculpteur was a son of Antoine; this is incorrect (see
Jal, *op. cit.,* p. 774).

9. F. Boyer, "Claude Lepautre, architecte,
pensionnaire du Roi à Rome, de 1667 à 1669," *BSHAF*
(1953), pp. 139–140.

first cited as Antoine's teacher in an eighteenth century text.[10] There can be little doubt that Antoine was heavily dependent upon his brother for the formation of his second (Baroque) stylistic phase, which was inaugurated in 1652/53 by the publication of the *Desseins de plusieurs palais* (see Chapter 3). But evidence is at hand which indicates that Antoine's first master may have been Étienne Martellange (1568/69–1641), the architect of the French Jesuits. Two etchings are preserved in Paris which depict front and side elevations and sections of Martellange's Jesuit Noviciate, Paris (1630–42; destroyed).[11] One bears the inscription "A. Lepaultre & sculp"[12] and both are signed with the following inscription in the hand of Martellange: "Orthographia interior et exterior Ecclesiae Novitiatus Soc[ietatis] Jesu Parisiis in Suburbio S. Germani, anno 1640." This material constitutes the earliest evidence of Le Pautre's artistic activity. It would appear that in 1640, when only nineteen years old, he was entrusted by Martellange with architectural drafting, and the question naturally arises as to whether Antoine's master may indeed have been the Jesuit architect. But we have no additional clues concerning this Martellange-Le Pautre relationship. Martellange died the very next year (1641); if Le Pautre worked in his studio, he would then have had to seek another master.

In the same year that Martellange approvingly ratified Antoine's etchings, a certain Adam Philippon was sent to Rome by Louis XIII, and probably took along with him at this time his apprentice and relation, the young Jean Le Pautre, the future print-maker.[13] Philippon (b. 1606), a *menuisier,* was but one of a number of Frenchmen who were dispatched to Italy in 1640 to seek out talented Italian artists to lure back to France, as well as to send back works of art. It was exactly at the same moment that Paul Fréart de Chantelou went to Rome to bring Poussin to Paris. This "talent hunt" was the idea of Sublet de Noyers, who had become Surintendant des Bâtiments du Roi in 1638.[14]

After having spent time in Rome and other places in Italy, Philippon was back in Paris by 1642, and in 1645 published a book of engravings entitled *Curieuses recherches de plusieurs beaus morceaus d'ornemens antiques, et modernes.* Tradition

10. *Oeuvres d'architecture de Jean Le Pautre, architecte, dessinateur & graveur du Roi,* I (Paris, 1751), "Avertissement": "Le célèbre Antoine Le Pautre . . . lui [to Jean] étoit redevable de son habileté dans l'architecture. Ce fut Le Pautre, le graveur, qui lui donna les premières leçons de son art, et lui communiqua ce goût mâle et nerveux que l'on admire dans ses édifices. Antoine Le Pautre apprit aussi de son frère l'art de graver à l'eau-forte. . . ." Cf. also J. F. Blondel (*Cours d'architecture,* III [Paris, 1772], p. 445 n. f): ". . . il [Antoine] s'étoit nourri dans son Art par les lumieres fort étendues de Pierre & de Jean le Pautre, ses deux freres, l'un Sculpteur [in reality, a son of Jean] & l'autre Graveur. . . ."

11. P. Moisy, *Les églises des jésuites de l'ancienne assistance de France,* II (Rome, 1958), p. xxiii, pls. LXXIV, LXXI; J. Vallery-Radot, *Le recueil des plans d'édifices de la compagnie de Jésus conservé à la Bibliothèque Nationale de Paris* (Rome, 1960), p. 167 (nos. 570, 571).

12. It is unlikely that "A. Lepaultre" refers to Antoine's father Adrien, since he was a joiner and is not known to have been involved in architectural drafting. Antoine's eldest brother Adrien (b. 1614) is not known to have been in the arts.

13. Philippon was married to Marie Le Pautre, who was the daughter of a Jean Le Pautre and Marguerite Mouchard (Laborde, nouv. acq. franç. 12168, fol. 53696). I have not been able to puzzle out who this Jean Le Pautre was, except that he died before 1649 and was father to another Jean, a master mason, and another daughter, Madeleine, who married Louis Chamblin, a master carpenter (M. Dumolin, *Études de topographie parisienne,* I [Paris, 1929], p. 379 n. 2).

14. See E. Magne, *Nicolas Poussin, premier peintre du roi* (Paris, 1928), pp. 132ff.; F. Haskell, *Patrons and Painters* (New York, 1963), p. 176.

attributes the engraving of the plates to Jean Le Pautre, and Kimball has rightly drawn attention to this publication as testimony of French interest in the contemporary Italian Baroque.[15]

The content of Jean Le Pautre's prints strongly suggests that he was in Italy with Philippon.[16] Jean published his first plates in 1643,[17] and from that date on until his death in 1682, this incredibly fertile artist produced a corpus of well over 2,000 prints of every variety imaginable.[18] Philippon's interest in contemporary Italian art was communicated to Jean, whose prints are permeated with the language of the Italian Baroque.

Returning to Antoine, we hear of him next in 1643 when, as godfather to the daughter of Richard Douval, joiner, he is referred to as "masson et architecte."[19] But the very next year he is termed "architecte des bastiments du roy" at the baptism of a son of Pierre Gouge, carpenter.[20] Antoine was to retain this title throughout the remainder of his career. Again there is a lapse of several years, but in 1646 he undertook the first two buildings of which we have knowledge, the Chapelle de Port-Royal and the Hôtel de Fontenay-Mareuil, both in Paris (see Chapters 1 and 2). From this time on we can closely follow his architectural career until his very last years.

Other important milestones in Antoine Le Pautre's career may conveniently be cited here. On January 27, 1648 he married Renée de Poix in Saint-Laurent, Paris,[21] and in 1652 or 1653 he published the *Desseins de plusieurs palais*.[22] In 1660, he was appointed architect to Philippe d'Orléans, the brother of Louis XIV, a post which he retained until his death.[23] In addition, Antoine was one of the founding members of the Royal Academy of Architecture, which first met on December 31, 1671. (His colleagues were François Blondel, director, and Libéral Bruant, Daniel Gittard, François Le Vau, Pierre Mignard, and François d'Orbay, architects.) He last attended the meetings on November 21, 1678,[24] and was paid for having served as a member during 1678 on January 15, 1679.[25] However, he had died shortly before this, on January 3, 1679, as is indicated in a recently-discovered inventory drawn up after his death.

15. Kimball, *op. cit.*, p. 12.

16. H. Destailleur, *Notices sur quelques artistes français* (Paris, 1863), pp. 69–70, 80–81.

17. His first plates depicted the baptism of Louis XIV on April 21, 1643 at Saint-Germain-en-Laye (*ibid.*, p. 80).

18. D. Guilmard (*Les maîtres ornemanistes*, I [Paris, 1880], p. 75) has counted 2,248 plates but there are assuredly more. Catalogues are furnished in *ibid.*, pp. 70ff. and in Destailleur, *op. cit.*, pp. 65ff.

19. Laborde, nouv. acq. franç. 12141, no. 42.481 (January 4, 1643).

20. Laborde, nouv. acq. franç. 12141, no. 42.482.

21. Jal, *op. cit.*, p. 773.

22. E. L. G. Charvet (*Lyon artistique: architectes* [Lyons, 1899], p. 220) credits Antoine as being the author of *L'art universel des fortifications* (Paris, 1667), but this in reality is a collection of five plates by Jean (Destailleur, *op. cit.*, p. 115).

23. Jal, *op. cit.*, p. 774. I have found no evidence for E. de Ganay's assertion that Antoine was architect to Philippe before 1660 (*André Le Nostre, 1613–1700* [Paris, 1962], p. 72).

24. Lemonnier, I, p. 251 n. 4. R. Blomfield (*A History of French Architecture from the Death of Mazarin till the Death of Louis XV, 1661–1774*, I [London, 1921], p. 115) suggests that Antoine ceased attending the meetings because he may have been dissatisfied with the decision rendered by the Academy concerning a legal wrangle which broke out between himself and Jean in 1678 (see the meetings held on June 6, 27, and July 4, 11, and 18, 1678 in Lemonnier, I, pp. 165, 167–168, 175–176). However, the Academy decided in favor of Antoine (*ibid.*, pp. 175–176).

25. Guiffrey, I, cols. 1085–1086. For payments to Le Pautre for his membership in the Academy see *ibid.*, cols, 648, 657, 713–714, 721, 781–782, 789, 857–858, 930, 990, 999, 1096.

He is cited in the document as "conseiller du Roy, architecte de son Académie Royale, et controleur des Batiments de son Altesse royale Monseigneur le duc d'Orleans."[26]

Like François Mansart, Louis Le Vau, and many other important seventeenth century French architects, Antoine is not known to have traveled to Italy, but apparently relied upon prints and drawings for his knowledge of southern architecture. Indeed, we can trace his presence in Paris during 1648, 1649, and 1650, the years between the completion of his first works and the emergence of his new Baroque style in 1652.[27]

Little is known of his personality, but Dezallier d'Argenville does report the following incident:

> On dit qu'il étoit grand mangeur. Le marquis de Louvois le trouva un jour seul, qui mangeoit un dindoneau dans la primeur. Il lui demanda s'il comptoit le manger en entier. *Quoi!* repartit le Pautre, *c'est de la viande creuse.*[28]

This personal weakness would seem to be confirmed by the engraved portrait of Antoine by Robert Nanteuil which graces the title page of the *Desseins de plusieurs palais.*[29]

---

26. Minutier, XVI (January 12, 1679); for this reference I am grateful to M. J. M. Thiveaud, a student at the École Nationale des Chartes, who is preparing a thesis on Le Pautre for presentation in December 1969. Le Pautre's date of death has traditionally but erroneously been cited as 1691 (first given by A. N. Dezallier d'Argenville, *Vies des fameux architectes depuis la renaissance des arts* . . . [Paris, 1787], p. 400), 1682 or 1681.

27. Documents which indicate Le Pautre's presence in Paris during 1648, 1649, and 1650 are in Paris: Laborde, nouv. acq. franç. 12141, nos. 42.352 (marriage to Renée de Poix on January 27, 1648), 42.353 (baptism of daughter Jeanne on October 17, 1648), 42.354 (baptism of son Claude on July 5, 1649), 42.483 (godfather on August 28, 1650). In addition, Le Pautre worked in the Hôtel de Guéménée in Paris during 1650 (see Appendix I).

28. Dezallier d'Argenville, *op. cit.*, p. 396.

29. C. Petitjean and C. Wickert, *Catalogue de l'oeuvre gravé de Robert Nanteuil*, I (Paris, 1925), pp. 226–228.

1

Chapelle de Port-Royal

Le Pautre's career as a practicing architect opened in 1646 when he began his first two buildings, the Chapelle de Port-Royal and the Hôtel de Fontenay-Mareuil, both in Paris. The Chapelle, in particular, was a challenging assignment for a young man of twenty-five because it was the first church ever erected for the French Jansenists. Le Pautre had had no previous architectural experience that we are aware of, except for drafting under Étienne Martellange and lessons in design and graphics from his elder brother Jean.[1] Why then did the Jansenists turn to this untried, fledgling architect? The answer may in part lie in the fact that one of the Le Pautre clan (Antoine's father Adrien or his uncle Jean) had worked in 1639 for Louis de Rohan in his Parisian *hôtel*.[2] Louis' wife, Anne, was closely associated with the Jansenists, and so the Le Pautre family was already known to this religious community when it

1. On Antoine's apprenticeship under Étienne Martellange and Jean Le Pautre, see Introduction, pp. 3ff.

Antoine published the designs of the Chapelle de Port-Royal in his *Desseins de plusieurs palais* (Figs. 1–4). Fig. 1 bears the inscription: "Plan de l'Esglise du Monastere du Port Royal Situé a Paris au Fauxbourg St. Iaques Conduit et Inventé par lAutheur." A print by Jean Marot (Fig. 5) cites Le Pautre as the architect, and numerous seventeenth and eighteenth century topographical and architectural writers, from Sauval to Dezallier d'Argenville, attribute the building to Antoine.

There exists a variant of Fig. 4 (see A. Gazier, *Port-Royal au XVIIe siècle* [Paris, 1909], pl. 25, bottom). Le Pautre also published his plates separately and dedicated them to Anne Geneviève de Bourbon-Condé, duchesse de Longueville (1617–79), a friend of the Jansenists (Paris, Archives de la Seine, Collection Lazare, vol. 97, fols. 1817–1821).

The chapel is located at 119, boulevard de Port-Royal and is part of the Hôpital de la Maternité.

2. The Hôtel de Guéménée, where Antoine later worked in 1650 (see Appendix I; L. Lambeau in *Procès-verbaux de la commission municipale du vieux Paris* [1902], p. 206).

decided to erect its church in Paris. The first stone was laid on April 1, 1646 and the chapel was apparently complete in all details by June 12, 1648.[3]

The Chapelle de Port-Royal enables us to define Le Pautre's stylistic position at the outset of his career, but the building takes on added significance as a monument which reflects the Jansenist attitude towards art.

Cornelis Jansen's posthumous *Augustinus*, the fundamental and initial treatise of Jansenism, appeared in 1640. In 1643, Antoine Arnauld (1612–94), the brother of Marie-Angélique Arnauld (1591–1661), the abbess of Port-Royal, published his *De la fréquente communion*, a strong attack on Jesuit probabilism, i.e., the ready giving of absolution without inquiry into the penitent's character or the sincerity of his repentance. Jansen's work, in Latin, reached a limited group of theologians; Arnauld's book, written in the vernacular, was read by a much wider audience and created a great storm. It is fair to say that after its publication the battle lines between Jesuit and Jansenist were drawn. Thus, Le Pautre's church was built at a critical moment of the struggle. In 1649, one year after its completion, Jansenist propositions were denounced to the Sorbonne, and in 1653 the Holy See condemned five of these.[4]

It is therefore astonishing to read a letter written by the abbess Arnauld in 1646 in which she proudly reveals that her new church "a été faite sur le modele des petits Jesuites."[5] She was here alluding to Martellange's Jesuit Noviciate (1630–42; destroyed). As will be subsequently analyzed, the abbess was absolutely correct: Le Pautre based his church to a large extent on this prototype. But why did the Jansenists choose to pattern their new house of God after that of their archenemies? The reason would seem to be that in architectural matters, considerations of an aesthetic nature far transcended those of denominational identification. Paradoxical as it may appear, the ascetic and sense-denying Jansenists seem to have been keenly aware of the latest issues involving artistic taste and aesthetic creed. But to understand this matter, we must examine certain artistic and intellectual events in France during the 1630's and 1640's.

Martellange's Jesuit Noviciate was one of the prime early works of a developing

---

3. For these dates see M. A. Arnauld, *Lettres de la révérende mère Marie-Angélique Arnauld, abbesse et réformatrice de Port-Royal*, I (Utrecht, 1742), p. 309 (Letter CLXXXVIII), p. 373 (Letter CCXXII), p. 375 (Letter CCXXIII). The church was dedicated on June 7, 1648 (J. A. Piganiol de la Force, *Description de Paris, de Versailles, de Marly, de Meudon, de S. Cloud, de Fontainebleau . . .*, new ed., VI [Paris, 1742], p. 316; A. M. Le Fèvre, *Description des curiosités des églises de Paris et des environs* [Paris, 1759], p. 332).

4. On Jansenism, see the bibliography in *New Catholic Encyclopedia*, VII (New York, 1967), p. 824.

5. Arnauld, *op. cit.*, I, p. 309 (Letter CLXXXVIII). The letter, dated September 21, 1646, was addressed to Marie de Gonzague, Queen of Poland, a friend of Port-Royal. The complete text is given here: "Puisqu'il vous plaît, Madame, par un excès de bonté, de savoir des nouvelles de votre petite Maison, je dirai à Votre Majesté que notre Eglise fut commencée le premier jour d'Avril, & que Monseigneur de Paris benit la premiere pierre. Elle est aujourd'hui presque achevée & si jolie que j'en ai de la confusion. Elle a été faite sur le modele des petits Jesuites; mais elle n'a que cinquante & un pieds de long, une croisée & trois petites Chapelles. Elle est si bien bâtie & tellement dans l'ordre de l'architecture, que tous ceux qui le voyent disent que c'est un petit chef-d'oeuvre. Nous avons fait aussi le côté du Cloître qui est bien clos, & dans lequel nous nous mettrons & y serons fort bien, jusqu'à ce que nous fassions notre Choeur, y ayant un grande grille dans la croisée. Notre eglise est dediée au très saint Sacrement, & Dieu nous a fait la grace d'obtenir une Bulle de Sa Sainteté [Innocent X] par laquelle la devotion du S. Sacrement sera transferée ceans, dont je m'assure que Votre Majesté sera bien aise." See also *ibid.*, I, p. 363 (Letter CCXVI) and p. 367 (Letter CCXVIII).

classicistic movement in seventeenth century France, a movement which eventually was to dominate and characterize the era of Louis XIV. Important figures in this current were François Sublet de Noyers, who became Surintendant des Bâtiments du Roi in 1638, and his cousins, the brothers Paul Fréart de Chantelou, Roland de Chantelou (Fréart de Chambray), and Jean de Chantelou. The painter and architect Charles Errard was also a member of this powerful coterie.

Sublet de Noyers believed that he had found in the person of Martellange precisely the right man to design a church that would exemplify the tastes and aesthetic convictions of this circle of connoisseurs. About 1629, Martellange had composed a document strongly critical of François Derand's plans for the church of Saint-Paul-Saint-Louis in Paris. Martellange had been appointed architect of this church in 1625, but had been replaced by Derand in 1629. In his attack, Martellange scored such features as engaged columns and columns engaged to pilasters, the latter "une monstruosité inconnue des anciens." [6] Martellange's pronouncements, which were critical of the sculpturally modeled wall, and his rationalizing spirit, which sought to harness architectural design by means of rules, must have appealed to Sublet de Noyers.[7] As a model for the Noviciate, Martellange chose Giacomo della Porta's S. M. dei Monti in Rome (1580), a church with a flat, pilaster façade and a ground plan derived from Vignola's Il Gesù, Rome.[8] The French architect slightly modified the ground plan, and created a façade marked by a lack of sculpture (except for a cartouche in the field of the pediment), the correct use of the orders (Ionic over Doric pilasters), and, in keeping with French taste, a greater vertical emphasis than was to be found in the Italian model. He adhered to spare and cold architectural decoration, avoiding the rich Baroque sculptural effects that Derand reveled in at Saint-Paul-Saint-Louis. The church was adorned with paintings by Poussin, Stella, and Vouet, the first two artists providing works of a cold, classical quality.[9] In 1643, the Jesuit College of Clermont published poems in Latin and French praising the Noviciate,[10] and the church was greatly admired by contemporaries. Paul Fréart de Chantelou's pride in the work, with which he had been closely associated, is expressed in a passage in his *Journal du voyage du Cavalier Bernin en France* in which Saint-Paul-Saint-Louis is held up as an object of scorn, a church filled with "vilains ornements,"

6. Martellange here anticipated by almost sixty years the Royal Academy of Architecture which, on August 8 and 14, 1687, criticized engaged columns and columns engaged to pilasters (Lemonnier, II, pp. 148–149). See also P. Moisy, "Martellange, Derand et le conflit du baroque," *BMon*, CX (1952), pp. 237–261; *idem, Les églises des jésuites de l'ancienne assistance de France*, I (Rome, 1958), pp. 438–450; H. Chardon, *Amateurs d'art et collectionneurs manceaux: les frères Fréart de Chantelou* (Le Mans, 1867).

7. In addition to his memorandum contra Derand, Martellange translated Jean Pélerin's (Viator's) *De artificiali perspectiva*, published in 1635 as a work by Mathurin Jousse. Martellange attempted to make Pélerin's text clearer. See Moisy, *Les églises des jésuites* . . . , I, p. 73–77.

8. On Martellange's dependence on della Porta's church, see E. J. Ciprut, "Les modèles de Martellange pour son Église du Noviciat de Paris," *XVIIᵉ siècle* (1954), pp. 583–593. See also *ibid.*, pp. 594–597 which contain an interchange of letters between Ciprut and Moisy. Ciprut points out in his article that Martellange probably also drew upon Onorio Longhi's façade of S. M. Liberatrice (1617), itself dependent on S. M. dei Monti.

9. Poussin: *The Miracle of St. Francis Xavier* (ca. 1641; Louvre); Stella: *Jesus among the Doctors* (Les Andelys, Notre Dame); Vouet: *The Madonna of the Jesuits* (1642; destroyed).

10. Moisy, *Les églises des jésuites* . . . , I, p. 445.

designed to please the multitude, and which is contrasted with the Noviciate, a building which pleases true connoisseurs.[11] Earlier, Fréart de Chambray in his *Parallèle de l'architecture antique et de la moderne* (1650) wrote that "cette Eglise est estimée la plus reguliere de Paris, & quoqu'elle ne soit pas chargée de tant d'ornements que quelques autres, elle paroist neantmoins fort belle aux yeux des intelligens, tout y estant fait avec une entente extraordinaire."[12] Indeed, Martellange's church came to be looked upon as a model of "bon goût" throughout the seventeenth and eighteenth centuries.[13]

Fréart de Chambray's *Parallèle* of 1650 contains the clearest and most important statement of this coterie's views in the field of architecture. He voiced unbounding praise for the Ancients, particularly the Greeks, whose orders "contiennent non seulement tout le beau, mais encore tout le necessaire de l'Architecture."[14] Of modern architects, Palladio and Scamozzi were to be followed, particularly the former. He attacked undisciplined fantasy and condemned modern inventions such as "des mascarons, de vilains cartouches, & de semblables grotesques ridicules et imperti nentes, dont l'Architecture moderne est toute infectée."[15]

Given this artistic and intellectual atmosphere, we can perhaps assume that Marie-Angélique, in noting that her new Jansenist church was based on the Jesuit Noviciate, was not thinking in terms of denominational identification but rather in terms of aesthetics: she and her order would be able to worship in a church equally in harmony with the newly formulated artistic beliefs of developing French classicism.

There was, however, another factor determining the choice of a model. In 1640 Le Pautre made measured elevations and sections of the Noviciate for Martellange — the earliest evidence of Le Pautre's artistic activity (see Introduction, p. 4).[16] This formative experience provided the young architect with a ready vocabulary which he could utilize and enlarge upon. Martellange's style as represented by the Noviciate was Le Pautre's architectural starting point.

Although the chapel was finished and blessed in 1648, Le Pautre in 1652/53 published designs which do not depict the building as it existed in reality, but which apparently show the architect's more ambitious but unrealized project.[17] In the text to the second (Jombert) edition of Le Pautre's designs, these differences are noted

11. P. Fréart de Chantelou, *Journal du voyage du Cavalier Bernin en France*, L. Lalanne, ed. (Paris, 1885), p. 253 (October 19, 1665).

12. R. Fréart de Chambray, *Parallèle de l'architecture antique et de la moderne* (Paris, 1650), "Epistre." On Martellange's church, see Moisy, *Les églises des jésuites . . .*, I, pp. 251–253, 348–349, 389–390, 535–536.

13. Marie-Angélique Arnauld wrote to the Queen of Poland in 1648: ". . . notre nouvelle Eglise laquelle, à ce que disent tous ceux qui la voyent, est la plus jolie & la plus devote de Paris, quoiqu'elle soit des plus simples" (Arnauld, *op. cit.*, I, p. 373 [Letter CCXXII]).

14. Fréart de Chambray, *op. cit.*, p. 2. He intended the Noviciate to be his place of burial.

15. *Ibid.*, p. 3. Apparently the cartouche in the field of the pediment was not considered objectionable. Concerning Palladio, Fréart de Chambray published a French edition of *I quattro libri dell'architettura* in 1650.

16. Moisy (*Les églises des jésuites . . .*, I, p. 445) believes that Le Pautre's etchings were propaganda instruments for the publicity campaign waged in favor of the Noviciate. This seems unlikely since the prints lack titles.

17. Le Pautre may have proceeded similarly in the case of the Hôtel de Fontenay-Mareuil (see Chapter 2).

and the writer surmises that Le Pautre's plans were simplified in execution in order to reduce expenses.[18] This may have been the case, but economy was surely not the sole motivating factor. The Jansenist attitude towards art was certainly a shaping force here.

It is certainly no coincidence that the Cistercians of Port-Royal, the followers of the ascetic Saint Bernard, became the representatives of the Jansenist position, which involved an attitude to sensory experience very similar to that of traditional Cistercianism. With reference to the arts, the Jansenists were strongly opposed to sensuous forms, and suspicious of, if not openly hostile to, all art in general. Pascal's "Quelle vanité que la peinture" [19] is an accurate reflection of the beliefs held at Port-Royal.[20] In their yearnings for direct mystical communion with the Divine, the Port-Royalists ideally sought to achieve this communication without any recourse to the senses. The contrast between this attitude and that of the Jesuits, the practitioners of Saint Ignatius Loyola's *Spiritual Exercises*, needs no elaboration.[21] In theory, Port-Royal rejected the fine arts, music, and, in general, the things of this world. "Cette règle est générale pour toutes les choses que plus on ôte aux sens, plus on donne à l'esprit" wrote Agnès Arnauld, the sister of Marie-Angélique, in 1648, thus summing up the Jansenist position.[22] Indeed, this same nun, who succeeded her sister as abbess in 1661, even rejoiced that she had lost her sense of smell when she was fifty-two and hence was unable to "prendre de la satisfaction dans les bonnes odeurs." [23] At times, the Jansenists consciously strove after ugliness, seen as a symbol of virtuous poverty.[24]

Nevertheless, the Jansenists never became iconoclasts, for by so doing they would have exposed themselves to the accusation of Calvinism. For this and practical reasons, their position was one of compromise. Art was permitted if it directly served religion, and painting and sculpture were recognized as gifts of God, given by Him to Bezalel and Oholiab (*Exodus* 31). Indeed, the Jansenists at times acknowledged the power of art as an aid to piety.[25] Art, when it was utilized, was to be an ascetic and spare art, forsaking virtuosity and sensuous appeal—the art of Philippe de Champaigne, the Jansenist painter par excellence.

This attitude towards art and this taste for restrained, sober forms prepared a meeting ground where French seventeenth century classicism and Jansenist sensibility could converge, and this inner affinity between the Jansenist "aesthetic" and

---

18. *Les oeuvres d'architecture d'Anthoine Le Pautre* (Paris, n.d.), p. 35: "Le dessein de cette Eglise . . . est different de l'ouvrage, en ce qu'il n'a point de porche ny de statuës, & que les trompes & la coupe en dedans n'ont point de sculture, ces ornemens ayant été retranchez pour éviter la dépense." On the author of the text of the Jombert edition, see Chapter 3, n. 1.

19. "Quelle vanité que la peinture, qui attire l'admiration par la ressemblance des choses dont on n'admire point les originaux!" (L. Brunschvicg, ed., *Pensées de Blaise Pascal*, II [Paris, 1904], p. 50 [no. 134]).

20. On Jansenism and the arts see B. Dorival, "Le jansénisme et l'art français," *Société des amis de Port-Royal* (1952), pp. 3–16; A. Hallays, "L'art et Port-Royal," in Gazier, *op. cit.*, pp. vii–xii.

21. See R. Wittkower, *Art and Architecture in Italy, 1600 to 1750*, 2d ed. (Baltimore, 1965), pp. 4–5.

22. Letter (1648) quoted in Dorival, *op. cit.*, p. 5.

23. Letter (1663) quoted in *ibid.*, pp. 4–5.

24. See, in particular, Marie-Angélique Arnauld's passage on poverty (August 27, 1652), quoted in *ibid.*, p. 7.

25. See the passages quoted in *ibid.*, pp. 8–9.

French classicism has been acutely noted by Dorival.[26] With reference to architecture, the *Constitutions* of Port-Royal explicitly stated: "Quand l'on fera quelque bâtiment au monastère, on aura égard que la structure soit le plus simple qu'il se pourra, pour la seule nécessité, & non pour l'ornement ni pour le plaisir."[27]

Because of these beliefs and attitudes, the Port-Royalists could certainly approve of the patterning of their new chapel after the recently completed Jesuit Noviciate, a church of a spare, economical design, which their young architect knew well and which was already enjoying a prestige among the rising circle of French classicists. Nevertheless, many architectural features projected by Le Pautre were rejected, undoubtedly in conformity with the Jansenist outlook towards art.[28]

An analysis of the plan and elevations of the chapel reveals how dependent Le Pautre was at the start of his career upon the French tradition, principally as represented by Martellange and Jacques Lemercier. In the plan (Fig. 1), Le Pautre made Martellange's layout of the Noviciate more compact by omitting one bay of the nave as well as the choir bay, so that the chapel took on a condensed form, consisting of one nave bay, the crossing, and the semicircular apse. Unlike the Noviciate, however, the small aisle bays flanking the nave bay do not communicate with the aisle bays which flank the crossing, and in this and in the omission of the choir bay Le Pautre's chapel is closer to the original prototype, della Porta's S. M. dei Monti. However, for the two oval chapels flanking the apse, Le Pautre apparently drew upon Mansart's Church of the Visitation in Paris (1632–34).[29]

Because the chapel is physically connected to the other buildings of the conventual establishment, a lateral entrance was necessary. In this instance, the prototype at hand was Lemercier's Church of the Sorbonne in Paris (begun 1635),[30] which has a lateral (northern) entrance in addition to the normal western one. Lemercier's church provided essential elements for the unrealized elevation of this façade (Fig. 2): the columnar portico of freestanding columns and the semicircular window.[31] Here, Le Pautre broke decisively with Martellange (who never used columns but always pilasters on his façades) and adopted a strongly sculptural, chromatic, and space-defining motif. However, Antoine omitted the pediment found on Lemercier's north façade, and instead turned to the older master's west façade, where a straight entablature is used.[32]

---

26. *Ibid.*, p. 16.

27. *Ibid.*, p. 13.

28. On these changes see also *ibid.*, pp. 13–14 and Y. Christ, "L'abbaye de Port-Royal de Paris," *Jardin des arts* (1959), p. 753.

29. These chapels would seem to constitute the sole borrowing from Mansart; hence it is not possible to agree with R. Blomfield, who considers Le Pautre's chapel to be a "variation" of the Visitation (*A History of French Architecture from the Death of Mazarin till the Death of Louis XV, 1661–1774*, I [London, 1921], p. 112). The chapels are sealed off from the space of the church by doors.

30. Noted by C. Gurlitt, *Geschichte des Barockstiles, des Rococo und des Klassicismus in Belgien,* *Holland, Frankreich, England* (Stuttgart, 1888), p. 131; Hautecoeur, II, i, p. 145.

31. Semicircular windows with vertical mullions, following the model of Roman thermae, were used by Martellange on the transepts of the Jesuit Noviciate and probably constituted details which appealed to Sublet de Noyers and his circle. Le Pautre dispensed with the Roman mullions and designed a window with a radiating pattern.

32. Le Pautre designed the lateral expanses of wall with portals surmounted by oval windows. Such windows, though with their long axes vertical instead of horizontal, were used on the flanks of the Jesuit Noviciate. They appear in Le Pautre's etching but not in the section published in the *Petit Marot* (cf. Moisy,

But this portico and the statues placed on its entablature were rejected, and the entire façade was reduced to a sober pilaster system, with a major Ionic order surmounted by dwarf Corinthianesque pilasters (Figs. 5, 6). The bold oval oculi over the lateral portals were diminished in scale, and the symmetry of the façade was upset by the insertion on the left side only of a segmental-headed window. Also expunged from the exterior were the balustrades, vases, and the elaborate base supporting the cross on the segmental pediment.[33] The roofing was also altered: archaic roofs of single slope took the place of double-sloped roofs.[34] On the interior, none of the rich decoration intended for the cupola, pendentives, and intrados of the crossing arches was executed, nor were the projected niches and statues realized (Figs. 3, 4). But Le Pautre also designed an elaborate altarpiece consisting of a central painting of the *Last Supper* (by Philippe de Champaigne; 1648, Louvre) flanked by monumental statues of the Virgin and Saint John the Baptist (by Philippe Buyster) which apparently was realized at least in part (Fig. 4).[35]

In the interior (Fig. 3), Le Pautre covered the square crossing with a circular dome on pendentives, not fully hemispherical, but far less depressed than Martellange's dome in the Jesuit Noviciate. Like the latter example, however, Antoine did not grant the dome exterior expression, but covered it with the sloped roofs. Here, both architects proceeded in a conservatively French and essentially non-classical path, for classical architecture, following the example of the Roman Pantheon, proudly displays the dome in the exterior elevation. (Indeed, during the Baroque era in Italy, the dome with its attendant drum tended to increase in height and boldness of silhouette at the expense of the substructure.[36])

The solitary nave bay is groin-vaulted (Fig. 8)—an austere and utterly bare form, traditionally found in French convent chapels.[37] Similarly, the apse is covered with a simple, unadorned half-dome (Figs. 3, 4, 7).

For the articulation of the walls (Figs. 3, 7), Antoine used unfluted Ionic pilasters which support a continuous entablature. The unifying horizontal entablature is echoed below by a molding which is a continuation of the imposts of the arches of the transept and nave bays. The entire design of these walls, with their framing bands, along with the half-dome of the apse, would seem to be directly based not on the Noviciate but on Lemercier's Church of the Sorbonne where, however, a Corinthian order is used. Lemercier's building also features coffered intrados, absent in the Noviciate, but, as noted, intended by Le Pautre.[38] Furthermore, in keeping with

Les églises des jésuites . . . , II, pls. LV A and LXXIV B). But since they were signed by Martellange himself, the Le Pautre etchings must be considered our most accurate guide to the appearance of the Noviciate.

33. The sculpture in the field of the upper segmental pediment is no longer extant but it is indicated in Fig. 5 in reduced scale. The same is true of the statues placed on the raking pediment of the central portal. It should be noted that Le Pautre varies sculptural elements from plate to plate (cf. Figs. 2, 4).

34. The façade of the Chapelle de Port-Royal, as executed, faintly recalls the center of Palladio's façade of S. Francesco della Vigna, Venice (ca. 1565): straight

entablature over the entrance portal, semicircular window above, heavy keystone.

35. H. Sauval, *Histoire et recherches des antiquités de la ville de Paris*, I (Paris, 1724), p. 425; L. Dussieux *et al.*, eds., *Mémoires inédits sur la vie et les ouvrages des membres de l'Académie royale de peinture et de sculpture*, I (Paris, 1854), p. 286.

36. Wittkower, *op. cit.*, pp. 142, 280–281.

37. Hautecoeur, II, ii, p. 761.

38. Absent in Le Pautre's prints, but present in Marot's prints of the Noviciate (cf. Moisy, *Les églises des jésuites . . .* , II, pls. LV A and LXXIV B). For the subsequent history of the chapel and the convent of

Jansenist sensibility, Le Pautre avoided polychromatic effects by building the church entirely of limestone from Saint-Leu.[39]

The chapel, as executed, fully satisfied the tastes of the Jansenists as well as those of French classicists, as may be seen in the unanimous praise which this church received from French architectural writers.[40]

As conservative and fully entrenched in the Martellange-Lemercier tradition as the church is, we should not ignore several features which point to the subsequent Baroque phase of the architect's career: the use of oval plans, the richness of the altarpiece and the intended sculpture, the *dessus de porte* with its bold cartouche and ample swags (Fig. 9), and the remarkable choir rail, with its convex-concave interplay (Figs. 1, 4). No trace of this remains, and it may never have been executed.[41]

The problem of Le Pautre's involvement with the other conventual buildings of Port-Royal de Paris must be considered.[42] The growth of Port-Royal des Champs under Marie-Angélique Arnauld (who became abbess in 1602), coupled with the insalubrity of the site, encouraged the nuns to seek an additional convent. Steps were taken in 1624–25 to secure property in the Faubourg Saint-Jacques in Paris, a favored area for nuns' convents. In January, 1626, the nuns were able to install themselves in the Maison de Clagny, the kernel of the new cloister. The buildings of the convent were gradually erected so that by ca. 1655 the cloister was complete on all four sides.[43] However, the cloister, as executed, did not follow the design indicated by Le Pautre in the *Desseins de plusieurs palais* (Fig. 4).[44] Here, the east façade of the cloister at least was to have had a ground story portico consisting of piers and semicircular

Port-Royal de Paris see H. Cordier in *Procès-verbaux de la commission municipale du vieux Paris* (1922), p. 75; M. Dumolin in *ibid.* (1931), p. 12; and *idem* and G. Outardel, *Les églises de France: Paris et la Seine* (Paris, 1936), p. 159.

39. A recent cleaning has restored the original blond tonality of the exterior. In total contrast to this ascetic coloristic conception, Le Pautre in 1657 (i.e., during his Baroque phase) began the façade of the Church of the Jacobins at Lyons, which was polychromatic (see Chapter 6).

40. G. Brice, *Description nouvelle de ce qu'il y a de plus remarquable dans la ville de Paris*, II (Paris, 1684), p. 98; G. L. Le Rouge, *Les curiositez de Paris, de Versailles, de Marly, de Vincennes, de S. Cloud, et des environs*, I (Amsterdam, 1718), p. 293; J. A. Piganiol de la Force, *Nouvelle description de la France*, 2d ed., II (Paris, 1722), p. 432. Sauval wrote (*op. cit.*, I, p. 425): "Au reste il n'y a rien de si propre, l'architecture en est très-agreable & des mieux entendües: sa manière à la verité est assés bisarre, mais fort galante & commode." I suspect that the latter half of this sentence was written with Le Pautre's later works and designs in mind.

Nicolas Poussin was the favorite contemporary painter of Sublet de Noyers and his circle. It is inter-

esting to note that Poussin's *Confirmation*, from the first series of the Seven Sacraments (ca. 1639; Duke of Rutland collection, Belvoir Castle, Grantham, Leicestershire), resembles the interiors of the Jesuit Noviciate and the Chapelle de Port-Royal. Blunt has recently noted that Poussin's architecture in *Confirmation* is based on another della Porta church, Sant'Atanasio dei Greci (1580–83), which stands directly across from Poussin's house in Rome. See A. Blunt, *Nicolas Poussin* (New York, 1967), I, pp. 189–190, fig. 153, II, pl. 130.

41. A plan of 1793 (facing p. 33 in P. Delauney, *La Maternité de Paris* [Paris, 1909]) shows a less convoluted arrangement of steps and choir rail, but this arrangement no longer exists today.

42. The following information is mainly drawn from Dumolin, *op. cit.* (1931), pp. 6ff.

43. *Ibid.*, p. 9. According to A. Gazier (*Histoire générale du mouvement janséniste depuis ses origines jusqu'à nos jours*, I [Paris, 1922], p. 55), the southern range of buildings was erected 1628–29. See also A. Boinet, *Les églises parisiennes: XVIIᵉ siècle* (Paris, 1962), pp. 274–276.

44. This is Le Pautre's only depiction of the cloister courtyard.

arches, the spandrels filled with wreathed medallions and swags.[45] Above is a story of rectangular windows separated by rectangular panels; dormer windows with alternating triangular and segmental pediments stand against the sloping roof. This design was evidently too sumptuous, and the cloister was provided with a totally bare and severe series of depressed arches forming the ground floor portico, with an equally spare elevation above (Fig. 10). In addition, Le Pautre also indicated a design for a building extending towards the north, perpendicular to the northern cloister range (Fig. 2). This *morceau* is an adaptation of the court elevations of Louis Le Vau's Hôtel d'Aumont in Paris (built, in part, before 1649).[46] But once again, Le Pautre's scheme was not followed, and the executed building was of barer form, with irregularly placed windows (Fig. 5).[47]

In sum, it would appear that Le Pautre bears responsibility for the chapel and nuns' choir alone.[48] He did provide designs for the conventual buildings, but these were not followed, and the executed structures are undoubtedly by other hands.

45. Le Pautre projected similar arcades for the court of the Hôtel de Fontenay-Mareuil.

46. C. Tooth, "The Early Private Houses of Louis Le Vau," *BurlM*, CIX (1967), p. 515 n. 22 (note by P. Smith).

47. This wing was demolished in the nineteenth century (Dumolin, *op. cit.* [1931], p. 10 and Delauney, *op. cit.*, pp. 67ff.). As noted by Hautecoeur (II, i, p. 146 n. 2), one of the *solitaires* of Port-Royal was Jean Bernard de Bel-Air (d. 1668), who was an architect of the convent (Gazier, *Histoire générale . . .* , I, p. 73). It is possible that he was responsible for the conventual buildings, but we lack further information on this point. The four-story building at the northeast corner which is still extant (Figs. 2, 5) appears to predate the chapel and does not seem to be by Le Pautre.

48. A nuns' choir was built in the main axis of the church, separated from the nave by a grille (see Fig. 3). According to Gazier (*ibid.*, p. 56), it was built in 1653. As it exists today it corresponds to Le Pautre's designs and is a simple, unadorned room. Le Pautre's church was the prototype for the plan and interior elevation of the Chapel of the former Convent of the Visitation in Moulins (Claude Collignon, 1648–55).

2

Hôtel de Fontenay-Mareuil

The Hôtel de Fontenay-Mareuil and the Chapelle de Port-Royal were both begun in 1646, and are Le Pautre's earliest works in architecture. They show the style of his initial, pre-Baroque, period, when he was committed to a relatively conservative and restrained French idiom.

In the case of the *hôtel*, Le Pautre's patron was François du Val, marquis de Fontenay-Mareuil (ca. 1595–1665), a distinguished courtier, soldier, and diplomat. He grew up in the company of the Dauphin (later Louis XIII), and fought in major campaigns from 1616 to 1629. From 1630 to 1633 he was the French ambassador to England, and served as the French ambassador to Rome from 1641 to 1643, and again from 1647 to 1649.[1]

We do not know how Antoine came to the attention of this man of the world, whose career had taken him all over western Europe. We do know, however, that on May 19, 1646, Fontenay-Mareuil signed a contract with Jacques Bruant, who acted as entrepreneur for Le Pautre.[2] The contract called for the erection of an *hôtel* near the corner of the rue Coq-Héron and rue Coquillière, to the east of the Palais-Royal, in a quarter which was then becoming fashionable due to its proximity to the latter building and to the Louvre. Construction was finished in May 1647;[3] on May 24 of that year, Fontenay-Mareuil left Paris for Rome to begin the second period of his ambassadorship.[4]

1. M. Dumolin, *Études de topographie parisienne*, II (Paris, 1930), p. 374; *idem*, "Notes sur quelques architectes du XVIIe siècle," *BSHAF* (1930), p. 16.

2. This contract is referred to in AN, Z^{ij} 266 (July 30, 1647). See Dumolin, *Études . . .* , II, p. 374; *idem*, "Notes . . . ," p. 16.

3. Dumolin, *Études . . .* , II, p. 376.

4. "Mémoires de Messire François Duval, Marquis de Fontenay-Mareuil," in J. F. Michaud and J. J. F. Poujoulat, eds., *Nouvelle collection des mémoires pour servir à l'histoire de France . . .* , V (Paris, 1837), p. 276.

Le Pautre dedicated the second part of his *Desseins de plusieurs palais* to his patron; three plates are devoted to the *hôtel* (Figs. 11, 14, 15). According to the text of the second (Jombert) edition, Antoine had been called upon to remodel a house dating from the early sixteenth century.[5] The Hôtel de Fontenay-Mareuil no longer exists, having been destroyed in the ninteenth century.[6]

We do not know the appearance of the older structure which Le Pautre refashioned. The site was irregular in that the rue Coq-Héron formed an oblique angle with the dividing wall which separated this *hôtel* from the neighboring lot. A wedge-shaped area also cut deeply into the site at the rear. Le Pautre arranged the *hôtel* around three sides of the rectangular court, closing the fourth (entrance) side with a thin, irregularly shaped section containing the entrance portal on the ground floor and a chapel and *cabinet* above.[7] The main living quarters on the ground floor were placed at the rear of the court, the traditional location of the *corps-de-logis*, but on the first floor these quarters were placed in the wings as well.

In plan, the Hôtel de Fontenay-Mareuil was traditional and undistinguished. The rooms were virtually all of square or rectangular plan, forms that are typical of French practice but which are in striking contrast to Le Pautre's designs of the 1650's, in which are found oval, circular, octagonal, and even trefoil room plans. Only on the first floor overlooking the rue Coq-Héron did Antoine design a small chapel and *cabinet* with curved walls, evidently carried on *trompes*. The resulting plan was sprawling and loose, lacking graduated spatial progressions.

There were, however, several features which indicate Le Pautre's up-to-date knowledge of contemporary innovations in French house design. These include the doubling of rooms in the right wing, creating greater flexibility;[8] the placement of the vestibule and stair in a far corner of the court, thus permitting an uninterrupted

---

Later names for the building were Hôtel de Gesvres and Hôtel Chamillart. After the death of Fontenay-Mareuil in 1665, the house was remodeled by his son-in-law, the Duc de Gesvres, as is indicated in *Les oeuvres d'architecture d'Anthoine Le Pautre* (Paris, n.d.), p. 19. However, contrary to Dumolin ("Notes . . . ," p. 17), there is no firm evidence that it was Le Pautre who remodeled the building at that time.

5. *Les oeuvres d'architecture* . . . , p. 19: ". . . le Sieur le Paultre avoit fait ces desseins pour Monsieur le Marquis de Fontenay-Mareüil, qui y vouloit faire des reparations & augmentations considerables, avec lesquelles il eût été difficile d'en faire une piece d'architecture, qui pût avoir rang entre celles qui se font distinguer par leur belle composition & decoration. Cette maison est d'une vieille maniere, & du temps que l'architecture commença à paroistra en France, y ayant plus de cent années de sa premiere construction, comme il est facile de le connoître par les ordres Dorique & Ionique sans proportion ny dessein, & par quelque chambranle de croisée tout à fait Gothique: ce qui a fait qu'on s'est contenté de la

rétablir dans ce qui étoit le plus necessaire, & la rendre de quelque utilité, en changeant la distribution des appartemens, ragréant les façades, & y faisant une porte neuve." For the authorship and dating of the text of the Jombert edition see Chapter 3, n. 1.

6. According to the Marquis de Rochegude and M. Dumolin (*Guide pratique à travers le vieux Paris*, new ed. [Paris, 1923], p. 240), the *hôtel* was destroyed in or before 1825 because in that year fragments of it were set up at the Passage Choiseul in Paris.

7. Probably not executed (see n. 14). Le Pautre's entrance portal is described in *Les oeuvres d'architecture* . . . , p. 19: "La grande porte qui a été faite dans le mur de face sur la ruë, est neuve, & un ordre Dorique en fait tout l'ornement; cet ordre a deux paremens, l'un sur la ruë, & l'autre sur la cour; & l'entablement qui est plus haut que le mur, en fait le couronnement."

8. The doubling of rooms in the urban *hôtel* was an innovation of Louis Le Vau: Hôtel Tambonneau, Paris, probably designed in 1639 (F. C. Tooth, *The Private Houses of Louis Le Vau* [Dissertation, University of London, 1961], p. 181).

sequence of rooms in the *corps-de-logis;* [9] and direct circulation through the court, the *basse-cour,* and the street.[10] The main stair was another interesting feature. It mounted along three sides of the cage, and the text of the Jombert edition supplies the following description: "Le grand escalier est aussi construit de neuf, & a plus de marches qu'il n'en paroît au dessein; il est couvert d'un dôme sur quatre trompes, qui est de charpente, lambrissé de plâtre; ce dome est un ovale fort long. L'escalier ne reçoit du jour que par une petite cour qui est à côté." [11] The domed staircase immediately brings to mind Mansart, who had immortalized the form at the Châteaux de Blois (1635–38) and Maisons (1642–46). Both domes are oval, the one at Blois considerably more so. At Maisons, light enters the dome through the lantern at its summit, whereas at Blois, light fills the dome from windows on the second floor, the low lantern being unpierced. The description in the Jombert edition indicates that Le Pautre's dome was closer to that at Blois, in that it was strikingly oval in form and did not receive light from above.

As noted in the Jombert edition, the elevations furnished by Le Pautre do not entirely correspond to the plans.[12] Fig. 14 does correspond except for the design of the stair, but Fig. 15 is very puzzling. It bears the inscription: "Fasse du costé du parterre de L'hostel de Fontenet a Paris . . . ," but it does not agree with the façades at either end of the garden.[13] For this reason, we may assume that Fig. 14 more closely reflects what was actually constructed.[14]

Antoine designed his elevations with clearly defined stories, each sharply demarcated from the other by complete and continuous entablatures. The garden façade of the *corps-de-logis* was articulated by means of Tuscan and Ionic pilaster orders,

9. This arrangement was used by Jean du Cerceau at the Hôtel de Bretonvilliers in Paris (1637–43; see Blunt, 1957, p. 99). Possible earlier examples were Lemercier's Hôtel de Liancourt (before 1637) and Mansart's Hôtel de la Vrillière (begun 1635), both in Paris (*ibid.,* p. 256 n. 13). See also J. P. Babelon, *Demeures parisiennes sous Henri IV et Louis XIII* (Paris, 1965), pp. 186–188, where this detail of planning is traced back to the sixteenth century.

10. An earlier example is again provided by the Hôtel de Bretonvilliers (Blunt, 1957, p. 98). According to Babelon (*op. cit.,* ch. IV), the *basse-cour* (or *cour des offices*) appeared in Parisian architecture ca. 1620–30.

11. *Les oeuvres d'architecture* . . . , pp. 19–20.

12. *Ibid.,* p. 19.

13. The two projecting pavilions in Fig. 15 suggest that we are looking towards the end of the garden, away from the *corps-de-logis.* But the ground plans (Fig. 11) and Fig. 14 indicate pavilions two bays in depth, while those in Fig. 15 are only one bay deep. The ground plan does not indicate a stair leading to the central portal. A stair does lead down from the garden façade of the *corps-de-logis,* but this façade lacks pavilions.

14. Plans exist of the various floors, dating from the eighteenth century (Estampes, Va 230, fols. 29–33 [our Figs. 12, 13]; fol. 30 is dated 1728), which bear the de Cotte inventory number 585. They reveal a number of changes in the building, some of which may have been due to the Duc de Gesvres (see n. 4). The wing containing the long gallery and the flanking pavilions at the rear of the garden are not indicated. The absence of these features corroborates the text in *Les oeuvres d'architecture* . . . , p. 20. If it is true that these elements were never built, then Le Pautre published unexecuted details of the building five years after its completion. Antoine proceeded in precisely the same way for the Chapelle de Port-Royal. Therefore Fig. 15 may be understood as another ideal elevation.

Figs. 12, 13 confirm the statement in *ibid.,* p. 19, that the *cour d'honneur* was irregularly shaped, without a chapel and *cabinet* on the street façade to regularize the court shape. We may assume that the chapel and *cabinet* were likewise never constructed. Fig. 13 also reveals that the bold *cabinet* on a *trompe* was not executed; the *cabinet* is indicated but it does not project beyond the line of the façade. These drawings also indicate changes in the interior room distribution, in the *basse-cour,* etc. These changes are cited in *ibid.,* pp. 19–20.

with sober moldings around the tall windows. This restrained ordonnance was enlivened by small-scale caryatid figures in the attic zone. Urns, also small in scale,
adorned the cornice, and a pediment with reclining figures on the raking cornices
stood against the double-sloped roof. This design was carried around the court, except that here the ground floor Tuscan order was replaced by heavy piers carrying
semicircular arches with consoles at the keystones. An arcade of identical form was
presumably present on the wall which defined the right side of the garden, and an
open arcade was also present on the left side of the *cour d'honneur*.[15]

The composition, particularly the rear of the *corps-de-logis*, strongly recalls the
court elevation of the southern wing of the Cour du Cheval Blanc at Fontainebleau,
built ca. 1540, perhaps by Pierre Chambiges (demolished in 1738 and replaced by
the present Aile Louis XV).[16] It would appear that Le Pautre, at this stage, was at-
tracted to this early French classical design, extremely planar and bland, with no
textural differentiation between floors, and dependent on the repetition of a limited
number of elements.

In the problematical Fig. 15, however, some of the window openings are in the
form of depressed arches, with console keystones, panels in relief, and ornamental
spandrels. Framing bands appear on the pavilions;[17] their roofs are curved, and
large-scale statues enliven the skyline.

Nevertheless, despite their decorative features, these elevations are flat, timid,
and conventional when compared with the designs of Le Pautre's next period.[18]
Here, in one of his first works, we see that Antoine's initial style was deeply entrenched in a traditional French mode, never displaying the dynamic Baroque language of his subsequent phase. This was true of the planning as well.

---

15. This arcade is similar to that planned by Le
Pautre for the cloister of Port-Royal de Paris (Fig. 4).
Le Pautre was fond of courtyard arcades (cf. Figs. 26,
37).

16. F. Gebelin, *Les châteaux de la Renaissance*
(Paris, 1927), pp. 97ff. This wing housed the Galerie
d'Ulysse.

17. Le Pautre used framing bands on the interior of the Chapelle de Port-Royal, and they appear
in subsequent designs (cf. Figs. 7, 27; *Les oeuvres
d'architecture* . . . , pl. 47).

18. The fragment of the façade erected at the
north entrance of the Passage Choiseul (see n. 6) is
related to the lower two stories of the left side of Fig.
14. But the attic story is absent, the windows have
straight hoods, and they are not as closely placed next
to the pilasters as in Fig. 14. Due to the fact that fragments of the *hôtel* were transported to the Passage
Choiseul and then re-erected in 1825, it would be
hazardous to decide to what extent Le Pautre's original work is preserved in this elevation.

3
Desseins de Plusieurs Palais

Le Pautre's book of designs bears a twenty year *privilège du roi* granted on December 28, 1652.[1] Hence the volume (issued "chez l'autheu") appeared at the very end of that year or sometime during 1653. It contains no text; instead, there are two dedication pages and an "Advertissement au Lecteur." The initial dedication page is addressed to Mazarin,[2] but there is another edition in which this page is directed to

1. The full title is: *Desseins de plusieurs Palais. Plans & Elevations en Perspective Geometrique, Ensemble les Profiles Elevez sur les Plans, le tout dessine et Inventez par Anthoine le Paultre, Architecte, et Ingenieur Ordinaire des Bastimens du Roy.* At a subsequent date, the Parisian publishing house of Jombert reissued Le Pautre's plates, accompanied by an analytical but anonymous text, as: *Les oeuvres d'architecture d'Anthoine Le Pautre.* Traditionally, this text has been ascribed to the French architect and theoretician Augustin Charles d'Aviler (1653–1700) on the basis of the following note from the anonymous "Avertissement" in the first volume of the *Oeuvres d'architecture de Jean Le Pautre, architecte, dessinateur & graveur du roi* (Paris, 1751): ". . . il [Antoine] publia un recueil de ses ouvrages . . . dont la première édition parut en 1652, sans aucun discours. Ce livre fut réimprimé après la mort de l'auteur, et les réflexions judicieuses que M. d'Aviler a ajoutées a chaque édifice, dans cette seconde édition, la rendent encore plus recommandable, et la feront toujours rechercher avec empressement par les amateurs de la bonne architecture."

It is possible to date the publication of the Jombert edition between 1697 and 1709 because it is dedicated to the "Prince de Conty," i.e., François Louis de Bourbon, prince de Conti (1664–1709). He is addressed in the dedication as "Son Altesse Serenissime," and therefore the edition cannot predate his (unsuccessful) appointment as King of Poland in 1697 by Louis XIV. On the other hand, if the text was indeed written by d'Aviler, then it was composed in or before 1700 (the year of d'Aviler's death), but not before 1682, because on p. 18 a reference is made to Desgodet's *Les édifices antiques de Rome*, published in that year. Another reference in the text confirms a seventeenth century date: on pp. 2–3, Salomon de Brosse and François Mansart are called "deux des plus grands Architectes de nostre siecle."

A facsimile edition of the Jombert edition was recently issued by the Gregg Press (1966).

2. It is highly likely that one of the reasons why Antoine dedicated his book to Mazarin was to counteract any adverse effects resulting from his brother Jean's folly in publishing an anti-Mazarin print earlier in 1652, during the Fronde. See Estampes,

Philippe d'Anjou (later Philippe d'Orléans), the brother of Louis XIV, and Le Pautre's subsequent Maecenas.[3] The second page of dedication is addressed in both editions to François du Val, Marquis de Fontenay-Mareuil, Le Pautre's early patron.

Of particular interest is the "Advertissement au Lecteur," which is here quoted in full:

> Lecteur, ce n'est pas mon dessein, de vous entretenir des Edifices des Anciens Romains, ni des Modernes. Ni de ce que Vitruve & les autres qui l'ont suivy en ont remarqué; Ie ne pretends pas aussi vous presenter un Livre des Regles de l'Architecture, & de tous les Ordres qui s'y pratiquent; d'autres en ont excrit assez amplement, & ie ne pourrois vous donner que des redittes. Ie vous fay un present tout simple de ces Desseins, que ie vous prie de ne pas rebuter. Ce sont des Enfans de mon Genie, & de mon experience. I'ay tasché de vous rendre facile l'execution de mes Desseins, & i'en puis donner des exemples par la conduite de quelques uns des Bastimens, que i'ay eslevez, tant pour les Grands que pour les particuliers. Mon principal but n'est que l'utilité publique, & la facilité de bastir. I'ay tasché d'observer le plus exactement qu'il m'a esté possible, les graces, les proportions des hauteurs, les Distributions des logemens, & toutes les commoditez necessaires. Si l'Ouvrage vous plaist, i'auray toute la satisfaction, que i'en espere, & ie m'efforceray de reconnoistre vostre Approbation, par les nouveaux Ouvrages, que ie vous destine.

Le Pautre's publication of a volume entirely devoted to his architectural projects, complete with the portrait of the architect, had precedents in the French architectural tradition.[4] But never before had an architect used a book as a means of dramatizing a personal stylistic revolution, and the change is underlined by the inclusion of plates depicting Le Pautre's two initial works.

In the *Desseins de plusieurs palais*, Le Pautre reveals his radically altered approach to architecture. His early style, embodied in the Chapelle de Port-Royal and the Hôtel de Fontenay-Mareuil, is rejected in favor of a bold and expansive idiom, characterized by a dramatic handling of space and a sculptural approach to mass.

Le Pautre's designs are outstanding within the context of French seventeenth century architecture with respect to their pronounced sense of weight and mass. This is in part conveyed by the extensive use of rustication, which links these designs to the Italian tradition and distinguishes them from the mainstream of French practice, with its typically texturally neutral and more fragilely articulated façades. The

Ed 42b, fol. 150 (bottom) and P. de Chennevières and A. de Montaiglon, eds., *Abécédario de P. J. Mariette . . .* ("Archives de l'art français," VI), III (Paris, 1854–56), pp. 186–187. Similarly, Jean published engravings in 1653 and 1654 which glorified the Peace (see H. Destailleur, *Notices sur quelques artistes français* [Paris, 1863], p. 72).

3. Philippe assumed the title of Duc d'Orléans in 1660 upon the death of his uncle, Gaston d'Orléans.

A copy with a dedication page addressed to Philippe d'Anjou is in Paris, Bibliothèque de l'Arsenal, Estampes 571. The page reads in part as follows: ". . . i'ose Monseigneur, esperer, que considerant cette Architecture, vous y remarquerez le grand avec l'utile, & un agreable meslange d'ordres, & orne-ments, Grecs, Romains & Francois, qui plaisent & sont commodes. Ie seray trop heureux, Monseigneur, si vostre Altesse agrée ces premiers Ouvrages de mon esprit, & si vous me permettez d'en commencer d'autres sous le glorieux tiltre d'un de vos Architectes & Ingenieux, en attendant que la continuation de mes emplois me fortifie de plus en plus, pour travailler quelque iour à un Palais aussi noble & rare que vous le meritez." Le Pautre's request was granted later in his career when he became Monsieur's architect (1660).

4. Cf. J. A. du Cerceau the Elder's *Livre d'architecture* of 1559, 1561, and 1582. Philibert de l'Orme published his portrait in his *Le premier tome de l'architecture* (1567).

rustication is used in several ways: in an over-all manner, covering wall surfaces and orders alike (Figs. 18, 26), intermingled with an unfluted order (Figs. 22, 30), confined to the *rez-de-chaussée* (Fig. 36), or appearing as a vertical angle (or quoining) strip (Fig. 27). But it must be emphasized that Le Pautre never follows the Italian tradition of conflicting rusticated patterning, but always treats the rustication as horizontal channeling, occasionally relieved by radial patterns above windows and arches. This more uniform treatment of rustication is typical of French architecture, which rarely indulges in the "savage brutality" sometimes encountered in Italian examples. Nevertheless, the degree of rustication and textural aggressiveness in these designs is outstanding within the French context, and demonstrates the architect's decisive break with the bland and conventional elevations of his early works.

In the First Design (Figs. 18, 19), Antoine has chosen as his model de Brosse's powerful Luxembourg Palace in Paris (begun 1615)[5]—a building exceptional in French architecture because of its heavy, rusticated elevations. This relationship is demonstrated by the domed entrance pavilion and the over-all rustication. But Le Pautre enriches this basic scheme on the garden façade by the use of freestanding columns, large semicircular concavities below the lateral windows of the ground floor, and smaller statue-filled niches. The latter reappear on the entrance façade, and on the entrance pavilion the architect indicates monumental caryatid figures on the ground floor boldly supporting a Doric frieze—a "licentious" mixture of the orders which undoubtedly was frowned upon by Fréart de Chambray and his circle.[6] In the Second Design (Fig. 22)—a variation on Palladio's Villa Rotonda[7]—we find Palladio's serene classical porticos replaced by gigantic Persians supporting heavy entablatures.[8] Strong textural values and contrasts are created by the channeled rustication which replaces Palladio's smooth, neutral wall surfaces. And more vigorous than their Palladian counterparts are the bold moldings of the high podium and the prominent four-sided dome.

In these designs Le Pautre uses superposed orders, which enhance the impression of each floor as a horizontal layer, heavily resting upon or supporting its neighbor. In the Fourth Design (Fig. 30), however, we find one of Antoine's rare experiments with the colossal order, which introduces a strong vertical tendency.[9] But the effect of weight is retained due to the moldings which divide the two stories and which interweave among the orders. This order, directly derived from Le Vau's Le Raincy (before 1645),[10] is characterized by very tall, slim pilasters intermingled with

5. Noted by C. Gurlitt, *Geschichte des Barockstiles, des Rococo und des Klassicismus in Belgien, Holland, Frankreich, England* (Stuttgart, 1888), p. 132. The Luxembourg is mentioned in the discussion of the First Design in *Les oeuvres d'architecture* . . . , p. 3.

6. Fréart emphatically warned against contaminating one order with elements of another: caryatids, being female, cannot be associated with the male Doric order. See R. Fréart de Chambray, *Parallèle de l'architecture antique et de la moderne* (Paris, 1650), Preface. This feature was also criticized in *Les oeuvres d'architecture* . . . , p. 4.

7. Le Pautre's dependence on Palladio in the Second Design is noted in *ibid.*, pp. 7–8; Gurlitt, *op. cit.*, p. 132; Blunt, 1957, p. 140.

8. This use of monumental figures recalls contemporary architecture in the south of France (cf. Hautecoeur, II, i, pp. 205–225, figs. 194, 201, 203).

9. Le Pautre considered using the colossal order in only one other project: a preliminary design for the Château de Seiglière de Boisfranc at Saint-Ouen (before 1672; Fig. 95).

10. Noted by Blunt, 1957, p. 140.

rusticated wall surfaces; these contrast dramatically with the channeled rustication of the great concavities, where the orders are absent. It is precisely here that the architect has adopted one of the recurrent themes of Baroque architecture: the curving façade, with its suggestion of movement and shaped, molded space.

In addition to these features of the elevations, Le Pautre's designs illustrate a new approach to spatial composition. We can find among these designs an axial coordination of varied units of planning which produces emphatic spatial sequences. The visitor is led through a series of contrasting spaces which continually varies and modulates his experience, providing crescendo and climax, decrescendo and pause.

In the Third Design (Figs. 24–26), for example, one enters through a long, dark, narrow passage to emerge into the shade of a portico, from which one continues directly into the increased light of the courtyard. Here, the *corps-de-logis* beckons, due to its greater height, broad, inviting steps, and curved walls which suggest movement towards the three central portals. The steps produce a change in level and one enters the trefoil vestibule, whose walls are articulated by statue-filled niches. Continuing on axis, one is then led by the curving walls to a further room, very bare and of different shape, in which the exterior light can again be glimpsed. There follows a columnar porch, flanked with niches; afterwards, one descends to the left or right into the garden. Throughout this journey there is never any repetition of spatial units. Each stage constitutes a new experience and adventure.

This type of planning reaches its culmination in the remarkable Fourth Design (Figs. 28, 29, 32). Here the visitor, after passing through a small introductory oval vestibule, immediately experiences the gigantic three-story domed octagonal salon, articulated by a colossal order of Corinthian columns and pilasters. To right or left, the same sequence obtains: a long, straight stair leads to a first landing of circular plan, covered by a dome. From here the stair climbs again on the same axis, reaching a second rectangular landing, flat-ceiled and with columns in the corners. At last one enters a vast barrel-vaulted hall, richly ringed with a series of coupled columns.

In these designs, we note that Le Pautre breaks away from the usual square and rectangular rooms of the French tradition, and uses circular, oval, and apsidal-ended units, as well as most unusual trefoil and octagonal plans. The eating into the walls by means of niches seems like a natural corollary of the dynamic suggestiveness of the spaces. Furthermore, the placement of columns within rooms adds to the aggressive character of the interiors.

If we refer back to the plan of the early Hôtel de Fontenay-Mareuil (Fig. 11), we can clearly grasp the revolution in Antoine's style which these designs represent. The traditional stringing-out of unintegrated rectangular spaces is replaced by correlated, interacting units. A thoroughly Baroque conception has emerged.

In addition to providing spaces for reception and display, Le Pautre has equipped his château and *hôtel* designs with the traditional French *appartements* — quarters destined for daily, practical living. These are always arranged in a flexible manner, with easy communication between the various rooms of specialized uses. In the Second Design (Fig. 21), the manner in which Le Pautre has transformed Palladio's plan of the Villa Rotonda is revealing. The strict biaxial symmetry of Palladio's plan has been drastically modified. Instead of stairs of identical form leading to identical spatial sequences on all four sides, we find entrances on only two opposite sides, thus giving a distinct axial orientation to the spatial progression.[11] The passage from low vestibule to high salon is present in the Villa Rotonda, but whereas Palladio's central room is followed by a vestibule identical to the first one traversed, Le Pautre's third unit of the sequence—a long, transverse gallery—is entirely different from the initial vestibule. Similarly, the second flight of steps differs from the first. In addition, the French architect is not solely concerned with creating an ideal pattern which is perhaps satisfying only on paper; instead, he creates spaces for practical living: *appartements*, a chapel, and corridors.[12]

Le Pautre's inventiveness in planning extends to staircase design as well. In the First Design (Figs. 16, 17) the major stairs are placed in the four corners of the court, a disposition which avoids any interruption of the main sequence of rooms, and which perhaps finds an echo in Bernini's third project for the Louvre (1665).[13] The Fifth Design (Fig. 33) incorporates a monumental stair with straight ramps placed immediately to one side of the entrance vestibule, at right angles to the main axis of the house. This is probably the first proposal of this scheme in France; the idea was realized in such later buildings as the Hôtel Aubert de Fontenay (Jean Boullier, 1656–61) and the Hôtel de Lionne (Louis Le Vau, 1662), both in Paris.[14]

The Sixth Design (Figs. 38–40) stands apart from the projects discussed above. Far from illustrating principles of Baroque composition, it foreshadows certain tendencies of the architect's last period, when he strove to reduce the Baroque content of his designs.

Aside from the vigorously rusticated portal (the composition of which is derived from Palladio's "interpenetrating" church façades),[15] the outer façades are extremely planar, without rustication or textural differentiation. They are generically related to the lateral expanses of the street façade of the Fifth Design (Fig. 35) and, like it, anticipate the severity of the Château de Clagny (1674; Fig. 97). The relatively long, low elevations strike a new note. They enclose a courtyard space of very different quality from the corresponding spaces in the First, Third, and Fifth Designs. The towering walls and vertical, shaftlike spaces of these examples are the antitheses of the more expansive, horizontal space of the Sixth Design. We shall see that Le Pautre further developed this type of courtyard during his final phase. The courtyard façades of the Sixth Design are of a tame, academicizing quality, with their strict use of repeated orders and arches, unrelieved by rustication or exuberant decorative motifs. This colder quality obtains as well in such details as the Pantheon coffering of the barrel-vaulted salon and the Greek wave motif which runs along the outer façades at the base of the *rez-de-chaussée*.

11. There is ambiguity concerning which stairs are the entrance stairs and which exit into the garden. The ground plan (Fig. 21) is oriented so that the double-ramp flight appears to be the entrance, but an elevation (Fig. 22) suggests the other alternative. In his Third and Fifth Designs, Antoine uses the double-ramp flight on the garden façades.

12. Fig. 21 is possibly the source for Lord Burlington's plan of Chiswick House (begun 1725).

13. On other aspects of Bernini's indebtedness to Le Pautre, see pp. 29–30, 30 n.34.

14. I am indebted to Prof. Sir Anthony Blunt for this observation.

15. R. Wittkower, *Architectural Principles in the Age of Humanism*, 2d ed. (London, 1952), pp. 80ff.

It is evident, therefore, that the *Desseins de plusieurs palais* is stylistically heterogeneous. The majority of the plates proclaim the architect's development of a new idiom of Baroque composition, very different from his two initial works which are included in the volume. But a few designs already point to his post-Baroque phase, which began about 1665.[16]

One of the most important features found in the *Desseins de plusieurs palais* is the use, in château and *hôtel* design, of domed rooms extending two or more stories in height.[17] The term *salon à l'italienne* was first applied by the French to this architectural form in the seventeenth century.[18] It is essential to study the origins and development of this architectural unit.

Earl Rosenthal has recently demonstrated that Andrea Mantegna's house in Mantua (begun 1476) was intended to contain as its central element a round, domed room, two stories in elevation.[19] This is the earliest example of the form of which we have knowledge, although Rosenthal indicates that Mantegna's design was anticipated in the sketches of Francesco di Giorgio. Mantegna's house is thus the prototype of that most famous and influential sixteenth century creation, Palladio's Villa Rotonda, near Vicenza (begun ca. 1550).[20] It should be noted at this point that the circular, domed two-story hall of Francesco di Giorgio, Mantegna, and Palladio is essentially a borrowing from ecclesiastical design, the incorporation in a secular context of the essential element of a centralized Renaissance church. The first architectural theorist of the Renaissance, Leone Battista Alberti, had sanctioned this type of transference from the ecclesiastical domain to the secular when discussing the de-

---

16. A number of other designs included in the *Desseins de plusieurs palais* call for brief comment (plate numbers refer to the Jombert edition):

Pl. 47 seems to be based on Palladio's Palazzo Chiericati, Vicenza (begun 1550). In both examples we find a bay organization of 3–5–3 on two floors, but the French architect closes in Palladio's open porticos, except for the central group of five bays on the ground floor. Le Pautre depends for the richness of effect on framing bands, decorative motifs (shells, swags), statuary (as in Palladio), but adds greater verticality and complexity through the roofing forms and the attic story.

The ground plan of pl. 49 seems to have been utilized by Le Brun in several of his architectural designs (see J. Guiffrey and P. Marcel, *Inventaire général des dessins du Musée du Louvre et du Musée de Versailles: École française*, VIII [Paris, 1913], nos. 8162, 8163, 8205).

Pl. 36 is strongly reminiscent of Michelangelo's Senators' Palace on the Capitoline Hill, Rome (this relationship is noted in *Les oeuvres d'architecture . . .* , p. 22).

Pls. 30(2) and 31(2) (ornamental designs) reflect the influence of Stefano della Bella (1610–64), who was in Paris 1639–50.

17. See Figs. 20, 23, 26, 32. In the first two examples the rooms are square in plan. In the third example the room is oval, in the fourth, octagonal.

18. H. Sauval (*Histoire et recherches des antiquités de la ville de Paris*, III [Paris, 1724], p. 4) speaks of *chambres à l'italienne* built by Le Pautre in the Hôtel de Guéménée in Paris in 1650 (see Appendix I). For formal definitions, see A. C. d'Aviler, *Dictionnaire d'architecture* (Paris, 1693), p. 226; J. F. Blondel, *De la distribution des maisons de plaisance et de la décoration des édifices en général*, I (Paris, 1737), pp. 31–32; C. E. Briseux, *L'art de bâtir des maisons de campagne*, I (Paris, 1743), pp. 21–22; C. F. Roland Le Virloys, *Dictionnaire d'architecture . . .* , II (Paris, 1770), p. 598. For d'Aviler and Briseux, the name derives from the fact that the room is domed; for Blondel, "sa grande élévation lui a fait donner le nom de Salon à l'Italienne" (p. 31).

19. E. E. Rosenthal, "The House of Andrea Mantegna in Mantua," *GBA*, s. 6, LX (1962), pp. 327–348.

20. See W. Lotz, "La Rotonda: Edificio civile con cupola," *Bollettino del centro internazionale di studi di architettura*, IV (1962), pp. 69–73. Palladio also used the domed central hall in his design for the Villa Trissino at Meledo.

sign of vestibules of private houses, and in the same lines he seems to have adumbrated the form used by Mantegna and Palladio:

> The Ancients, before their Houses made either a Portico, or at least a Porch, not always with straight Lines, but sometimes with curve, after the Manner of the Theatre. Next to the Portico lay the Vestibule, which was almost constantly circular; behind that was the Passage into the inner Court, and those other Parts of the House which we have already spoken of. . . . Where the Area is round it must be proportioned according to the Design of the Temple; unless there be this Difference, that here the Height of the Walls must be greater than in the Temple. . . .[21]

Alberti also called for the placement of such rooms in the very center of the house, as in the Renaissance examples cited above:

> . . . Vestibules, Halls, and the like Places of publick Reception in Houses, ought to be like Squares and other open Places in Cities; not in a remote private Corner, but in the Center and the most publick Place, where all the other Members may readily meet. For here all Lobbies and Staircases are to terminate; here you meet and receive your Guests.[22]

This Italian Renaissance tradition was adopted by Le Pautre in his Second Design (Figs. 21–23), which, as noted above, is modeled after the Villa Rotonda, although Le Pautre's central hall is square, not circular. As in the Italian examples, the two-story room is immured within the fabric of the building, and can only find exterior expression through its dome, which in Antoine's design is of the French, four-sided variety. Similarly, in the First and Third Designs (Figs. 20, 26), square and oval halls are revealed on the exterior by their domes, although these rooms do not occupy the central points of their plans due to the fact that both buildings are laid out around courtyards.[23] But in his Fourth Design (Figs. 30, 32), Antoine departs from this tradition, and allows the *salon à l'italienne* to be expressed throughout the entire height of the elevation as a projecting mass flanked by concave walls. This immensely plastic, Baroque conception had a prototype, not Italian but French. It was Louis Le Vau, that much underrated master, who, at the Château du Raincy, first granted the *salon à l'italienne* an exterior expression throughout its entire elevation. This great work of Le Vau (erected before 1645 but destroyed in the early nineteenth century)[24] has never been recognized for its immense significance in the history of architecture. Plates in the *Petit Marot* and a late eighteenth century description[25] inform us that the central pavilion consisted of an oval vestibule filled with a forest of freestanding columns on the ground floor. Above this, extending through the

21. L. B. Alberti, *Ten Books on Architecture*, J. Leoni, trans., J. Rykwert, ed. (London, 1955), p. 190 (ix. 3).

22. *Ibid.*, p. 84 (v. 2).

23. In the Fifth Design (Figs. 34, 37), a room in the *corps-de-logis* marked "chambre" is suggestive of a *salon à l'italienne*, but it receives no light from the exterior in its upper level as do the other examples. Le Pautre designates the *salon à l'italienne* as "salle"

or "porch." The "chambre" of the Fifth Design does not project and is not distinguished on the exterior by a dome.

24. For the dating see Blunt, 1957, pp. 135, 266 n. 83.

25. L. V. Thiéry, *Guide des amateurs et des étrangers voyageurs dans les maisons royales . . . aux environs de Paris* (Paris, 1788), pp. 178–179.

first and second stories, was the internally domed, oval *salon à l'italienne*, its walls articulated with painted *trompe-l'oeil* pilasters. This large, oval central pavilion bulged out from the body of the château on both court and park façades, forming great convex projections. Later in his career, Le Vau re-employed this form (with variations) at the Châteaux de Meudon (after 1654) and Vaux-le-Vicomte (1656–61), and in his east façade of the Louvre (construction halted in 1664). But before Le Vau turned to these later achievements, Le Pautre had published his Fourth Design, which, proceeding directly from Le Raincy, developed an octagonal hall through not two but three enormous stories.

Le Vau also employed the *salon à l'italienne* in the urban *hôtel*,[26] and Le Pautre incorporated this feature in the Hôtel de Guéménée, Paris, in 1650 (see Appendix I), and proposed the form in his Third (*hôtel*) Design (Fig. 26).

An essential element of the *salon à l'italienne* as used by Le Vau and Le Pautre is its associated vestibule, which serves as a decorous overture to the subsequent splendor of the main room. At Le Raincy, Le Vau placed these two units in vertical communication, salon over vestibule, and this system was followed by Le Pautre in his First and Third Designs (Figs. 20, 26).[27] In the Second and Fourth Designs (Figs. 23, 32) vestibule and salon communicate horizontally, being placed on the same floor, and this system was in turn taken up by Le Vau at Vaux-le-Vicomte. Whereas Le Vau always used freestanding Doric or Tuscan columns in his vestibules and lighter pilasters in the salons, Antoine used no orders of any sort in his introductory rooms, but reserved them for the salons, usually articulated with columns (Figs. 20, 23, 26, 32).

In all of these systems, the effect was dramatic and dynamic. The visitor first entered a grave, soberly decorated, one-story environment and then passed into a brilliantly adorned, expansive space of much greater height, domed and receiving light from above. Here was Baroque spatial movement and climax. Here, too, were lavish painted vault decorations. At Vaux-le-Vicomte, for example, Le Brun intended to fill the cupola with *The Palace of the Sun*, depicting "Apollo sending out his torch-bearer to the new star of Fouquet, crowned by Mars and Jupiter and supported by Saturn with his promise of immortality."[28] The dome, the age-old symbol of heaven, was thus used for the purpose of secular glorification.[29] Although Le Pautre's designs do not indicate specific programs, it is not unreasonable to imagine his cupolas filled with similar decorations.

Thus, the external projection of the salon in elevation, its dramatic correlation

26. Le Vau used the *salon à l'italienne* in his Hôtel Hesselin (ca. 1640–ca. 1644), Hôtel d'Aumont in the Place Royale (1640's), and perhaps in the Hôtel Tambonneau (probably designed in 1639), all in Paris. See F. C. Tooth, *The Private Houses of Louis Le Vau* (Dissertation, University of London, 1961), p. 96.

27. Le Vau then used the same system at Meudon (after 1654).

28. J. Montagu, "The Early Ceiling Decorations of Charles Le Brun," *BurlM*, CV (1963), p. 405.

29. The program at Vaux-le-Vicomte was an-

ticipated at Pieter Post's Huis ten Bosch in The Hague (1645–51). The building, derived from the Villa Rotonda, contains a central domed hall, decorated from 1647 with paintings representing *The Triumph of Frederik Hendrik*, the Stadholder. See H. Rose, *Spätbarock: Studien zur Geschichte des Profanbaues in den Jahren 1660–1760* (Munich, 1922), p. 168; J. Gamer, "Jean Marot in den Diensten des Kurfürsten Karl Ludwig von der Pfalz," *Heidelberger Jahrbücher*, VI (1962), p. 79.

with a spare, introductory vestibule, and the use of noncircular plans constitute the specifically French Baroque transformations of Italian Renaissance forms. The influence of the French version of the *salon à l'italienne* upon later Baroque architecture in Europe was vast. One has only to think of such masterpieces as Guarini's Palazzo Carignano in Turin (1679–92) or Neumann's Residenz at Würzburg (begun 1719) to realize the stunning effect of Le Vau's and Le Pautre's potent designs.[30]

Another influential motif found in the *Desseins de plusieurs palais* is the drum-without-dome. This appears in the Fourth Design (Figs. 30–32), the most extraordinary creation in Le Pautre's *oeuvre*. I have discussed elsewhere [31] the appearance of this motif in the designs of many leading architects, including Louis Le Vau, François Mansart, Bernini, Hildebrandt, Fischer von Erlach, Boffrand, Boullée, Ledoux, and the American Thomas U. Walter.[32] As used by Le Pautre, the motif is a purely formal invention, inspired by depictions of St. Peter's in the course of construction (between 1564 and 1588), with its drum still lacking the great dome. In the designs of Hildebrandt and Fischer von Erlach, however, the motif was used as a monumentalized representation of the "open" crowns worn by these architects' patrons, a further instance of the enlargement of symbols of rank and power to full architectural scale in the Baroque period.[33] It was in these terms that Colbert criti-

30. On the *salon à l'italienne* see also: Rose, *op. cit.*, pp. 167–169; J. Cordey, "Le grand salon ovale de Vaux-le-Vicomte et sa décoration," *La revue de l'art ancien et moderne*, XLVI (1924), pp. 237–238; P. Du Colombier, *L'architecture française en Allemagne au XVIIIᵉ siècle*, I (Paris, 1956), p. 75; R. Strandberg, "Le château de Champs," *GBA*, s. 6, LXI (1963), p. 98 n. 10, p. 99 n. 22.

Related to the *salon à l'italienne* is the *sala grande*, a rectangular hall, also of two stories, as in such Italian examples as the Palazzi Farnese, Quirinale, Borghese, and Barberini (all in Rome). Due to their rectangular plans, these halls were not covered with the dome, and thus lacked this specific architectural symbol of glorification. Nevertheless, their ceilings frequently served as fields for painted hymns of praise for earthly potentates, as in Pietro da Cortona's ceiling in the Palazzo Barberini representing *The Glorification of the Reign of Urban VIII* (1633–39). The rectangular plan, however, precluded convex protrusions in the elevations; such halls usually were expressed by crowning features which rose above the adjacent roofs. Perhaps the first *sala grande* so treated was Flaminio Ponzio's Salone da Ballo (Sala del Concistoro pubblico) in the Quirinal Palace (1605–12), where a belvedere rises above the roof line. See J. Wasserman, "The Quirinal Palace in Rome," *AB*, XLV (1963), pp. 232–233.

31. R. W. Berger, "Antoine Le Pautre and the Motif of the Drum-without-Dome," *JSAH*, XXV (1966), pp. 165–180.

32. A few additional examples of the motif may

be cited here: Nicolas Tessin the Younger (?): Sketch for a "Lusthaus" (H. Sedlmayr, *Johann Bernhard Fischer von Erlach* [Vienna and Munich, 1956], pl. 307); M. J. Peyre: Project for an academy (E. Kaufmann, *Architecture in the Age of Reason* [Cambridge, Mass., 1955], fig. 98 [On the influence of the Fourth Design on the plan for this project see Berger, *op. cit.*, p. 165 n. 2.]); C. De Wailly: Project for a French Pantheon (Paris, Bibliothèque des arts décoratifs, album 55); William Thomas: Design for a mausoleum, 1781 (Kaufmann, *op. cit.*, fig. 30); Joseph Bonomi: Roseneath, Dumbartonshire, 1803–6 (J. Summerson, *Architecture in Britain, 1530 to 1830*, 4th ed. [Baltimore, 1963], pl. 187a).

33. See, e.g., the depiction of "closed" crowns in designs by Hildebrandt, Rainaldi, and Borromini (Berger, *op. cit.*, figs. 8, 16, 17; cf. also fig. 18 to a print by Stefano della Bella depicting the procession of the Holy Sacrament in Paris in which a monumental royal French crown is upheld by angels in a similar fashion, in H. Nasse, *Stefano della Bella* [Strassburg, 1913], pl. 4, top). In 1666 F. Dubois submitted a project for the royal chapel of the Louvre which was topped by the royal French crown (E. Sekler, *Wren and his Place in European Architecture* [New York, 1956], pl. 34a). Roseneath (see n. 32) was built for the Duke of Argyll, but the domeless-drum form is not used as a representational motif in this instance since English dukes wear crowns of "closed" form (see H. G. Ströhl, *Heraldischer Atlas* [Stuttgart, 1899], commentary for pl. XVI, fig. 6).

cized Bernini's first Louvre project as an inexact representation of the royal French crown, since that crown was of "closed" form, and Bernini had used the domeless-drum idea, indicative to Colbert of an "open" crown.[34] But it must be stressed that there is no evidence that Le Pautre used the motif as a depiction of an "open" crown. He did not indicate that the Fourth Design was intended for a specific patron or rank.

The drum-without-dome has a bizarre and fantastic quality, in harmony with the vast scale and intricate plan of the Fourth Design. The motif is an eloquent indication of the new-found energy and bold imagination of the architect.[35]

There is a drawing in Stockholm of the ground plan of a large château (Fig. 41)[36] which seems like a page taken out of the *Desseins de plusieurs palais*. The design includes a number of elements typical of Antoine's Baroque style: entrance vestibule and associated salon, with the orders characteristically reserved for the salon; oval rooms; bi-columnar porticos (cf. Figs. 21 [columns replaced by Persians], 38); massive blocks of masonry. In addition, the four complex niche arrangements on the entrance side of the court, in the pattern a–B–a, recall the Sixth Design (cf. Fig. 38), and the stair is of the same form as found in Fig. 33. Most unusual is the diagonal placement of the two stables, which creates a pattern of radial avenues. Behind the château is an enormous circular basin enclosed by massively thick walls molded into giant niches. There can be little doubt that this drawing is by Le Pautre; however, to assign it a precise date is impossible. All we can say is that it must have been created during the architect's Baroque period, that is, between ca. 1652 and ca. 1665.

Why did Le Pautre change to a Baroque style? This question is more easily posed than answered. Unfortunately we have very little information which can grant

---

34. In Berger, *op. cit.*, pp. 170–171, I argued that Bernini's first Louvre project was directly inspired by Le Pautre's Fourth Design. I would like to suggest here that the *logge* which are present on the central and flanking concave portions of Bernini's façade may also have been derived from Antoine's design. Cf. Fig. 29 with Bernini's plan (R. Wittkower, *Art and Architecture in Italy, 1600 to 1750*, 2d ed. [Baltimore, 1965], fig. 9). In 1666, Bernini alluded to the domeless-drum idea in his design for the apse of S. M. Maggiore, Rome (H. Brauer and R. Wittkower, *Die Zeichnungen des Gianlorenzo Bernini* [Berlin, 1931], I, p. 163, II, pl. 182).

35. In *Les oeuvres d'architecture . . .*, p. 18, the commentator describes the domeless drum as follows: "La hauteur du grand Portique s'élevant au dessus de l'ordre fait paroistre un Attique avec pilastres & bossages, & huit fenestres qui éclairent la voute du plain Cintre, elle est de maçonnerie sans charpente au dessus, & aprés des retraites en forme de degrez ou sieges comme ceux du Pantheon, il y a une grande terrasse avec des dales de pierre à joints recouverts dont le profil de l'appuy est comme celuy du siege de marbre qui est au pied du mur de face du Palais Farnese; ce profil ressemble à un balustre continu." It is evident that this text attempts to ac-

count for the sources of the upper elements of the domeless drum and not for the total form itself. It is interesting to note, however, that St. Peter's is mentioned in the course of the discussion of this design (p. 17).

The Fourth Design was influential in other respects as well. Sir Christopher Wren was probably influenced by the plan (Fig. 29) when designing the Greek cross plan for St. Paul's (noted by Blunt, 1957, p. 266 n. 93). Wren owned a copy of Le Pautre's book (Sekler, *op. cit.*, p. 118 n. 3). In a letter written during his Parisian sojourn (1665–66), Wren cited Le Pautre as one of the best architects in France, after Bernini, Mansart, Le Vau, and Gobert (M. Whinney, "Sir Christopher Wren's Visit to Paris," *GBA*, s. 6, LI [1958], p. 237).

The lateral elevations of the Fourth Design (Fig. 31) seem to have influenced Vanbrugh's garden façade of Blenheim Palace (1705–24; Vanbrugh's indebtedness to Le Pautre was noted by R. Blomfield, *A History of French Architecture from the Death of Mazarin till the Death of Louis XV, 1661–1774*, I [London, 1921], p. 112 and Blunt, 1957, p. 266 n. 94).

36. Stockholm, Nationalmuseum, CC 2109. It bears the inscription: "Plan generalle du Chateau de plaisence."

insights into his mind and personality, but something can be said concerning the fact that Le Pautre's stylistic change occurred during the era of Jules Cardinal Mazarin, who had succeeded Richelieu as First Minister in 1642.

The Italian cardinal had inherited from his supporter, Pope Urban VIII Barberini (1623–44), a passion for rich and sumptuous art forms.[37] In 1643, soon after his accession to power in France, he forced the resignation as Surintendant des Bâtiments du Roi of Sublet de Noyers, the leader of a classicist, pro-Poussin clique, and replaced him with the weaker Le Camus, whom the cardinal could dominate.

A brief review of Mazarin's activities as art patron is revealing. In 1643 he acquired as his Parisian residence the Hôtel de Chevry-Tubeuf (subsequently the Hôtel Mazarin), which had been begun in 1635 in a traditional brick-and-stone manner.[38] But to decorate the two superposed long galleries,[39] Mazarin called upon the Italians Romanelli and Grimaldi, who introduced a version of Pietro da Cortona's manner into Paris (1646–48). This was the first appearance of a decorative mode that, in the hands of Le Brun, was to characterize the interiors of Vaux-le-Vicomte and Versailles.

In architecture, Mazarin made no effort to dislodge the First Architect, Lemercier, who often worked in an Italianate manner. Upon the death of Lemercier in 1654, Mazarin chose Louis Le Vau to succeed to the high post,[40] and thereby selected a vigorous, experienced master whose Hôtel Lambert in Paris (begun ca. 1640) and Château du Raincy (before 1645; destroyed) pointed the way to a French Baroque style. Additional evidence of Mazarin's tastes in architecture is provided by the façade of SS. Vincenzo ed Anastasio in Rome (Martino Longhi the Younger, 1646–50), commissioned by the cardinal, which is an outstanding example of Baroque sculptural vigor and decorative fantasy. Mazarin was also responsible for the introduction into France of Italian opera, with its elaborate scenographic constructions,[41] and he patronized the Theatines, who were famous for their use of theatrical and dramatic procedures in their services.[42]

37. On Mazarin and the arts see P. Du Colombier, "Le premier ministre se fait l'ambassadeur de l'art italien," in G. Mongrédien, ed., *Mazarin* (Paris, 1959), pp. 112–151; F. Haskell, *Patrons and Painters* (New York, 1963), pp. 180ff.

38. On this building see R. A. Weigert, "Le Palais Mazarin, architectes et décorateurs," *Art de France*, II (1962), pp. 147–169. The initial architect was Jean Thiriot.

39. The wing (also in brick-and-stone) which houses these galleries was begun in 1645 by François Mansart, who was replaced in 1646 by Le Muet. See *ibid.*

40. In 1654, Colbert, then secretary to Mazarin, proposed the names of Le Muet, Mansart, and Louis Le Vau as candidates for undertaking the design of the new buildings of the Château de Vincennes. Mazarin chose Le Vau. Le Muet was undoubtedly too *retardataire* and Mansart seems to have aroused the displeasure of the cardinal in 1646 when he was dismissed from the Hôtel Mazarin. Colbert, however, did not suggest Le Pautre, perhaps because of his youth, the bad politics of his brother Jean (see n. 2), Antoine's professional association with the Jansenists (see Chapter 1), or the style of the *Desseins de plusieurs palais*, which may have been too strong for Colbert. But we are left with mere speculation concerning this matter. See J. Cordey, "Colbert, Le Vau et la construction du Château de Vincennes au XVIIᵉ siècle," *GBA*, s. 6, IX (1933), p. 274.

41. The first Italian opera produced in Paris was Sacrati's *Finta pazza* (1645) with machine effects by Torelli. See M. F. Bukofzer, *Music in the Baroque Era from Monteverdi to Bach* (New York, 1947), pp. 147–149; V. L. Tapié, *The Age of Grandeur* (London, 1960), pp. 87–92; P. Bjurström, *Giacomo Torelli and Baroque Stage Design* (Stockholm, 1961), pp. 115ff.

42. The Theatines were invited to France by Mazarin in 1644. Money from Mazarin's will paid for Guarini's Sainte-Anne-la-Royale (begun 1662), but it is problematical whether Mazarin (who died in 1661) had any influence concerning the choice of architect. See D. R. Coffin, "Padre Guarino Guarini in Paris," *JSAH*, XV (1956), pp. 3–11. It is interesting

There can be no doubt, then, that Mazarin directly encouraged the mid-century period of Italian Baroque influence, which was particularly evident in the fields of architecture and architectural decoration.[43] Then, too, Antoine's brother, Jean, had probably been in Rome during the early 1640's and had experienced at first hand the throbbing artistic atmosphere of the developing Baroque capital. These factors give us some understanding of the context in which Antoine worked, and the *Desseins* and the monuments to be discussed in the ensuing chapters reveal his new language of Baroque form.

to note that although Mazarin purchased two of Poussin's early masterpieces (*Inspiration of the Poet* in the Louvre; *Diana and Endymion* in Detroit), he did not patronize the painter during his later, more

classical period (Haskell, *op. cit.*, pp. 180–181).

43. F. Kimball, *The Creation of the Rococo* (Philadelphia, 1943), pp. 11ff.; Hautecoeur, II, i, p. 227–248. See also Tapié, *op. cit.*, pp. 69–160.

4

Saint-Laurent: Choir Decoration

In 1654 Le Pautre was called upon to refashion the choir of Saint-Laurent, a fifteenth century Flamboyant Gothic church in Paris.[1] The architect declined to design in the older style or in a spirit of compromise with it; instead, he treated the choir in his newly formed Baroque style, which forms a vivid contrast to the older work.[2] This church, as well as the Hôtel de Beauvais (also designed in 1654), provided Le Pautre with the first opportunities to work in his new manner after publication of the *Desseins de plusieurs palais.*

1. Saint-Laurent was constructed during the first quarter of the fifteenth century; the choir was dedicated in 1429 (M. Dumolin and G. Outardel, *Les églises de France: Paris et la Seine* [Paris, 1936], p. 79).

A document dated March 31, 1654 names Le Pautre as the designer of the new main altar (AN, LL 815, fol. 13); the appearance of the original altar of 1442 which Le Pautre's replaced is not known (L. Brochard, *Histoire de la paroisse et de l'église Saint-Laurent à Paris* [Paris, 1923], p. 154).

Modern writers have given Le Pautre responsibility for the entire decoration of the choir, and this is clearly supported by the internal, stylistic evidence provided by this extant composition. See *Inventaire général des richesses d'art de la France. Paris: monuments religieux,* I (Paris, 1876), p. 49; Brochard, *op. cit.,* pp. 154ff., 181–182; G. Huisman, *Pour comprendre les monuments de Paris* (Paris, 1925), pp. 179–180;

Dumolin and Outardel, *op. cit.,* pp. 81–82; Y. Christ, *Églises parisiennes* (Paris, 1947), p. 41; A. Boinet, *Les églises parisiennes: Moyen-Age et Renaissance* (Paris, 1958), pp. 312–313, 315–316.

François Blondel is sometimes linked with Le Pautre as co-designer of the decoration. There is absolutely no foundation for this assertion.

Saint-Laurent was Antoine's parish church. He was married there in 1648 (A. Jal, *Dictionnaire critique de biographie et d'histoire,* 2d ed. [Paris, 1872], p. 773) and baptized two of his children in the church (Laborde, nouv. acq. franç. 12141, nos. 42.353 and 42.354).

2. Transept and nave vaults, fully in the Gothic style, were erected in 1654/55–59, but there is no evidence that Le Pautre was involved in this work (see Brochard, *op. cit.,* p. 151). Dumolin and Outardel (*op. cit.,* p. 82) have pointed to some small details

Le Pautre replaced the pointed and broadly spaced arches of the fifteenth century with dense, sculptural forms, which effectively block any possibility of visual penetration through the arcade of the rear of the choir into the ambulatory beyond (Figs. 42, 43). Only by lifting his eyes to the stained glass above can the spectator glimpse the exterior luminosity beyond the architecture of the church. This treatment is very unusual in France and virtually unknown in Paris. For example, all of the extant Parisian churches with complete ambulatories erected during the sixteenth and seventeenth centuries permit views through the choir into the ambulatory, whether the choir supports consist of Gothic piers (as in Saint-Eustache) or classical ones (as in Saint-Nicolas du Chardonnet).[3] But at Saint-Laurent this tradition was violated. Gothic practice favored this vista of penetration, which is an additional manifestation of the diaphanous quality of Gothic architecture.

It is significant that this Gothic principle of "dégagement," which emphasized views through the rows of interior supports to spaces beyond, came to be specifically cited as a quality to be abstracted from Gothic buildings in order to be embodied in modern (i.e., seventeenth and eighteenth century) architecture. The late seventeenth and eighteenth century writers who called for this process of abstraction and reutilization of Gothic architectural ideas were responsive to Gothic aesthetic qualities and sympathetic to many features of this older style.[4] It is evident that Le Pautre was not similarly disposed towards the great medieval style; not only did he design forms which speak an entirely different language in themselves, but he violently interfered with a spatial effect which had survived the Gothic period and which was subsequently praised by French theoreticians.

The altar (baldachin) which Le Pautre designed is no longer extant, but is known to us through an early eighteenth century engraving (Fig. 42).[5] It consisted of four

which they attribute to Le Pautre: "Le double bandeau qui coupe les supports au-dessous de la naissance des voûtes date des enjolivements de 1654, comme les ornements ajoutés sous les clefs circulaires des voûtes." Also at this time (according to these writers), the mullions were removed from the high windows. The molding, consisting of a double band, is placed so as to suggest a capital and to negate the Flamboyant effect in which the ribs penetrate directly into the shafts without encountering any horizontal feature. This is a very interesting detail. If it is indeed by Le Pautre, it demonstrates his negative attitude towards this Flamboyant form, which strongly accentuates vertical continuities. However, not all of the shafts of the choir have this feature.

3. Extant sixteenth and seventeenth century Parisian churches with complete ambulatories around their choirs: Saint-Étienne du Mont (1492–1626), Saint-Eustache (1532–1637), Sainte-Élisabeth (1628–30), Saint-Jacques du Haut-Pas (1630–84), Saint-Roch (1653–1736), Saint-Sulpice (1655–1777), Saint-Nicolas du Chardonnet (1656–1763), Saint-Louis-en-l'Ile (1664–1726). In Saint-Étienne du Mont the choir screen (ca. 1545) does not interfere with this view because of its height.

Fig. 42 shows grilles filling the arches to the right and left rear of the choir of Saint-Laurent; today these arches are walled up and decorated with wreaths and palm branches (see Fig. 43). Even if Fig. 42 reflects the original arrangement, it is evident that a spectator would not have been able to glimpse the ambulatory due to the curvature of the choir and the adjacent piers which effectively block out these arches when they are viewed from the nave.

4. See W. Herrmann, *Laugier and Eighteenth Century French Theory* (London, 1962), pp. 91ff.; R. D. Middleton, "The Abbé de Cordemoy and the Graeco-Gothic Ideal: A Prelude to Romantic Classicism–Part I," *JWarb*, xxv (1962), pp. 278–320; *idem*, "The Abbé de Cordemoy and the Graeco-Gothic Ideal–Part II," *JWarb*, xxvi (1963), pp. 90–123.

5. The altar disappeared ca. 1800 (*Inventaire général . . .* , I, p. 45). The existing central motif of the choir—a pedimented entablature supported by two Corinthian pilasters—is a nineteenth century replacement of the original baldachin.

Brochard (*op. cit.*, p. 155) points out that the scenes depicted above the portals in Fig. 42 were tapestries, and that portraits filled the medallions above the doors (replaced at an undetermined date by the initials of Saint Laurence).

Corinthian columns on high pedestals which supported an entablature and triangular pediment. This construction formed a baldachin for a sculptural group representing the Resurrection, the work of Gilles Guérin (1606–78).[6]

Le Pautre conceived of the choir decoration as a twofold system: first, the central, pedimented baldachin with the Resurrection group as the focus, extending higher than the surrounding features due to the high pedestals on which its columns rested; second, a complex sequence of wall decoration which follows the contours of the choir and wraps around the central baldachin. In both parts of the composition, Antoine used a Corinthian order but omitted the frieze and greatly emphasized the dentils of the cornice. The treatment of the dentils creates an insistent staccato effect, paralleled by the use of the consoles in the ground floor frieze of the courtyard of the Hôtel de Beauvais (Fig. 55); both are examples of Baroque boldness and exaggeration in the handling of details.

Le Pautre begins the sequence of wall decoration with portals (Fig. 44). The actual door frames are of conventional form and are surmounted by wreathed medallions which enclose the portraits of saints (now replaced by the initials of Saint Laurence). But these features are included within a rich composition consisting of pilasters and quarter-columns, supporting an entablature and segmental pediment. The prominent dentils are carried into the pediment, the field of which is filled with a cherubim's head, a cartouche, and festoons.[7] The portals are linked to the rear of the choir by narrow bays (Fig. 44) — architectural bridge passages — which continue the truncated entablatures, here surmounted by small, unmolded semicircular arches cut into the thickness of the wall, and filled with shells. These narrow bays lead to the rear, curved portions of the choir. Here, Le Pautre was able to create a broad, Baroque contrast of concave wall decoration played off against the dominating baldachin. Above the curved sections, the architect placed the richest part of the decoration (Fig. 45): rectangular panels, filled with ecclesiastical symbols,[8] are framed by very vigorous, projecting moldings with cherubims' heads at the summits. The panels are placed on blocks, the curvatures of which are emphasized by the broken crowning cornices. Volutes decorated with acanthus frame these panels, and heavy festoons hang down from above; piles of shells and leaves surmount the design.

In these panels in particular, Le Pautre put into practice decorative ideas which he enunciated two years before in the *Desseins de plusieurs palais*. The moldings and decorative forms display the plasticity, richness, and fantasy that one finds in the ceiling designs published in the *Desseins* (Figs. 45, 46).

6. L. Dussieux *et al.*, eds., *Mémoires inédits sur la vie et les ouvrages des membres de l'Académie royale de peinture et de sculpture*, I (Paris, 1854), p. 265. The north and south transepts of Saint-Laurent contain identical bas-reliefs which depict angels holding wreathed medallions which enclose the initials of Saint Laurence. The *Inventaire général* . . . , I, p. 49, attributes these reliefs to the campaign of Le Pautre and hence to Guérin. Brochard (*op. cit.*, p. 181) tends to believe that the reliefs are posterior to Le Pautre's activity. The quality of these reliefs is not equal to that of Guérin's known works, and hence I do not believe that they can be attributed to him. Guérin lived in the parish of Saint-Laurent and was buried in the church in 1678.

7. It is interesting to compare this portal composition to Roland Fréart de Chambray's account of how a modern architect of corrupt taste would redesign the tabernacles within the Roman Pantheon (*Parallèle de l'architecture antique et de la moderne* [Paris, 1650], p. 82, pl. p. 83).

8. These include an aureole, a Bible, and three Papal symbols: the tiara, the keys, and the triple cross.

5
Hôtel de Beauvais

The Hôtel de Beauvais in the rue Saint-Antoine (now the rue François-Miron) in Paris was attributed to Antoine Le Pautre by numerous seventeenth and eighteenth century topographical and architectural writers.[1] The *hôtel* was built for Catherine Henriette Bellier, *première femme de chambre* to Anne of Austria, and wife, since 1634, of Pierre Beauvais, a ribbon merchant.[2] This ugly and lascivious woman bears the delicate distinction of having provided the young Louis XIV with his first hetero-sexual experience. This incident probably took place in 1654, and since the economic fortunes of Madame de Beauvais rapidly rose from that year on, we may safely con-clude that her adventure with the King immediately redounded to her own advan-tage.[3] In 1654, she acquired the site of her future residence.[4] On December 23, 1654, the Bureau des Finances granted permission to Pierre Beauvais to construct three boldly projecting balconies for "la maison rue Saint-Antoine, dans la longueur du mur de façade sur la rue."[5] Since Beauvais's application was accompanied by plans

1. G. Brice, *Description nouvelle de ce qu'il y a de plus remarquable dans la ville de Paris*, 2d ed., I (Paris, 1694), p. 169; F. Le Comte, *Cabinet des singularitez d'architecture, peinture, sculpture, et gravure*, I (Paris, 1699), "Sommaire historique d'archi-tecture et des architectes" (unpaginated); G. L. Le Rouge, *Les curiositez de Paris, de Versailles, de Marly, de Vincennes, de S. Cloud, et des environs*, I (Am-sterdam, 1718), p. 166; A. N. Dezallier d'Argenville, *Voyage pictoresque de Paris* (Paris, 1749), p. 157; J. F. Blondel, *Architecture françoise*, II (Paris, 1752), p. 121; A. C. d'Aviler, *Dictionnaire d'architecture*, new ed. (Paris, 1755), p. 173; P. de Chennevières and A. de

Montaiglon, eds., *Abécédario de P. J. Mariette . . .* ("Archives de l'art français," VI), III (Paris, 1854–56), p. 182; A. N. Dezallier d'Argenville, *Vies des fameux architectes depuis la renaissance des arts . . .* (Paris, 1787), p. 396. The address: 68, rue François-Miron.

2. On Madame de Beauvais see J. Cousin, *L'hôtel de Beauvais: rue Saint-Antoine* (Paris, 1864).

3. *Ibid.*, p. 16.

4. *Ibid.* The main owner of this site and two of its medieval houses was the Surintendant des Fi-nances, Nicolas Fouquet (*ibid.*, pp. 18–19).

5. See n. 17. As indicated in *ibid.*, p. 16 n. 2, Cousin had access to the original documents concern-

of these balconies, we may conclude that Le Pautre designed the building during that year. Construction was evidently begun at the very end of 1654 or during 1655, and was finished not before 1657, because in that year Nicolas Legendre and Pierre Hutinot undertook the façade sculpture.[6] The site lay within the Marais district, which during the seventeenth century was one of the richest and most fashionable residential areas of Paris.

The property acquired by Catherine was occupied by three medieval houses.[7] These were demolished to make way for the new construction, but their foundations were reutilized in a special way which will shortly be analyzed. In order to secure building materials, Catherine actually succeeded in persuading Anne of Austria to make an outright grant to her of a large quantity of stone originally intended for the Louvre.[8] Thus, Le Pautre had at his disposal the finest French materials. Madame de Beauvais repaid her patroness by authorizing a program of façade sculpture that glorified the Queen Mother.

Le Pautre not only preserved the medieval foundations; he exploited them. Like Leonardo gazing at stains on a wall for the suggestion of new forms, Le Pautre must have let the outlines of these foundations speak and suggest the design of the superstructure. A survey of the medieval foundations taken by Du Seigneur[9] reveals that several important features of the ground plan were directly inspired by the underlying structures: the placement of the *corps-de-logis* along the street front, the circular vestibule, the passage from the court to the rue de Jouy, the semicircular ending of the court, and the stair at the left rear of the court (cf. Figs. 47, 49). But if these foundations suggested elements of the plan, they did not dictate it, and Le Pautre's brilliant achievement in producing this plan to fit the difficult site between the rue Saint-Antoine and the rue de Jouy represents a triumph of the architectural imagination.[10]

As Gurlitt has noted, the plan had no precedent in the history of architecture.[11] Nevertheless, its component features can be analyzed in terms of architectural tradition, along with the elevations.

The placement of the *corps-de-logis* on the street front instead of at the rear of

ing the Hôtel de Beauvais, which in 1864 were in the possession of the proprietor, M. Adolphe Jouet. Cousin published résumés of some of these documents (*ibid.*, pp. 73ff.), but they were never consulted by later writers, and my own efforts to locate them have been fruitless. On the dating of the Hôtel de Beauvais see *ibid.*, pp. 16–25.

6. See n. 20.

7. Cousin, *op. cit.*, pp. 16ff.

8. This incident is reported in P. Bonnefon, ed., *Mémoires de Louis-Henri de Loménie, comte de Brienne dit le jeune Brienne*, II (Paris, 1917), pp. 8–9. This incident greatly angered Mazarin and may have contributed to his feelings against the Le Pautre brothers (see Chapter 3, n. 2).

9. M. Du Seigneur, "L'hôtel de Beauvais," *La construction moderne* (1886), pp. 378–379 and pl.

61; see also Cousin, *op. cit.*, p. 22. It is not possible to adequately explore the *caves* today because of the blocking of numerous passages.

10. J. F. Blondel, *Cours d'architecture*, III (Paris, 1772), p. 445: ". . . le Plan distribué dans un terrein fort irrégulier, laisse voir ce que peut le génie d'un homme de mérite, lorsqu'au vrai talent de l'Architecture, il fait joindre le raisonnement & le goût de son Art." The plans of the ground floor and the first floor, by Jean Marot (Figs. 47, 48), are accurate insofar as they can be verified by the existing structures. Marot's plans provide our only knowledge of the interior room distribution, which was disturbed as early as 1706 (see n. 27).

11. C. Gurlitt, *Geschichte des Barockstiles, des Rococo und des Klassicismus in Belgien, Holland, Frankreich, England* (Stuttgart, 1888), p. 131.

the court is unusual in France in the case of a great *hôtel,* but is by no means un-known. As Hautecoeur has pointed out, this arrangement was common in modest buildings, but also appeared in a number of important seventeenth century Parisian *hôtels.*[12] More unexpected, however, are the four shops which occupy the *rez-de-chaussée* (Figs. 47, 50, 52). The coupling of a private residence with public shops is a survival of the ancient Roman *insulae* with *tabernae,* and Le Pautre's use of mez-zanine windows over these shops is again fully within this ancient tradition, which had been very much alive during the late Quattrocento in Tuscany and the High Renaissance in Rome.[13] In Paris, this practice was relatively rare, but an important model was provided by the houses of the Place Dauphine (begun 1607), which Le Pautre also drew upon for the A–b–A rhythm of the lateral ranges of his *rez-de-chaussée.*[14]

Like many other French *hôtel* façades of the seventeenth century, the façade of the Hôtel de Beauvais (Figs. 50, 52) has no orders, depending instead upon vertical strips of channeled rustication and horizontal moldings to define the major lines of articulation.[15] Le Pautre's solution for the entrance portal is noteworthy. By con-tinuing the channeled strips through the attic floor, the architect allows the portal composition to be read in three ways: as extending through the entire height of the façade, as extending through the *premier étage* (in which case it is crowned by the triangular pediment and frames the entrance arch and the central window of the main floor), or as reaching only through the *rez-de-chaussée* and framing the en-trance arch alone. In this way, Le Pautre has designed a large unit which is satis-factorily proportioned to the entire expanse of the façade, but which can be sub-divided by the eye to relate to the smaller divisions.[16]

The central balcony is built on a *trompe,* and so daring was its degree of pro-jection into space that, as noted previously, Pierre Beauvais had to obtain special permission from the Bureau des Finances to allow its construction.[17] Although the rue Saint-Antoine was one of the wider streets of mid-seventeenth century Paris, the aggressive, sculptural effect of this *trompe,* moving out into space, would not have been lost on visitors traveling along the street. The lateral windows of the main

12. Hautecoeur, II, i, p. 181.

13. On the use of shops and mezzanines in Ital-ian Renaissance architecture see H. Hibbard, "The Architecture of the Palazzo Borghese," *Memoirs of the American Academy in Rome,* XXVII (1962), pp. 17ff. with bibliography; A. Boëthius, *The Golden House of Nero: Some Aspects of Roman Architecture* (Ann Arbor, 1960), pp. 129ff.

14. Noted by J. P. Babelon, *Demeures parisi-ennes sous Henri IV et Louis XIII* (Paris, 1965), p. 90. For other Parisian examples of *bottega* design pre-dating the Hôtel de Beauvais see *ibid.*

Marot's plan (Fig. 47) indicates that a shop was also located on the rue de Jouy. Blondel specifically praised Le Pautre's solution as beneficent for the gen-eral life of a city (*Architecture françoise,* II, p. 122).

15. See Blondel, *Cours d'architecture,* III, p.

446 for a passage extolling this aspect of the façade.

16. On this problem see Hibbard, *op. cit.,* pp. 19–21. See also Blondel, *Architecture françoise,* II, p. 123; *idem, Cours d'architecture,* III, pp. 446–447.

17. Cousin, *op. cit.,* p. 77: "23 décembre [1654] —Sentence du bureau des finances qui permet au sieur de Beauvais de faire construire, à ses frais et dépens, un balcon qui sera élevé jusqu'au premier étage de la maison rue Saint-Antoine, dans la longueur du mur de façade sur la rue, lequel aura 11 pieds ½ de long sur 4 pieds d'avance sur la rue; ainsi que deux autres balcons aux deux côtés de la dite maison. Le tout conformément au plan figuré cy-après.—Plan figuré des dits balcons, signé et paraphé *ne varietur.*" On this *trompe* see Blondel, *Architecture françoise,* II, p. 123; *idem, Cours d'architecture,* III, p. 447.

floor also have their individual balconies and balustrades, but these are not built on *trompes;* the central windows of each group of three are accentuated by balconies of bolder projection, consoles, entablatures with brackets, and sculptural decoration.[18] By placing these windows over the minor openings below (narrow shop entrances and mezzanines), Le Pautre complicated the façade rhythms and upset the vertical correspondences. In the upper reaches of the elevation, repose was restored by the equal accents of attic and dormer windows, held together by the unifying roof. It must be noted, however, that whereas the ground floor openings faithfully reflect the spaces behind (shops, shop entrances, main entrance), those on the first floor do so only partially: the group of three windows at the left corresponds to the *grande salle*, but no such arrangement can be found on the right. The symmetry of the façade composition is not realized in the room arrangement behind, and this flexible approach to design is reflected in the plans of the ground and first floors (Figs. 47, 48), which go their own ways with a minimum of vertical correspondence.[19]

The entire sculptural program of this façade was a glorification of Madame de Beauvais's patroness, Anne of Austria: the Victories on the central pediment displayed her heraldic emblems, her portrait was enclosed by a medallion held by putti on the surface of the *trompe,* and the baskets of fruit over the lateral windows of the *premier étage* undoubtedly alluded to Anne's fertility in having given birth to Louis XIV.[20] Hence it was most appropriate for the Queen Mother to have occupied the central balcony during the procession of Louis and Marie-Thérèse on August 26, 1660.[21]

A drawing in Stockholm, which is an elevation of Le Pautre's façade (Fig. 51),[22] is highly finished except for the roof; its bare outlines are faintly indicated in pencil. Although quite close to the definitive version (Fig. 50), it differs from it significantly in several details: the Victories on the pediment are posed differently, the lateral windows of the *premier étage* bear military trophies as sculptural adornment, the *rez-de-chaussée* contains arched openings instead of square shop openings with semicircular mezzanines above, only three *mascarons* are indicated instead of seven, and, most important, only two of the lateral windows of the main floor have balconies,

---

18. See *ibid.,* pp. 447–449.

19. The latter point is noted in Blunt, 1957, p. 139.

20. The iconography is explained by Guillet de Saint-Georges; see L. Dussieux *et al.,* eds., *Mémoires inédits sur la vie et les ouvrages des membres de l'Académie royale de peinture et de sculpture,* I (Paris, 1854), pp. 410–411. The two large Victories were the work of Nicolas Legendre (1657), who also sculpted the decoration over the two lateral windows of the first floor. He was assisted by Pierre Hutinot. See also Cousin, *op. cit.,* pp. 24–25.

The pediment with cartouche is very similar to the one in Fig. 36 (from the *Desseins de plusieurs palais*).

21. Cousin (*op. cit.,* p. 26) notes that Marot's prints show the pediment-cartouche filled with the arms of France and Navarre. This was probably a temporary alteration on the occasion of the royal entry. On this entry see the *Gazette de France,* September 3,

1660, pp. 785–816; J. Marot, *Histoire de la triomphante entrée du roy et de la reyne dans Paris le 26. d'aoust, 1660* . . . (Paris, 1665); G. Mourey, *Le livre des fêtes françaises* (Paris, 1930), pp. 131–134; V. L. Tapié, *The Age of Grandeur* (New York, 1960), pp. 94–102. On June 5, 1662, the Hôtel de Beauvais was again used for a carrousel in honor of the birth of the Dauphin (Mourey, *op. cit.,* pp. 134–142).

The plan of the Hôtel de Beauvais necessitated the placement of the entrance portal slightly to the right of the central vertical axis of the façade. Le Pautre skillfully adjusted for this factor by designing symmetrically around the portal and masking the narrow excess strip of façade on the left by setting it back slightly from the line of the façade. This detail was noted by Blondel, who recommended Antoine's solution as a model for this type of difficulty (*Architecture françoise,* II, p. 123).

22. Stockholm, Nationalmuseum, THC 6513.

instead of all six.[23] It is difficult to understand these deviations from the executed building unless the drawing is, indeed, a preparatory study by Le Pautre himself, or at least from the hand of an assistant. In this respect, it is essential to recall that the license granted by the Bureau des Finances on December 23, 1654 specifically mentioned only two balconies on the *premier étage*, aside from the central one.[24] This may have been because only two of the six lateral balconies subsequently built projected farther than the others.[25] On the other hand, the Stockholm drawing may depict the state of the façade design in December, 1654, a design which only envisaged three balconies *in toto*. The presence of military trophies is puzzling until one notes their presence in the executed decoration of the stair cage (Fig. 63). Thus, Le Pautre may have indicated them as a conventional form of decoration before the specific sculptural program to the glory of Anne of Austria was conceived, but afterwards retained the motif in the stair.[26] Noteworthy is the indication of the play of light and shade on the façade, particularly on the curve of the *trompe*. The Victories are rendered with broad freedom in a thoroughly Baroque, pictorial style.[27]

The visitor makes his way into the building via a long barrel-vaulted passage which presents a slightly ascending slope.[28] This leads to the flat-ceiled circular vestibule, the perimeter of which is defined by six Doric columns placed on tall pedestals. Although circular vestibules had been used in French architecture before,[29] Le Pautre's scheme broke decisively with tradition by the manner in which the vestibule projects into the space of the court, thereby creating a fluid and dynamic relationship between vestibule space and courtyard space. Steps lead from the vestibule, those on the left to the main staircase, those on the right to the kitchen and service areas. These stairs are of a singular, undulating plan, directly based on those in Mansart's Church of the Visitation, Paris (1632–34)—a plan which suggests movement, and hence appealing to a Baroque-minded architect.[30]

23. In addition, the cartouche in the pediment is of a different form, the portrait-medallion is not held by putti, and the strip of façade on the left is not indicated.

24. See n. 17.

25. In this respect we note that Brice (*op. cit.*, I, p. 168) describes the façade as adorned with *three* balconies.

26. Military trophies also appear in the trefoil vestibule of the Third Design from the *Desseins de plusieurs palais* (Fig. 26) and in the courtyard elevation of the Fifth Design (Fig. 36, end bays).

27. The actual entrance doors are superb examples of seventeenth century *menuiserie* (Fig. 53). These doors are slightly concave, in response to the convexity of the balcony above. According to Cousin (*op. cit.*, p. 24), an eagle with outstretched wings was replaced by the cartouche which bears the house number (not shown in Fig. 53), probably in 1706; the claws of the eagle still remain, resting upon the swag in the tympanum (*ibid.*). A similarly posed eagle still remains in the stair cage (Fig. 61). Both may refer to Louis XIV (see n. 36). The bucrania prepare the visitor for the rams' heads within the building, just as the

scales and triglyphs of the *trumeau* hint at details of the ground floor of the court.

On the subsequent changes which the building underwent in 1706, see Cousin, *op. cit.*, pp. 46–48; Estampes, Va 249c.

28. The long entrance corridor to a rear court can be found in Roman High Renaissance architecture: e.g., Peruzzi's Palazzo Massimi (begun 1535); designs by Antonio da Sangallo the Younger, particularly a plan for his house in the via Giulia (G. Giovannoni, *Antonio da Sangallo il Giovane*, II [Rome, n.d.], fig. 311). This bears additional relationships to the Hôtel de Beauvais in that the court terminates in an apse and there is a spiral stair in the left rear of the court.

29. Cf., e.g., the vestibule in Louis Le Vau's own house in Paris (3, quai d'Anjou; 1640–42) and that in the Luxembourg Palace. Blondel juxtaposed the plan of the latter vestibule with Le Pautre's, thus indicating the identical paired spacing of the columns (Blondel, *Cours d'architecture*, IV, pl. XXXIX).

30. Today the steps on the right are straight as a result of a subsequent alteration. Antoine had indicated this type of stair in the *Desseins de plusieurs palais* (Figs. 28, 38).

The plan of the courtyard is extraordinary due to the convergence of the sides which lead to the broad semicircular apsidal ending. There was no precedent in *hôtel* design for converging court walls, but Le Pautre could have drawn upon a convenient Parisian landmark, the Place Dauphine (begun 1607), for inspiration. Standing at the base of the triangular space that was the Place Dauphine, the spectator's attention would have been forcefully led by the converging sides towards the open space at the apex, permitting a view of the equestrian statue of Henri IV.[31] Similarly, at the Hôtel de Beauvais, the lateral walls concentrate the visitor's focus upon the hemicycle and, specifically, the Ionic portico behind which the chapel was located (Figs. 48, 55). Behind the conceptions of the Place Dauphine and the Hôtel de Beauvais lay the tradition of Renaissance and Baroque scenography, which often drew upon the device of converging lateral walls to concentrate attention upon a distant object.[32]

The concave termination of the court had forerunners at the Château de Grosbois (ca. 1600) and the Stable Court at Fountainebleau (Rémy Collin, 1609), both of which may be dependent on a design of the elder du Cerceau.[33] But the artistic value of the conception resides not in these possible links with earlier monuments but in the synthesis of the apsidal ending with the converging lateral walls, and the powerful effect of this termination which echoes and amplifies the intrusion of the circular vestibule into the space of the courtyard. It is as if the space contained within the court were endowed with a wall-shaping power: when disturbed by the outward protrusion of the vestibule, the space responded by pushing back towards the rear of the court, molding the walls with a magnified intensity and pressure.[34]

The courtyard elevations (Figs. 55, 56) have been seriously disturbed, but the *rez-de-chaussée* is apparently intact, and the disposition of the upper floors can be seen in Du Seigneur's reconstructions (Figs. 58, 59).[35] The Doric columnar order of the circular vestibule is transformed, through the transitional device of flanking Doric pilasters, into a progression of channeled piers which continue around the perimeter

31. On another relationship between the Hôtel de Beauvais and the Place Dauphine, see. p. 39.

32. It is important, in this context, to recall that Italian opera, stagecraft, and scenography flourished in Paris from 1645 on under Mazarin's sponsorship. See Tapié, *op. cit.*, pp. 87ff.; P. Bjurström, *Giacomo Torelli and Baroque Stage Design* (Stockholm, 1961), pp. 115ff.

It is interesting to note that the courtyard of the Hôtel de Beauvais has certain affinities with one of Torelli's stage sets (set for *Bellerofonte*, Venice, 1642; reproduced in *ibid.*, p. 62, top). Common features include converging lateral walls leading to a focal hemicycle, rusticated ground floor piers, a heavy entablature in the hemicycle, an aedicular structure over the hemicycle, freestanding columns on the first story of the hemicycle, and stairs at the rear of the court. Torelli's set depicts a palace courtyard.

33. J. A. du Cerceau the Elder, *Livre d'architecture* (Paris, 1582), pl. VI. See Blunt, 1957, pp. 100, 257 n. 18.

34. The coach passage leads from the court and exits in the rue de Jouy; this type of solution was also used by Antoine at the Hôtel de Fontenay-Mareuil. See also Blondel, *Architecture françoise*, II, p. 123.

35. During the French Revolution a new owner, Maurin, destroyed the original fenestration in order to divide the first floor into two floors. The results of this mutilation are evident in the present condition of the court, but the interrupted entablatures of the *corps-de-logis* and the first two bays of the lateral walls are original and are not the results of the addition of an intermediate upper floor. Hautecoeur is in error in assuming that Le Pautre designed the intermediate floor (II, i, p. 150). See Cousin, *op. cit.*, p. 63; and below, n. 39. Maurin's alterations are also evident in the street façade (cf. Figs. 50, 52).

of the court. These piers recall the channeled strips of the façade, but their column-like proportions render a heavier effect, and in the hemicycle of the court the piers are revealed as possessing depth, thus accentuating the feeling of weight and support. Shell-headed niches on the lateral walls are surrounded by vigorous channeling, and the entire *rez-de-chaussée* is powerfully unified by a continuous series of heavy, scale-encrusted consoles in the frieze of the entablature. Only on the entablature of the vestibule do the traditional Doric metopes and triglyphs appear. The sculptural and chromatic values created by the consoles are enhanced on the *corps-de-logis* by the insertion between the consoles of sculpted rams' and lions' heads,[36] the former alluding to Madame de Beauvais (Catherine Bellier [bélier = ram]) (Fig. 57).[37] This massive, sculptural entablature effectively demarcates the ground floor from the stories above. In this courtyard design, Antoine used a rusticated, sculptural elevation to serve as a secure podium for the more lightly articulated superstructure, a system which he first adopted in his *Desseins de plusieurs palais*.[38]

The *premier étage* is defined by a sequence of Ionic pilasters; Corinthian pilasters are used for the second floor, which is limited to the *corps-de-logis* and the first two bays of each of the lateral walls of the court. It is important to note that Antoine discontinued the Ionic entablature on these façades so that the vertical continuity between the two stories would be accentuated.[39] The fragments of interrupted entablature, thus created, produce a disquieting, Mannerist effect.[40]

The curve of the circular vestibule is carried through the entire elevation, forming a striking convex mass emerging from the wall of the *corps-de-logis*. Opposite this is the chapel, the focus of the entire court. It is prefaced by a portico of two Ionic freestanding columns bearing a straight entablature, reminiscent of Le Pautre's intended portico for the Chapelle de Port-Royal.[41]

---

36. J. Hillairet (*Connaissance du vieux Paris: rive droite* [Paris, 1963], p. 67) surmises that the lions' heads may symbolize Louis XIV. See also n. 27 and 49.

37. Four of these heads also appear on the entablature of the circular vestibule. Its remaining metopes are filled with rams' heads in bas-relief and the monogram PCHB (intertwined), standing for Pierre Beauvais and Catherine Henriette Bellier (Cousin, *op. cit.*, p. 27). In the stair cage this monogram appears, surmounted by a baron's crown; Pierre Beauvais received the title of baron about 1654 (*ibid.*, p. 16). Le Pautre's use of animal heads is an adaptation of classical bucrania to the demands of contemporary symbolism.

Concerning the *mascarons* of the hemicycle, Du Seigneur surmises (*op. cit.*, p. 391): "On suppose que la seconde tête à gauche pourrait bien être le portrait de Mme de Beauvais, et la tête d'homme surmontant l'entrée du petit escalier ovale, celle de noble homme Pierre de Beauvais." This cannot be confirmed because there are no known portraits of the Beauvais.

38. Cf. especially Figs. 36, 37. Oval windows,

used in the hemicycle of the Hôtel de Beauvais, also appear in these designs.

39. This is the present condition of these orders, and Du Seigneur indicated the same system in his reconstruction. The entablatures break back smoothly to the wall without any indication of having been subsequently mutilated for the addition of the intermediate upper floor (see n. 35).

40. Blondel, *Architecture françoise*, II, p. 123: "La décoration des bâtimens de cette cour est un peu trop tourmentée. . . ." It is questionable to what extent the dormer windows overlooking the court reflect the original design.

41. The present construction above this entablature is a modern intrusion. Du Seigneur has indicated a small lantern, very similar to the one covering the chapel in a *hôtel* design from the *Desseins de plusieurs palais* (Figs. 37, 59). The placement of the chapel in this location was a radical break with the architect's earlier practice of placing it over the entrance (Hôtel de Fontenay-Mareuil, Third and Fifth Designs).

It was J. F. Blondel who first called attention to the unusual visual effect granted to the spectator who stands within the entrance passage of the Hôtel de Beauvais and peers past the vestibule into the court:

> . . . de l'entrée de ce porche . . . l'on jouit peut être du plus beau coup d'oeil qu'il soit possible d'imaginer par l'aspect de l'Architecture qui décore le fond de la cour au premier étage. Comme cet étage se trouve rétreci par l'obliquité des murs collatéraux de cette même cour, & orné dans son pourtour de colonnes, de pilastres, & de membres d'Architecture distribués avec beaucoup de goût, cet assemblage forme une perspective réelle au-dessus de toute description. . . . le coup d'oeil dont je veux parler, . . . mérite a bon droit d'être examiné sur le lieu. C'est pourquoi j'y renvoye expressément nos jeunes Dessinateurs & Peintres d'Architecture, tant pour leur faire connoître le pouvoir de l'optique & l'effet que produit le clair obscur, que pour leur apprendre à rendre la vérité des tons, des lumieres, des teintes & des ombres.[42]

Despite the mutilations which the building has suffered, this effect can still be enjoyed thoroughly today (Fig. 54). In this view, the columns of the vestibule stand as dark objects boldly silhouetted against the back cloth of the court. Le Pautre has brilliantly succeeded in creating a purely scenographic and chromatic effect rarely paralleled in French architecture.

The only part of the original interior that is extant is the stair cage.[43] From the circular vestibule the visitor passes through a portal to the stair on his left (Fig. 60). The sober Doric of the vestibule now modulates to the brilliant Corinthian order. Two pairs of freestanding columns serve as supports for the landing above (Figs. 61–63). Before ascending, the visitor is tempted to explore the small, niche-flanked areas placed beneath one of the flights on a direct line with the entrance portal. Here, a stone bench can be found for repose.[44] The straight flights ascend around a rectangular cage with an open well in the center, a type of stair used previously by the architect at the Hôtel de Fontenay-Mareuil. The visual environment is activated by a balustrade of unusual design, which consists of interlacing S-shape and reverse-curve segments of considerable complexity (Fig. 64).[45]

The rich sculptural decoration of the cage was executed by Martin Desjardins (1640–94),[46] but several modern writers have suspected the mind of Jean Le Pautre behind the design of the forms.[47] This is almost certainly the case because of the

42. Blondel, *Architecture françoise*, II, p. 122.

43. The interiors indicated by Du Seigneur are imaginary, as he himself notes (*op. cit.*, p. 391).

Cousin (*op. cit.*, p. 65 n. 1) wrote in 1864: "Nous avons parcouru les logements actuels de l'hôtel de Beauvais, et nous n'avons trouvé d'autre trace de son ancienne décoration, que quelques mètres de la corniche sculptée de la grande galerie, perdus aujourd'hui dans une cuisine en soupente. On y distingue encore, au milieu de rinceaux élégants, des enfants et des singes jouant de divers instruments de musique." This fragment no longer exists today.

44. Niches and stone benches were used by Le Pautre in the stair vestibule of his Hôtel de Fontenay-

Mareuil. See *Les oeuvres d'architecture d'Anthoine Le Pautre* (Paris, n.d.), p. 19.

45. Since the stair at the Hôtel de Fontenay-Mareuil was covered by a dome, it is open to question whether Antoine proceeded in like manner at the Hôtel de Beauvais. But the demolition of the interiors and the lack of evidence do not permit a solution.

Le Pautre's balustrade is closely related to Louis Le Vau's at the Hôtel Lambert. See also n. 48.

46. Dussieux *et al.*, eds., *op. cit.*, I, p. 387.

47. Cousin, *op. cit.*, p. 29; Du Seigneur, *op. cit.*, p. 379; J. Vacquier, *Les vieux hôtels de Paris. Le quartier Saint-Paul* (Paris, 1914), p. 10; Hautecoeur, II, i, pp. 315–316.

youthfulness of Desjardins at the time and because a comparison of many of the motifs with those of the Hôtel Lauzun (decorated at the same time [1656–57] by Jean Le Pautre) reveals very close similarities.[48] Here one meets the rich and exuberant Baroque decorative style of the elder brother, which heightens the effect of the Corinthian order. Here we are truly transported into the world of Jean's prints.[49]

The plan of the Hôtel de Beauvais is an outstanding example of the ingenuity and flexibility achieved by French seventeenth century architects in residential design. The distribution of rooms on the ground floor and the first floor, as indicated by Marot's prints (Figs. 47, 48), constituted an ingenious adaptation to the irregularities and constraints of the difficult site, and writers have unanimously applauded Le Pautre's brilliant adjustment of the rooms to the available space. Noteworthy features on the first floor were the passageways, the long gallery with apsidal ends, the hanging garden, the grotto and chapels (all of trefoil plan), and the terrace which encircled the court.[50]

In this building, the architect put into practice the new language of forms which he had first promulgated in the *Desseins de plusieurs palais* of 1652. In the Third Design (Fig. 24) we find specific features which recur at the Hôtel de Beauvais: the long entrance passage; the curved termination of the court, behind which is a room of trefoil plan (ground floor vestibule in Fig. 24; first floor chapel in the *hôtel*). As in the Third Design, we find in the Hôtel de Beauvais room shapes of non-rectangular form, with their attendant suggestions of spatial motion. A dynamic spatial sequence on the main floor, consisting of grand cabinet–gallery–chapel, is matched by the sequence, passageway–vestibule–court, the latter space of powerful, dynamic effect. The court elevation, with its massive, rusticated ground floor, renders that feeling for weight and mass which most directly relates Antoine's architecture of this period to contemporary Italian practice. The Hôtel de Beauvais is Le Pautre's masterpiece.[51]

48. The responsibility of Jean Le Pautre for the decoration of Louis Le Vau's Hôtel Lauzun was demonstrated by F. Kimball ("Authorship of the Decoration of the Hôtel Lauzun," *GBA*, s. 6, XLV [1955], pp. 45–52). The decorations were published by L. Dimier, *Le style Louis XIV: L'hôtel Lauzun* (Paris, 1912). Cf. the putti in his pls. 2–5, 21 to the putti of the Hôtel de Beauvais; his pl. 14 (rams' heads, female heads, garlands) to those of the Hôtel de Beauvais; his pl. 22 (interlace motif in niche) to the balustrade of the Hôtel de Beauvais. The last comparison suggests that Jean may have been responsible for the balustrade design. A variant of the pattern appears in one of his undated prints (*L'oeuvre de Lepautre*, IV [Paris, n.d.], pl. 342).

49. The eagle over the niche in the stair cage recalls the eagle which formerly adorned the entrance portal (see n. 27). Both may refer to Louis XIV (Cousin, *op. cit.*, p. 29 and Vacquier, *op. cit.*, p. 10).

50. The grotto of the Hôtel de Beauvais seems to be the first in France to have been integrated into the living quarters of a residence. Before this, grottos were either placed in gardens or in the basements and ground floors of buildings. In the plan of the *sous-sol* of the Fifth Design (from the *Desseins de plusieurs palais*), Le Pautre marked one room "Vestibule ou Grode."

Also noteworthy is the oval spiral stair at the left rear of the court which provided direct access to the chapel.

51. The Hôtel de Beauvais influenced Cottard's Hôtel Amelot de Bisseuil in Paris (1657–60; C. Sellier, *Anciens hôtels de Paris* [Paris, 1910], p. 103) and Fischer von Erlach's Trautson Palace in Vienna (begun 1710; H. Aurenhammer, *Johann Bernhard Fischer von Erlach* [Vienna, 1956], pp. 145ff.).

On the subsequent changes which altered the Hôtel de Beauvais, see n. 27.

Bernini visited the Hôtel de Beauvais on October 14, 1665, and Chantelou's account reveals Bernini's admiration for what he saw: "A la sortie de là l'on est allé chez Mme de Beauvais, qui a montré avec grand soin et plaisir sa maison au Cavalier. L'on est entré par un grand appartement que le Cavalier a dit être de belle proportion pour les largeurs et les hauteurs. Après, il a loué l'esprit de la maîtresse sur sa belle entente, distribution et dégagement de la maison. Du grand appartement l'on a passé dans la gallerie, au bout de laquelle est la chapelle, de là dans le jardin et puis dans la grande allée . . . ; de là l'on est allé dans l'autre aile, tout était dans une propreté extrême. Le Cavalier a dit qu'il ne croyait pas qu'il y eût maison à Paris où les appartements fussent de si belle proportion et si commodes. Mme de Beauvais l'a prié de le dire au Roi. Il lui a dit que le Roi devrait la prendre pour y venir quelquefois, qu'au Louvre il n'y avait pas de tels appartements. Elle a dit qu'au premier achat la maison lui coûtait 30,000 écus, qu'elle s'était assujettie à ce qui était fait, qu'elle eût sans cela pu faire quelque chose de plus beau; que de tout abattre, sa famille eût crié contre elle" (P. Fréart de Chantelou, *Journal du voyage du Cavalier Bernin en France,* L. Lalanne, ed. [Paris, 1885], p. 237). Earlier

that year, Bernini had criticized Le Pautre's cascade at Saint-Cloud (see Chapter 7). Bernini must have admired the circular entrance vestibule at the Hôtel de Beauvais where visitors could mount to and descend from coaches while under cover (see remarks in *ibid.,* pp. 109, 188, which reveal Bernini's predilection for this feature).

Mme. de Beauvais's last lines, as recorded by Chantelou, seem to reveal her awareness of the role of the medieval foundations in the creation of the house (see p. 38); there is no indication that the superstructures of the medieval buildings were retained. By "premier achat," Mme. de Beauvais was probably referring to the major transactions of 1654, because in 1657 the Beauvais purchased part of a house in the rue de Jouy to complete their site (Cousin, *op. cit.,* pp. 19, 77). This minor addition was made while the Hôtel de Beauvais was rising, since the façade sculpture was being undertaken that year (see p. 38).

6

Church of the Jacobins, Lyons: Façade

That a chapter of Dominicans in far-off Lyons called upon Le Pautre to design a new façade for their Gothic church is proof of the architect's growing fame during the 1650's.[1] Work on the lateral (northern) façade of the late fifteenth century church was begun in 1657, but the construction seems to have been left entirely in the hands of local masons and to have dragged on over a number of years.[2] The church was

1. The façade was attributed to "Le Pautre" by A. Clapasson (*Description de la ville de Lyon* [Lyons, 1741], p. 39) and by F. Z. Collombet ("Église et couvent des Jacobins, aujourd'hui Hôtel de la Préfecture," in L. Boitel, ed., *Lyon ancien et moderne*, II [Lyons, 1843], p. 361). A. N. Dezallier d'Argenville specifically cites Antoine as the architect (*Vies des fameux architectes depuis la renaissance des arts . . .* [Paris, 1787], p. 400). However, "J. le Pautre" is named as the designer in an anonymous, undated woodcut (Estampes, Va 176, vol. ix). Among Jean's numerous architectural prints is one (undated) which is related to the Lyons façade (Estampes, Ed 42c, fol. 38, bottom right), particularly its left half. But as far as we know, Jean never practiced as an architect.

The lateral façade provided the main entrance to the church.

2. The date 1657 is given by: Collombet, *op. cit.*, p. 361; C. Bauchal, *Nouveau dictionnaire biographique et critique des architectes français* (Paris, 1887), pp. 361–362, 501; A. Vachet, *Les anciens couvents de Lyon* (Lyons, 1895), p. 393; M. Cormier, *L'ancien couvent des Dominicains de Lyon. I-Description-Plans-Vues diverses* (Lyons, 1898), p. 23; E. L. G. Charvet, *Lyon artistique: architectes* (Lyons, 1899), pp. 220, 332, 337; J. B. Martin, *Histoire des églises et chapelles de Lyon*, I (Lyons, 1908), p. 46; A. Kleinclausz, *Lyon des origines à nos jours* (Lyons, 1925), p. 171; Hautecoeur, II, i, pp. 152–153. However, Dezallier d'Argenville (*op. cit.*, p. 400) gives the date 1674, which also appears on the anonymous woodcut cited in n. 1. But Dezallier errs when he describes the façade as adorned with Corinthian and Ionic orders; other sources indicate that the Corinthian and Composite orders were used. Hence, this inaccuracy may indicate that Dezallier's dating is untrustworthy.

According to Collombet (*op. cit.*, pp. 361–362), construction was begun in 1657 under Robert Rogier, who was replaced after a legal process by Jean Turrin and Jean Vallançot. The capitals were sculpted

destroyed in 1816;[3] Le Pautre's façade is known to us only through graphic evidence and written descriptions.[4]

In general, the façade conformed to a type popularized by Giacomo della Porta's façade of Il Gesù in Rome (1575), consisting of two stories of orders, the second narrower than the lower and linked to it by volutes (Fig. 66). But because Le Pautre applied this façade to the flank of a basilican church instead of using it to form the western entrance, the form lost its structural meaning. Originally devised to correspond to and reflect the nave and side aisles of basilican churches, this type of façade appeared in Lyons as a monumental, decorative screen; the upper story corresponded to no structural feature and was not physically attached to any part of the Gothic church (Fig. 65). Thus, Le Pautre was determined to adorn church and square with an up-to-date Italianate form, even at the cost of constructional logic.

Three large niches adorned Le Pautre's façade, filled with statues of the Virgin and Child (upper story, center), Saint John the Baptist (lower story, left), and Saint Dominic (lower story, right).[5] The orders chosen were Composite over Corinthian,[6] and Collombet informs us of the polychromy of the façade: the frieze (apparently of the upper and lower orders) was of red marble of Savoy, as were two pilasters (it is not clear whether the pilasters referred to were those in the lower story or those flanking the Virgin's niche). In addition, at least four of the columns were of jasper, and the capitals were of white Seyssel stone.[7]

The façade (Fig. 66) is extremely Italianate and, specifically, Roman. In the lower story there is the typically Roman increase in the value of the orders from pilasters at the extremities through engaged and freestanding columns next to the portal.[8] This progression and the accompanying forward breaks of the entablature create a powerful High Baroque emphasis on the center, underlined by the heavy pediment over the portal. This stepwise arrangement of the orders serves to enclose bays (the lateral bays which contain the niches; the central bay which contains the portal)— another characteristic of the Roman Baroque façade. The upper story is similarly organized.[9] The emphatic Baroque quality of the composition is also achieved through

by Jacques Mimerel in 1660; Alexandre Richard directed the work until 1676; sculptural work was still being undertaken in 1687.

3. Martin, *op. cit.*, I, p. 47. In 1843 Collombet reported (*op. cit.*, p. 362) that remnants of the façade existed in the rue Sully, in the Brotteaux section of Lyons, but I was unable to find any trace of them in 1963.

4. Fig. 66 seems to be the most reliable visual source for several reasons: (1) it is the clearest and most detailed representation; (2) it shows pilasters at the extremities of the lower story, a detail which is confirmed by the woodcut cited in n. 1 and by a plan published in Cormier, *op. cit.*; (3) Fig. 66 and the woodcut correspond more closely with one another than does either with Fig. 65. But the latter has the virtue of depicting the façade in its relation to church and square.

5. The Virgin and Child were sculpted by Nicolas Bidaut, the others by Guillaume Simon; they date from the 1680's. The arms of the archbishopric of Lyons were placed in the pediment over the entrance portal. See Clapasson, *op. cit.*, p. 39 and Collombet, *op. cit.*, pp. 361–362.

6. Clapasson, *op. cit.*, p. 39; Collombet, *op. cit.*, p. 361. These writers are confirmed by the visual evidence.

7. Collombet, *op. cit.*, pp. 361–362.

8. For the principles concerning the organization of Italian Baroque façades see R. Wittkower, "Carlo Rainaldi and the Roman Architecture of the Full Baroque," *AB*, XIX (1937), pp. 242ff. and *idem, Art and Architecture in Italy, 1600 to 1750*, 2d ed. (Baltimore, 1965), *passim*.

9. I assume that the outer columns of the upper order are engaged and not freestanding.

the use of bold, sculptural motifs and an avoidance of unified, planar wall surfaces. The emphasis on the column, too, is consistent with the evolution of Roman façades at this date.[10] However, accompanying these elements are others which serve to complicate the work. In the lower story, the outer bays are framed by orders of unequal value (pilaster and engaged column), with a resultant asymmetry at entablature level. Furthermore, the engaged columns perform a dual function: they frame the lateral bays in conjunction with the pilasters, and they support the second plane of entablature which occupies the center of the lower story. In the upper level, a pilaster order of discordant scale supports an entablature and pediment which overlap the main entablature. These features—unsymmetrical bay framing, dual function of orders, juxtaposition of small and large orders, and superimposition of motifs—constitute Mannerist elements which interpenetrate the High Baroque framework in a manner typical of mid-century Roman practice.[11] Only details are specifically French: the entrance portal in the form of an arch on piers[12] (a motif repeated in smaller scale around the Virgin's niche), and the touch of Gallic delicacy and elegance provided by the foliage which lies on these arches.[13]

Le Pautre's façade presupposes an up-to-date knowledge of Baroque architecture in Rome. Specifically, the Lyons façade bears a strong similarity to that of S. Nicola da Tolentino (Fig. 67). There are important differences: the Roman work has columns at the extremities of the lower order, lacks a large pediment over the central bay of the ground story, has curved screens in place of scroll volutes, etc. Nevertheless, no other Roman façade is so close to Le Pautre's, and the question of direct influence arises. The façade of S. Nicola was begun in 1655, and construction continued into the 1660's.[14] Due to the fact that the lateral façade of the Church of the Jacobins was begun in 1657, it seems probable that, if Le Pautre did indeed use S. Nicola as his model, the Frenchman had knowledge of the plans and hence access to its architect's studio. However, the designer of the façade of S. Nicola is unknown, although the name of Alessandro Algardi has been improbably connected with it.[15] It is by no means absolutely certain that we are, in fact, dealing here with a case of direct influence. There seems to be greater likelihood that similar results were arrived at independently, through the process of manipulating common elements of architectural grammar and syntax which were being diffused throughout Europe as the Baroque style evolved.

Be that as it may, a comparison of the Lyons façade with those (ideal and realized) of the Chapelle de Port-Royal may serve as an index of the revolution in Antoine's style after his conservative beginnings. At Lyons, we find neither the

10. Wittkower, "Carlo Rainaldi . . . ," p. 290. However, columnar orders in all stories are features of such well-known earlier French works as Saint-Gervais (1616, de Brosse) and Saint-Paul-Saint-Louis (1634, Derand), both in Paris.

11. Wittkower, *Art and Architecture . . . , passim.*

12. Popularized by such influential works as those cited in n. 10.

13. This treatment is paralleled in Le Pautre's projected design for the east side of the cloister of Port-Royal de Paris (Fig. 4).

14. F. Fasolo, "La 'fabbrica' della chiesa di S. Nicola da Tolentino," *Fede e arte*, XI (1963), pp. 81ff.

15. *Ibid.*, pp. 89ff. The building activity was supervised by Giovan Maria Baratta, but he does not appear to have supplied the design. Wittkower has argued against the possibility of Algardi having been a practicing architect (*Art and Architecture . . . , p. 366 n. 36 [viii]).

classical pretensions of the projected façade nor the timid flat quality of the executed work. Instead, we are struck by the entirely Baroque nature of the composition: the use of sculptural motifs, dramatic incident, and central climax.[16] Once again, as in the choir of Saint-Laurent, Le Pautre chose to adhere to a modern conception and refused to adjust to the medieval style in any way.

16. Hautecoeur (II, i, p. 153), followed by J. Evans (*Monastic Architecture in France from the Renaissance to the Revolution* [Cambridge, 1964], p. 111), attributes the monastic buildings to Le Pautre, but I have found no evidence to support this. The convent was reconstructed 1714–42 (Kleinclausz, *op. cit.*, p. 171).

7
Cascade at Saint-Cloud

The *grande cascade* at Saint-Cloud is one of Le Pautre's most outstanding creations. It deserves to be better known because of its intrinsic high quality and the role which it played during the celebrated Parisian sojourn of Gianlorenzo Bernini in 1665.

Saint-Cloud, which is situated west of Paris, had been the country residence since 1658 of Philippe d'Orléans, the younger brother of Louis XIV.[1] In 1660, Monsieur (as Philippe was called) chose Le Pautre as his personal architect,[2] and Antoine's first task was to create a monumental cascade worthy of the elaborate hydraulic structures which had already made the park of Saint-Cloud famous. What Le Pautre produced was the most dramatic piece of garden furniture ever seen in France (Figs. 69–73).

A number of modifications and restorations have altered the original appearance of the cascade, but a contemporary drawing by Perelle (Fig. 68) enables us to grasp the details of Le Pautre's design.[3] The cascade originally emptied into a curved basin at its foot. This was amplified in 1698–99 by Jules Hardouin-Mansart, who created a

1. On Saint-Cloud and its Maison de Gondi see Vicomte de Grouchy, "La maison de Gondi à Saint-Cloud," *Bulletin de la société de l'histoire de Paris et de l'Ile-de-France*, XVIII (1891), pp. 45–48 and E. Magne, *Le château de Saint-Cloud* (Paris, 1932), *passim*.

2. A. Jal, *Dictionnaire critique de biographie et d'histoire*, 2d ed. (Paris, 1872), p. 774.

3. There exist several drawings probably executed in 1699 by Alexandre Le Blond immediately after the restoration of the upper cascade and the alteration of the lower had been carried out by Jules

Hardouin-Mansart (see R. Strandberg, "André Le Nôtre et son école. Dessins inédits ou peu connus dans la collection Tessin-Hårleman, au Musée National de Stockholm," *BSHAF* [1960], pp. 125–126). These drawings clearly show the series of low cascades in the lower basin which Mansart created to empty the waters into the newly created long canal. See also *Dessins du Nationalmuseum de Stockholm, collections Tessin & Cronstedt* (Paris, 1950), p. 55, pl. XXX; *Dessins du Nationalmuseum de Stockholm: Versailles & les maisons royales* (Paris, 1951), pp. 49–50.

long canal leading from the lower basin to an oval pool at the far extremity, the resultant expanse of water enlivened by spouting jets. This composition still exists today (Fig. 69).[4] The figures of the Seine and the Loire are depicted in Fig. 68, reclining upon the crowning balustrade. These statues were replaced between ca. 1730 and 1734 by the existing figures of the Seine and the Marne, which create a greater central emphasis than one finds in the original disposition.[5] Essentially, however, Le Pautre's creation has come down to us intact, still operative in its delightful setting.

The cascade at Saint-Cloud (Figs. 70, 71) is a great water machine, an evidently man-made device geared to channel and display running water. Its architectonic form constitutes a compact, monumental construction, clearly demarcated from the surrounding natural world. Only the conventionalized panels of stalactites (or dripping water) and the strips of channeled rustication (Fig. 72) suggest the natural and the rustic.[6] When operating, the cascade presents a variety of effects: the circular basins spout individual jets, the outer ramps offer rivulet-like flows, low waterfalls descend from the arched openings. The main effect is seen in the center, where a powerful

CC 2104 (bearing the inscription "Pr Mr. Le Notre") is listed in the latter catalogue under "Château de Saint-Cloud," and E. de Ganay (*André Le Nostre, 1613–1700* [Paris, 1962], p. 72) describes it as a design for the lower part of the cascade at Saint-Cloud, preceding the project of J. H.-Mansart. This hardly seems possible; the drawing has nothing to do with Le Pautre's cascade.

Le Nôtre is said to have been appointed gardener to Monsieur in 1665 (G. Poncet de la Grave, *Mémoires intéressans pour servir à l'histoire de France . . .* , III [Paris, 1789], p. 182).

4. This work was attributed to Hardouin-Mansart and dated 1699 in the *Mercure galant*, July 1699, pp. 243–244. The same source tells of a restoration of the upper (Le Pautre's) cascade. H. de Longeville implies that Mansart's design was executed in 1698 (*Description des grandes cascades de la maison royale de Saint-Cloud* [Paris, 1706], p. 2). See also E. Soulié *et al.*, eds., *Journal du Marquis de Dangeau*, VI (Paris, 1856), p. 393.

5. The identification of the original figures as the Seine and the Loire is found in Longeville, *op. cit.*, pp. 5–6 and in G. L. Le Rouge, *Les curiositez de Paris, de Versailles, de Marly, de Vincennes, de S. Cloud, et des environs*, II (Amsterdam, 1718), p. 500. The cascade was restored ca. 1730–34, at which time the sculptor Lambert Sigisbert Adam created a new central group of the Seine and the Marne (J. Lebeuf, *Histoire de la ville et de tout le diocèse de Paris*, III [Paris, 1883], pp. 35–36). A. N. Dezallier d'Argenville explains that "la Figure de la Marne paroît dans une attitude suppliante, pour obtenir que la Seine veuille bien recevoir ses eaux" (*Voyage pittoresque des environs de Paris*, 4th ed. [Paris, 1779], p. 57). Fig. 68 depicts a shield with the emblems of Monsieur between the two figures. The central water-

fall originally began at the top of the uppermost ramp; the present arrangement, whereby the water issues forth from an urn placed between the Seine and the Marne, must date from the eighteenth century restoration. In addition, Fig. 68 reveals that the upper wall of the cascade was originally flanked by screening walls with niches and rectangular openings (?). These were removed apparently in 1698–99 and replaced by the extant curved buttresses, since the latter are indicated in several drawings by Le Blond (e.g., Stockholm, Nationalmuseum, THC 383; see above, n. 3).

Longeville (*op. cit.*, pp. 4, 7, 13) indicates that the crowning balustrade was occupied by figures of Hercules and the Fauns, and that the four lower statues represent the Winds.

In addition to the restorations of 1698–99 and ca. 1730–34, others were carried out in 1773–74 (P. T. N. Hurtaut and Magny, *Dictionnaire historique de la ville de Paris et de ses environs . . .* , II [Paris, 1779], p. 364; *Curiosités du château de Saint-Cloud* [Paris, 1783], p. 4) and in the 1830's under Louis-Philippe (*Château de Saint-Cloud. Domaine de la couronne* [Paris, 1839], p. 26). The exact nature of the work in these cases is not known. The cascade was restored between 1945 and 1954 by M. Félix Brunau, Conservateur du Domaine de Saint-Cloud. (See below, n. 6, 7.)

6. Fig. 68 clearly indicates that Le Pautre used alternating bands of stalactite drippings and smooth wall around the two central arches. In their present form, these arches are entirely surrounded by the drippings. The keystone masks recall one of Antoine's earlier fountain designs (Fig. 75). The naturalistic rocks beneath the statues of the Seine and the Marne, as well as the water dragons, are due to Adam (see above, n. 5); they do not appear in Fig. 68.

descent of water resembles a violent cataract. The whole is enlivened with spouting, grotesque masks, aquatic creatures, turtles, and frogs. The open arches, admired by Tessin,[7] invite the spectator to peer into the remote accesses of the cascade, as if to penetrate to its secret source.

A key element of Le Pautre's conception is the wall with arched openings which defines the upper vertical plane of the cascade. This is used to gain greater elevation for the sources of the central and lateral cataracts (the latter are fed by the circular fountains at the upper extremities). By means of this device, the intensity and violence of the descent of the waters are considerably increased. The open arches allow glimpses past the wall into two distant enclosed chambers, open to the sky, where the architect has placed the outlets of the intermediate rivulets: basins set in rusticated niches, capped with Tritons riding dolphins (Fig. 73). From the top of the wall [8] begins the descent of the central and outer ramps, a series of aggressive horizontal blocks tumbling down the hillside. The lowest ramp in the center, of convex form, suggests movement towards the lower basin, where its shape is echoed.

The cascade, while providing a view toward the Seine from its upper terraces, was also designed to be viewed from afar, as the terminal feature of a long vista leading from a terrace overlooking the Seine towards the château (Figs. 69, 79).[9] Even before the additions of Mansart, this *allée* existed, flanked by narrow canals and low waterspouts (Fig. 78). From the distance, the cascade forms a striking chromatic accent, its warm buff tones and silver cataracts contrasting with the enveloping green. Thus, every device has been employed to emphasize the architectural and man-made quality of the cascade, set down in the midst of nature but clearly distinct from her.

Precisely when was Le Pautre's cascade constructed? Because of the loss of the account books of Philippe d'Orléans,[10] an answer is not immediately available. It is usually stated, however, that the *grande cascade* was finished in 1667.[11] As far as I can determine, the first writer who suggested this terminal date was Poncet de la Grave,

7. "Relation de la visite de Nicodème Tessin à Marly, Versailles, Clagny, Rueil et Saint-Cloud en 1687 (suite et fin)," *Revue de l'histoire de Versailles et de Seine-et-Oise*, XXVIII (1926), p. 298: ". . . les deux arcades qui percent entre les trois cascades font un assez bel effect. . . ." These arches are of flattened form today, but Fig. 68 shows them closer to semicircular form.

8. The balustrade which surmounts the wall is functional since the cascade supports terraces which afford views towards the Seine (Poncet de la Grave, *op. cit.*, III, pp. 47–48; the terraces are indicated in Fig. 79).

9. When Le Pautre's cascade was constructed, the Château de Saint-Cloud was not yet built, and the site was still occupied by the Maison de Gondi. Perelle's engraving (Fig. 78) shows the new château. On the Château de Saint-Cloud see Chapter 8.

10. V. Champier and G. R. Sandoz, *Le Palais-Royal d'après des documents inédits (1629–1900)*, I (Paris, 1900), p. 152.

11. Magne, *op. cit.*, p. 63; Hautecoeur, II, i, p.

162; A. Marie, *Le palais de St-Cloud* (Paris, 1952), p. 12; Ganay, *op. cit.*, p. 72.

The *grande cascade* was cited as being a work by Le Pautre by the Swedish architect Nicodemus Tessin the Younger when he visited Saint-Cloud in 1687 ("Relation de la visite . . . ," p. 298). During the eighteenth century a number of writers also attributed the cascade to Antoine: Longeville, *op. cit.*, p. 2; T. Corneille, *Dictionnaire universel, géographique et historique* . . . , III (Paris, 1708), pp. 322–324; A. Antonini, *Memorial de Paris et de ses environs à l'usage des voyageurs*, new ed. (Paris, 1744), p. 198; Dezallier d'Argenville, *op. cit.*, p. 57; *idem, Vies des fameux architectes depuis la renaissance des arts* . . . (Paris, 1787), p. 396; J. A. Dulaure, *Nouvelle description des environs de Paris*, 2d ed., I (Paris, 1787), p. 111; L. V. Thiéry, *Guide des amateurs et des étrangers voyageurs dans les maisons royales . . . aux environs de Paris* (Paris, 1788), p. 327; Poncet de la Grave, *op. cit.*, III, p. 47. I have not found any evidence to support Ganay's assertion that the Francini were responsible for the *jeux d'eau* (*op. cit.*, p. 72).

who wrote in 1789: "Le 7 Mai [1667], Sa Majesté fut à la promenade à Saint-Cloud, avec Monsieur, son Frere unique, qui, a cette occasion, fit jouer toutes les Eaux, ainsi que les Cascades *nouvellement construites*" [my italics].[12] This passage apparently prompted Magne to write in 1932: "Le 6 mai 1667 [correcting Poncet de la Grave], il y est convié à voir la grande cascade enfin terminée." [13] Poncet de la Grave's passage is based on an entry in the *Gazette de France* dated May 7, 1667, which reports events which occurred on the preceding day:

> . . . le Roy vinst à la promenade à Saint Clou, en la délicieuse Maison de Monsieur: où Sa Majesté, apres avoir vû les Cascades, & les autres beautez du Lieu, fut régalé par leurs Altesses Royales. . . .[14]

Here there is no mention of "les Cascades nouvellement construites," an interpolation by Poncet de la Grave. We could perhaps conclude that this passage from the *Gazette de France* at least provided a *terminus ante quem*, but the problem is complicated by the fact that another cascade already existed at Saint-Cloud before the creation of the *grande cascade*. This was the Gondi cascade (Fig. 80); the use of the plural ("les Cascades") could have been a reference to this older cascade alone, since it was composed of multiple basins. In order to assign a precise date to Le Pautre's work, it is necessary to introduce some contemporary evidence of primary importance—Gianlorenzo Bernini's comments on Saint-Cloud as reported by Paul Fréart de Chantelou in his *Journal du voyage du Cavalier Bernin en France.*

The first mention of Bernini's interest in Saint-Cloud occurs under the date July 26, 1665:

> L'après-dînée, il [Bernini] a été à Saint-Cloud, dont il a trouvé la situation extrêmement belle à cause de la vue et des eaux. Il a trouvé qu'on pourrait faire une cascade rustique au carré où est le grand jet d'eau, laquelle parmi des choses si ajustées serait d'une grande beauté.[15]

In this passage no mention is made of an existing cascade, but by the "carré où est le grand jet d'eau" Chantelou is referring to a basin of water which still exists at Saint-Cloud and which is indicated in Allegrain's panoramic view of the site, dating from the early eighteenth century (Fig. 79, lower left center). This basin, which still features a central water jet, famous for its height, was one of the older attractions of the park of Saint-Cloud. The basin was described by Brackenhoffer in 1644, and in the same passage we are informed of a composition composed of spouting masks and water basins which corresponds to the modest cascade which appears on Allegrain's view and whose details can be clearly discerned in a print by Silvestre (Fig. 80): [16]

> . . . il y avait une très belle pièce d'eau, carrée, entourée d'une balustrade de pierre; il y avait là-dessus un pilier et un Cupidon enlacés, artistement sculptés

12. Poncet de la Grave, *op. cit.*, III, p. 183.
13. Magne, *op. cit.*, p. 63.
14. *Gazette de France* (1667), p. 438.
15. P. Fréart de Chantelou, *Journal du voyage du Cavalier Bernin en France*, L. Lalanne, ed. (Paris, 1885), p. 70.
16. The Silvestre print bears the inscription:

"Veüe et Perspective de la Cascade du Jardin de l'Illustrissime Archevesque de Paris a sainct Cloud." This is a reference to Jean François de Gondi, the proprietor from 1625 to 1654. Hence the print was probably made before the death of Gondi in 1654. The precise location of the Gondi cascade was pointed out to me by Prof. Peter Collins of McGill University.

en pierre, qui donne à ce lieu un charme singulier. En bas, contre la paroi, sur un côte de la pièce d'eau, il y a neuf grands masques grimaçants, joliment taillés dans la pierre, qui rejettent l'eau dans une conque marine en pierre, placée sous chacun d'eau. Au milieu de la pièce d'eau, où il y avait alors beaucoup de cygnes, se dressait un Neptune, qui faisait jaillir l'eau par cinq ouvertures, à la hauteur d'une maison.[17]

It is true that Brackenhoffer mentions nine spouting masks and a central Neptune whereas Silvestre indicates only six masks and a female figure.[18] Nevertheless, the concordance between the traveler's description and the artist's view is sufficient to establish the fact that Bernini, when he visited the *grand jet* on July 26, must have seen the Gondi cascade (Fig. 80) — an anonymous work built sometime before 1644.[19]

Chantelou's entry tells us that Bernini conceived the idea of creating "une cascade rustique" for this particular location. The only possible point for such an addition would have been on the higher, sloping ground behind the Gondi cascade which is filled in with a dense grove (Fig. 80).[20]

Chantelou's journal then supplies us with the following entry (August 2):

S. E. [Cardinal Antonio Barberini] lui [to Bernini] a dit qu'elle avait su qu'il avait été à Saint-Cloud. Il lui a répondu qu'il avait trouvé la situation, le jardin et les eaux fort belles. S. E. lui ayant demandé ce qu'il lui avait semblé de la cascade, et si elle ne lui avait point paru trop belle, il lui a dit que c'en était le défaut; qu'il faut cacher l'art davantage et chercher de donner aux choses une apparence plus naturelle, mais qu'en France généralement en tout on fait le contraire.[21]

News of Bernini's pointed criticisms soon reached the ears of Monsieur himself. Chantelou wrote on August 18 as follows:

S. A. R. m'a appelé et m'a dit à l'oreille: "Est-il vrai que le cavalier a trouvé à Saint-Cloud ma cascade trop ajustée?" Je lui ai dit qu'oui. Monsieur a repris et dit: "Boisfranc[22] m'a rapporté que le Cavalier trouvait que de mon bouillon d'eau [the *grand jet*] l'on peut faire quelque chose de beau. Je serais bien aise que vous lui demandiez un dessin pour cela, comme de vous-même." J'ai assuré Monsieur que je le ferais, que j'avois déjà prié le cavalier d'y travailler. A quelque temps de là, S. A. R. m'a rappelé et m'a dit: "Peut-être faudrait-il pour cela qu'il

17. E. Brackenhoffer, *Voyage de Paris en Italie, 1644–1646* (Paris, 1927), p. 43.

18. John Evelyn also visited Saint-Cloud in 1644, but he refers to the figure as a Laocoön: "... above all that fountaine of the Laocoon in a very ample square poole or Piscina, casting waters neere 40 foote in height, and having about it a multitude of Statues and basines, is a most glorious & surprizing object. ..." (*The Diary of John Evelyn*, E. S. de Beer, ed., II [Oxford, 1955], p. 107 [February 27, 1644].)

19. This cascade no longer exists save for one of the water basins.

20. In Allegrain's painting (Fig. 79) this wood has been partially cleared to reveal a small fountain and basin. This feature is specifically mentioned in Dezallier d'Argenville, *Voyage pittoresque* ..., p. 58, where it is attributed to André Le Nôtre, whose

activity at Saint-Cloud is said to date from 1665 (see above, n. 3). However, a traveler's diary of 1664 seems to contain a reference to this fountain (E. Browne, *Journal of a Visit to Paris in the Year 1664*, G. Keynes, ed. [London, 1923], p. 18 [June 2, 1664]): "A square Pond, in the Middle of which the water spirteth up continually; *one fine fountaine standes above this pond* [my italics] and another beneath it and nine basons with fountaines at the upper side pouring into it. ..." If Browne's description is accepted as accurate, then Bernini in 1665 saw the composition recorded in Allegrain's view (Fig. 79).

21. Fréart de Chantelou, *op. cit.*, p. 80.

22. Joachim Seiglière de Boisfranc, treasurer to Monsieur. Le Pautre later built a château for him at Saint-Ouen and a *hôtel* in Paris in the rue Saint-Augustin (see Chapter 9 and Appendix I).

retournât encore une autre fois à Saint-Cloud?" Je lui ai dit que, s'il était nécessaire, je l'y mènerais exprès.[23]

Not until September, however, was Saint-Cloud discussed again (September 3):

Monsieur ensuite m'a demandé à l'oreille si j'avais parlé au Cavalier de ce dessin de Saint-Cloud. Je lui ai répondu qu'oui, qu'il m'avait promis de le faire, et que je le mènerais sur le lieu exprès.[24]

On September 13, Chantelou spoke to Bernini:

. . . je l'ai prié que nous repassassions par la maison de S. A. R. à Saint-Cloud pour revoir le lieu, où il a jugé que l'on pourrait faire une cascade naturelle et la dessiner. Il a reparti qu'il n'y avait pas du temps suffisamment, qu'il fallait qu'il demeurât sur le lieu une heure ou deux.[25]

On September 26, Chantelou recorded the following conversation:

Je l'ai prié que la première fête il voulût bien que nous allassions à Saint-Cloud. Il m'a dit qu'il irait, fête ou non, mais que, quand il me dit qu'il y avait quelque chose de beau à y faire, il n'avait pas vu la cascade qui y est; que son dessein était d'y en faire une naturelle; que depuis, ayant fait réflexion, il avait jugé qu'un semblable ouvrage ne plairait pas ici, et que déjà Monsieur y avait fait la dépense d'une cascade. Je lui ai reparti qu'il était bon de nous montrer en France comment ces choses se doivent faire. Il m'a dit qu'il le ferait, puisque je le souhaitais.[26]

Here is the key passage. The first part of the second sentence reads in translation: "He [Bernini] told me that he would go, holiday or no, but that, when he told me that there was something fine to make there [the rustic cascade], he had not seen the cascade which is there. . . ." The implication is clearly that Bernini, after having told Chantelou of his cascade idea on July 26, did so *before* he had seen Le Pautre's cascade (which he then must have viewed immediately afterwards since the two cascades were directly adjacent [Fig. 79]).

At this point we must investigate the history of the site now occupied by the *grande cascade*. It is frequently asserted that Le Pautre transformed or remodeled a pre-existing cascade.[27] No specific evidence to support this claim has been advanced, but Hautecoeur has published a plan of Saint-Cloud which shows the *grande cascade* in completed form (Fig. 76).[28] This plan also indicates the Maison de Gondi before its transformation into the Château de Saint-Cloud (see Chapter 8), and Hautecoeur has dated the plan 1658, the year in which Monsieur purchased the old build-

23. Fréart de Chantelou, *op. cit.*, p. 104.

24. *Ibid.*, p. 132. Two days later, on September 5, a royal visit took place at Saint-Cloud: "La Compagnie y prit d'abord le divertissement des Cascades. . . ." (*Gazette de France* [1665], p. 898.)

25. Fréart de Chantelou, *op. cit.*, p. 156.

26. *Ibid.*, p. 182.

27. A. E. Brinckmann, *Baukunst des 17. und 18. Jahrhunderts in den romanischen Ländern*, 4th ed. (Berlin-Neubabelsberg, 1922), p. 322; "Relation de

la visite . . . ," p. 298 n. 91; Magne, *op. cit.*, p. 56; Hautecoeur, II, i, p. 162. Magne states that Le Pautre's cascade was built on the site of the Gondi cascade; this is obviously untrue.

28. As far as I can determine, the indication "Maison a Monsieur Fouquet" (lower left center) does not refer to Nicolas Fouquet, the Surintendant des Finances, because he did not own property at Saint-Cloud.

ing and its park.[29] Hautecoeur's dating implies that the *grande cascade* already existed before Le Pautre's entry on the scene in 1660.[30] However, there is no evidence to support the 1658 dating, and it is entirely possible that this plan was drawn up sometime during the 1660's, just after the completion of the *grande cascade* but before the construction of the new château (south wing finished by 1671; see Chapter 8).

Nevertheless, it is entirely possible that a cascade of some sort did exist on the site of the *grande cascade* before 1660. In 1644, John Evelyn visited Saint-Cloud. After describing the basin of the *grand jet*, he wrote:

> . . . but nothing is more esteem'd than the Cascada falling from the greate stepps into the lowest & longest Walke from the Mons Parnassus, which consists of a Grotto or shell house erected on the summit of the hill; & herein are divers waterworkes, and unlucky contrivances to wet the Spectators: This is coverd with a fayre Cupola, the Walls paynted with the Muses, statues placed thick about it, whereof some antique and good.[31]

It is very likely that Evelyn is here referring to that now-vanished domed structure (labeled "Ancienne Grotte" on Mariette's map of Saint-Cloud, 1738) which is visible in Figs. 78 and 79, adjoining the *grande cascade*.[32] Evelyn's description clearly indicates that a cascade of some sort was located near this grotto. Furthermore, in 1664, another Englishman, Edward Browne, left this description of the park:

> Here are a great many water-workes; the most remarkable are these upon the Side of a hill, forty two basons placed seven abrest, which have all fountains in them.[33]

If Browne is here describing the cascade indicated by Evelyn—and it is evident that he is *not* talking about the Gondi cascade—then we can form an approximate idea of its configuration: six rows of basins, seven abrest, each basin perhaps identical to the circular ones with small spouting jets which now adorn the *grande cascade* (Fig. 70).

Browne's account, therefore, seems to indicate that Le Pautre's cascade was not in existence when he visited Saint-Cloud on June 2, 1664; the site was occupied by an older construction which Le Pautre subsequently transformed. It is entirely likely, I believe, that Le Pautre began his work shortly after Browne's visit, that activity continued during the remainder of 1664 and into 1665, and that the *grande cascade* was completed by the end of July 1665, when Bernini first saw it. The passages from Chantelou's journal quoted above indicate 1665 as the terminal date, as does the next entry, which describes in great detail Bernini's second and last visit to the site on October 4, 1665. In this passage, the *grande cascade* is clearly the object of Bernini's scrutiny and criticism:

29. Hautecoeur, II, i, p. 157.

30. This view contradicts Hautecoeur's own statement (II, i, p. 162): "Le Pautre refit la cascade, qui était déjà fort avancée, lorsqu'en 1665 le Cavalier Bernin visita Saint-Cloud, et qui était achevée en 1667."

31. *The Diary of John Evelyn*, II, pp. 107–108.

32. This grotto is also described by Brackenhoffer (*op. cit.*, p. 44), but he does not mention a cascade. Hautecoeur's attribution of the grotto to Le Pautre (II, i, p. 162) must be rejected.

33. Browne, *op. cit.*, p. 18. Browne then continues with a description of the basin of the *grand jet*; see n. 20.

Après dîner, nous sommes allés à Saint-Cloud où le Cavalier a dessiné une forme de cascade naturelle, qu'on pourrait faire vis-à-vis du grand jet d'eau à l'endroit où est la balustrade.[34] Il a bien été une heure à faire son dessin, après il me l'a montré et me l'a donné à entendre, puis il a ajouté: "Je m'assure que cela ne plaira pas. L'on n'est pas ici accoutumé à ces choses naturelles; on en veut de plus ajustées et plus petites, comme sont les ouvrages des religieuses." L'abbé Butti lui a demandé s'il avait vu la cascade qui était là: il a dit qu'oui, et qu'elle était de la sorte qu'il venait de dire. Il m'a dit là-dessus: "Ce que je viens de faire n'est que pour ceux qui ont le goût des belles et grandes choses. Je ne doute pas qu'on ne trouve l'autre plus belle que ce que j'ai fait, mais je l'ai fait pour l'amour de vous. S'il était bien exécuté, je crois bien qu'on ne pourrait plus regarder l'autre; en tout cas, il y en aurait deux de manières différentes, mais il faudrait que cela fût bien exécuté et pour cela en faire un modèle auparavant."[35]

In the above passage, Bernini has been designing at the basin of the Gondi cascade; hence Butti's question and Bernini's response logically apply to the *grande cascade*. The passage continues:

1   Après, nous sommes allés voir la cascade; il y avait grand monde pour la voir, pour ce qu'elle ne joue qu'avec un billet de S. A. R. M. Billon, concierge, a dit au Cavalier de se tenir au pied des escaliers, mais le Cavalier a voulu descendre en bas. L'on a mis l'eau qui a commencé petit à petit à se répandre partout.
5   Le Cavalier est encore descendu plus bas, afin d'en voir mieux l'effet. Ayant bien considéré l'espace qui est entre le premier bassin au pied des rampes et le second, il m'a dit qu'on pourrait faire une espèce de lunette entre ces deux bassins qui enrichirait encore la cascade, et qu'on pourrait encore donner à ce canal environ vingt pieds de large; le reste de l'espace des deux
10 côtés le gazonner en pente douce, et qu'à la lunette il suffirait de donner cinq palmes de profond, qui sont trois pieds et quelques pouces. L'abbé Butti a dit qu'on pouvait la continuer dans toute sa longueur, jusques à la balustrade qui est sur le chemin. Après que la cascade a eu joué, nous sommes remontés par à côté. Le Cavalier s'est un peu arrêté à considérer les figures dont cette cas-
15 cade est ornée, qui sont d'un jeune homme protégé du cardinal Antoine [Barberini]. L'abbé a dit qu'elles étaient comme d'après Michel-Ange. Il a répondu que quand l'on voit des noix, l'on jugeait que c'était de sa manière. Le Cavalier a dit au concierge: *È bella, è bella;* qu'à Rome cela serait estimé beau, mais qu'en France cela pouvait passer pour merveilleux. Puis il s'est
20 tourné et m'a dit: "Vous pourrez le dire vous-même, et à Madame, la pensée que j'ai eue pour elle." Je lui ai dit que je n'avais pas voulu aller chez Monsieur qu'il (que le Cavalier) n'eut retourné à Saint-Cloud et fait ce qu'il venait de faire.
    Nous en revenant, il m'a dit en chemin qu'il avait envie de faire peindre
25 la chose, afin qu'elle pût mieux paraître. L'abbé Butti a dit que le Bourson la viendrait peindre devant lui, et qu'il l'en avertirait. Je lui ai dit que le plus nécessaire était un profil. Il en est demeuré d'accord et m'a dit qu'il le ferait.[36]

Several details in this passage point to Le Pautre's cascade. First, in lines 3–5 Chantelou is evidently referring to the lateral short dummy flights of steps at the foot of the *grande cascade* (Fig. 68). It is true that the basin of the Gondi cascade was flanked by monumental stairs (Fig. 80). However, if Chantelou was referring to this

---

34. That is, at the rear of the basin, on the sloping land above the Gondi cascade (see Fig. 80 and n. 20).

35. Fréart de Chantelou, *op. cit.*, p. 199.
36. *Ibid.*, pp. 199–200.

cascade, it is by no means easy to understand why the concierge asked Bernini to stand at the *foot* of the stairs rather than *on* them, where he could have observed the waters from closer range; nor, if this was the case, why Bernini went further down, away from the cascade (line 5). This last maneuver is more comprehensible in relation to the *grande cascade*, which is effectively seen at some distance.

Second, lines 6–13 must be dealt with. In my estimation they cannot possibly be applied to the Gondi cascade, but they are comprehensible in relation to Le Pautre's: by "l'espace qui est entre le premier bassin au pied des rampes [a feature of the *grande cascade*, not the Gondi cascade!] et le second," Chantelou is probably referring to the *allée* which stretched from the curved basin at the foot of the cascade to a circular basin farther to the east (see Fig. 78, where the circular basin appears between the cascade and the Seine). Thus, Bernini's proposal would seem to be the germ of the idea later realized by Hardouin-Mansart.[37]

The next day (October 5), Chantelou reported the following events:

> Après que Sa Majesté a été partie, nous avons été au Louvre et y avons trouvé M. de Boisfranc, qui avait appris que le Cavalier avait été à Saint-Cloud. Il a été dire à Monsieur, qui était avec la Reine mère, que j'étais là. S. A. R. m'ayant fait passer dans les bains m'a demandé ce qu'avait dit le Cavalier de sa cascade; je le lui ai dit. Il m'a demandé après si le Cavalier avait entré dans sa maison, j'ai dit que non, qu'il n'en avait pas eu le temps. "Il venait de Versailles? m'a-t-il demandé. — Il est allé à Saint-Cloud exprès, lui ai-je répondu, pour dessiner ce qu'il estimait être à faire au lieu où est le grand jet d'eau." — "Qu'est-ce donc?" — Je lui ai dit: Une cascade plus naturelle et rustique, et que j'aurais soin de faire peindre son dessin, afin qu'on pût mieux connaître sa pensée; que s'il plaisait à S. A. R. de voir le Cavalier, il était dans l'antichambre, et que je le ferais entrer. Il est sorti et l'est allé trouver. Le Cavalier lui a aussitôt dit qu'il n'avait pu s'empêcher de voir encore une fois Saint-Cloud; que s'il demeurait à Paris, ce serait son lieu de plaisir, par le congé de S. A. R. Monsieur a dit qu'il en serait ravi. Il lui a répété ce que je lui avais rapporté de son sentiment touchant sa cascade, et que son dessin était pour une autre cascade qui serait belle aussi, quoiqu'extrêmement différente de l'autre. Il lui a parlé ensuite du canal à faire entre les bouillons d'eau, et que les jets qu'on y ferait allassent en arc, pour les différencier des autres qui sont vus sur une ligne droite.[38]

On October 9, Philippe asked Chantelou when he could see the plans of Bernini's cascade, and was reassured that they were being drawn up.[39] On October 10, Chantelou saw the designs for the cascade, but failed to describe them. Bernini expressed his belief that his design would be successful but felt that a model was needed.[40] Finally, on October 17, Chantelou brought the design for the proposed cascade to Monsieur. After reminding Philippe where the cascade was to be located, and after assuring him that the *grand jet* would be preserved, Chantelou informed Monsieur that Bernini had promised to construct a model after his return to Rome.[41] We

37. In ll. 14–16, reference is made to statues decorating the cascade, but both the Gondi cascade and Le Pautre's were so adorned. Le Pautre's name is not mentioned in these extracts from Chantelou's diary, but the architect's name also fails to appear in the account of Bernini's visit to the Hôtel de Beauvais (pp. 45–46, n. 51).

38. *Ibid.*, pp. 201–202.
39. *Ibid.*, p. 218.
40. *Ibid.*, p. 221.
41. *Ibid.*, p. 240.

hear no more of this project; apparently, Bernini never executed the model, and the whole idea was dropped.[42]

Bernini's feelings about Le Pautre's cascade are explicit: it was "trop belle," "trop ajustée," and not natural or rustic enough. The whole conception was too artificial, whereas what was demanded was above all a naturalistic form. Le Pautre's creation was to Bernini yet another example of inferior French taste, which delighted in works of art "de plus ajustées et plus petites, comme sont les ouvrages des religieuses." After reading Chantelou, one has the impression that the Italian was fascinated by the cascade but nevertheless could not approve of it aesthetically, for it was, to an emphatic degree, a work which did not *hide* art. Bernini's final sarcasm is memorable: "*È bella, è bella;* qu'à Rome cela serait estimé beau, mais qu'en France cela pouvait passer pour merveilleux."

Although Bernini's design for his rival cascade has not survived, we can be quite certain from Chantelou's diary that its most outstanding characteristic was its naturalistic rock formations, over which the water would have flowed. We possess, however, a supplementary clue to the appearance of this unexecuted work. In 1661, only four years before his trip to France, Bernini had built a cascade at the Villa d'Este at Tivoli. This work, the Cascade of the Water Organ, no longer exists, but its appearance is recorded in an engraving by Venturini (Fig. 81).[43] It is at once apparent that this naturalistic conception corresponds in general to the outlines of the Saint-Cloud project as it emerges from the pages of Chantelou's journal, and that here, in graphic form, is perhaps an indication of the approximate appearance of the proposed Saint-Cloud cascade.

Bernini's attitude towards petrous forms can be more precisely defined by an examination of some of his other works.[44] In the Fountain of the Four Rivers (1648–51) he had created a thoroughly naturalistic rock formation. Natural rock patterns continued to interest him (Fontana del Moro, 1653–55, also in the Piazza Navona), and with the Palazzo Montecitorio (from 1650), he began to introduce these forms in a most interesting way into monumental architecture. In this building, he used massive, roughly hewn quoins to frame the ground floor bays of the lateral sections of the façade. But even more astounding was the use of coarse slabs of rock to serve as sills and friezes of the windows in this part of the façade. Bernini even included sculptured plant growths among these rocks. After his arrival in Paris in 1665, he continued to be absorbed with these forms in connection with the Louvre project. The third design shows heavily rusticated window surrounds and a central portal on the west façade, and a basement course of "natural" rock, creating a rugged, craggy podium for the superstructure.[45] Later in his career, Bernini also planned to use rock forms for the ill-fated equestrian statue of Louis XIV, as is indicated by a drawing in Bassano. The rocky base was meant to represent the Mountain of Virtue.[46]

Clearly, then, Bernini was personally fond of such forms, but what is most

42. Bernini's designs for the cascade are lost.

43. On this cascade see D. R. Coffin, *The Villa d'Este at Tivoli* (Princeton, 1960), p. 113; C. Lamb, *Die Villa d'Este in Tivoli* (Munich, 1966), pp. 56–58.

44. On Bernini's use of natural rock forms in connection with the cascade at Saint-Cloud see also

R. Pane, *Bernini architetto* (Venice, 1953), pp. 92–93.

45. For Bernini's comments on his use of rock forms in the third Louvre design see Fréart de Chantelou, *op. cit.*, pp. 36, 41, 203.

46. See R. Wittkower, "The Vicissitudes of a Dynastic Monument. Bernini's Equestrian Statue of

significant is his individualized treatment of them. For example, the preparatory drawings for the Fountain of the Four Rivers indicate the great attention which he devoted to the conception of the rocky base.[47] Yet the final result in the Piazza Navona hardly suggests as its source the mind and skill of man. The rough, unsymmetrical rock seems shaped by the random forces of nature, not by human endeavor. This is true also of the other examples reviewed here.

Le Pautre also showed an interest in such forms before he built his cascade. In the *Desseins de plusieurs palais,* he had included two plates depicting rustic fountains (Figs. 74, 75).[48] The quality of the rustication here is more rugged and coarse than at Saint-Cloud, but Le Pautre's rock forms are in fact an epidermis, applied to underlying architectural and decorative forms; here and there, this subcutaneous structure shows through the rock-encrusted veneer. Unlike the Italian, the Frenchman is careful to stress the symmetry of the composition and the elegance of the silhouette. Extraordinary as Le Pautre's fountain designs are within the context of French seventeenth century architecture, they differ fundamentally from Bernini's organically naturalistic conceptions.

Similarly, at Saint-Cloud, the conventionalized strips of channeled rustication and the crisply demarcated panels of stalactites (or dripping water) constitute the sole references to the realm of nature. The rest of the cascade is composed of forms found in traditional architecture: a balustrade with statues, regularized arches, wall surfaces, steps, etc. These elements must have recalled to Bernini the world of man-made forms, which he evidently wished to banish when designing a cascade.

The artificial character of Le Pautre's water machine is accentuated by its site. Standing with his back to the Seine, the spectator first perceives the cascade at the end of a long corridor defined by cliff-like walls of clipped trees (Figs. 77, 78). As he approaches the basin at the foot of the cascade, the space expands laterally to left and right, but is again carefully limited by the greenery. Finally, the aggressive form of the cascade makes its full impact, placed in a box-like space bounded by tall trees, like a statue in a niche. Thus, the spaces of the total composition are crisply defined. All of this forms the sharpest possible contrast to Bernini's cascade at the Villa d'Este. Here, although the cascade could be viewed from afar along the cross axis formed by the fish ponds, the greenery was not arranged to carefully close in and define the cascade (Fig. 81).[49] Instead of a projecting, sculptural body, Bernini formed a theater-like concavity of rough boulders and earth, and created the impression that the water boiled up out of the living rock. In front of Le Pautre's cascade, on the

Louis XIV," in M. Meiss, ed., *De Artibus Opuscula XL: Essays in Honor of Erwin Panofsky,* I (New York, 1961), pp. 497–531.

47. R. Wittkower (*Art and Architecture in Italy, 1600 to 1750,* 2d ed. [Baltimore, 1965], p. 351 n. 18) notes that "surviving drawings prove that the rock was designed with the greatest care. . . ." See H. Brauer and R. Wittkower, *Die Zeichnungen des Gianlorenzo Bernini,* II (Berlin, 1931), pls. 25b, 26–28.

Bernini's love of water is indicated in Fréart de Chantelou's entry (*op. cit.,* p. 78) for July 31.

48. The possible borrowing of motifs from

Bernini may here be noted: in Fig. 75 we find two Tritons blowing conch shells who are perhaps direct quotations from the Fontana del Tritone in Rome (1642–43); in Fig. 74 the inverted dolphins of that fountain reappear at the summit, and the horses below seem to be closely dependent upon the figure of the horse (Danube) from the base of the Fountain of the Four Rivers (1648–51), finished just before the publication of the *Desseins de plusieurs palais.*

49. See Lamb, *op. cit.,* fig. 89 for a view across the fish ponds, looking away from Bernini's cascade; no distant view from the opposite direction is avail-

other hand, a spectator is made lucidly aware that the water has been artificially brought to a height in order to plunge downwards in a spectacular display intended for his delight and amusement. The stone aquatic creatures, turtles and frogs, are a fitting accompaniment to Le Pautre's cascade; only live fauna would have been the appropriate inhabitants of Bernini's.

From the preceding discussion it would appear that, when confronted with the task of building cascades, Le Pautre and Bernini differed on fundamental issues. Le Pautre's attitude towards the relationship between architecture and nature is essentially within the classical tradition, which demands that art be an improvement on nature, not a mere imitation of her. Vitruvius, in his account of the origins of human civilization (II, 1, 1–3), wrote that after the discovery of fire and the subsequent development of social intercourse, early man initially made shelters which were literal imitations of natural forms. He dug caves in hills, fashioned mud and wattle to form nests like those of swallows, or simply used leaves to form a covering. But the Roman architect made clear that progress towards a higher architecture was brought about by virtue of man's reason and skill, resulting in buildings containing order and arrangement, proportion, symmetry, decorum, and distribution (I, 2, 1)— qualities very rarely, if ever, found in nature. This basic postulate of the classical viewpoint perhaps explains why Renaissance theorists looked upon rough Antique rustication as unfinished work.[50] And Le Pautre's cascade, with its essentially architectonic structure tinged with stylized references to natural forms, undoubtedly pleased such strict classical theoreticians like d'Aviler, who explicitly recommended (with reference to grottos) that "l'ordre qui les décore par dehors, doit estre rustique, & le dedans enrichi d'ornemens maritimes, de petrifications, de glaçons, de masques, & de festons de coquillages sans confusion, afin que l'architecture ne perde point sa forme nonobstant la Rocaille."[51]

On the other hand, Bernini's Saint-Cloud project, as it is reported by Chantelou and reflected in the Tivoli cascade, seems to have stressed the imitative capacity of art: a man-made cascade is to be a simulation of a natural one. In Italy, a tradition for this conception already existed in the sixteenth and early seventeenth centuries, as at Tivoli (Fig. 83) and Frascati.[52] We know, however, that at the moment in his career when he designed a naturalistic cascade for Saint-Cloud, Bernini firmly professed his faith in the classical view that art must be a refinement upon nature. In his famous address to the Royal Academy of Painting and Sculpture in Paris, he emphasized the need to study Antique sculpture before studying nature, and declared that the latter was almost always "faible et mesquine."[53] A more careful examination of the Tivoli cascade (Fig. 81) reveals, indeed, that the central torrent was carefully balanced

able. Nevertheless, Venturini's engraving reveals a more variegated treatment of greenery, which is less space-defining than at Saint-Cloud.

50. Cf., e.g., A. Palladio, *I quattro libri dell'architettura*, I (Venice, 1570), x. Bernini did not challenge Chantelou's belief that rough rustication was a modern invention, unknown to the Ancients (Fréart de Chantelou, *op. cit.*, p. 41).

51. A. C. d'Aviler, *Cours d'architecture*, I (Paris, 1694), p. 199.

52. Tivoli: Fountain of Rome, begun 1567–68 (see Coffin, *op. cit.*, pp. 23ff.); Frascati: rustic cascades at the Villa Aldobrandini (C. D'Onofrio, *La Villa Aldobrandini di Frascati* [Rome, 1963], figs. 72, 73). The cascades at the Villa Aldobrandini are the work of Carlo Maderno and Giovanni Fontana, 1603–4.

53. Fréart de Chantelou, *op. cit.*, entry for September 5.

on either side by smaller cataracts; by means of this compositional arrangement, Bernini undoubtedly intended his cascade to be an improvement upon nature, not a literal imitation, as at first glance it may appear to be.[54] Furthermore, this tripartite composition echoes the main lines of Le Pautre's cascade, with its central and flanking ramps (cf. Figs. 70, 81): in both instances, seventeenth century designers have adhered to the common notion of a symmetrical design with an accented center. It would appear, therefore, that both Le Pautre and Bernini subscribed to classical theory, but since their respective creations are poles apart stylistically, we must search for other factors to account for their contrasting conceptions.

In approaching this problem we must recognize that Le Pautre and Bernini drew upon differing traditions of cascade design. Le Pautre's cascade traces its ancestry back to the formalized, architectonic cascade which had been developed in Italy during the sixteenth century[55] and codified in the main cascade of the Villa Aldobrandini at Frascati (1603–4). The artificiality and stylization of these cascades and their progeny in France[56] represent a process of architectural abstraction of natural forms, which satisfies the basic demands of classical thought outlined above. But, as already noted, the Italian sixteenth century also spawned the naturalistic cascade, which allowed architects to closely imitate nature through naturalistic rock formations and asymmetry (Fig. 83). What is most significant is that this type of cascade was never adopted in France until the introduction of the *jardin anglais* in the second half of the eighteenth century; until then, only the architectonic type appeared in French gardens. This more restrictive situation suggests a relationship to the tradition of French classicism—more orthodox than the Italian—with its pronounced emphasis on structural clarity, whether in the fine arts, literature, or philosophy. And the appearance of naturalistic elements in severely stylized form corresponds to the contemporary French insistence on the idealization of nature, as realized in the works of Poussin and Racine.

The greater degree of stylization of the rustic features of the cascade in comparison with the fountain designs of 1652 (cf. Figs. 71, 72, 74, 75) is indicative of Le Pautre's stylistic position, for by 1664–65 he was on the threshold of his final, less Baroque period. Nevertheless, the violence, drama, and movement of the waters at Saint-Cloud were not emulated in France, and Le Pautre's cascade was never chosen as a model. Instead, the emphasis turned to serene or delicately playful forms, which graced the gardens of Le Nôtre.

54. Of course, the structure at the top of Fig. 81 is not due to Bernini; it is the Water Organ, begun in 1568 by Lucha Clericho (Luc LeClerc?) and Claude Venard (Coffin, *op. cit.*, p. 17). The balustrade probably dates from the sixteenth century; see the map (1573) by Étienne Dupérac where a railing is indicated at this point (*ibid.*, fig. 1). According to Lamb (*op. cit.*, p. 56), the lateral cataracts of Bernini's cascade were never executed, but Venturini's engraving probably indicates the intended design.

55. Villa Lante, Bagnaia (Vignola?, ca. 1566); Casino, Caprarola (ca. 1586?); Stairs of the Bubbling Fountains, Villa d'Este, Tivoli (begun 1567); Villa d'Este, Cernobbio (Pellegrino Pellegrini, 1570); Villa Cicogna, Bisuschio. Another important early Baroque formalized cascade is at the Villa Torlonia (Ludovisi-Conti) at Frascati (Carlo Maderno, from 1607).

56. Cascade at Rueil (Jacques Lemercier and Jean Thiriot, begun 1632); Le Pautre's cascade at Saint-Cloud. Other stylized French seventeenth century cascades were descended from the Viale delle Cento Fontane at the Villa d'Este, Tivoli: Fontainebleau (Rémy Collin, 1606–9?); Gondi cascade, Saint-Cloud (Fig. 80, before 1644); Liancourt (Jacques Lemercier, finished before 1637); Vaux-le-Vicomte (between 1656 and 1661, authorship uncertain). The

cascade at Rueil (Fig. 82), built for Richelieu, was the model for Le Pautre's cascade, but the water was used in a less dramatic, more decorative, fashion. Lemercier's cascade was also less sculpturally aggressive, lacked the upper arcaded wall, and was not as rich in fantasy of conception. Begun in 1632, the cascade was paid for in 1639; the executant was Jean Thiriot. It was destroyed in the nineteenth century. See A. Cramail, *Le château de Ruel et ses jardins sous le Cardinal de Richelieu et sous la Duchesse d'Aiguillon* (Fontainebleau, 1888), pp. 6, 75.

8

Château de Saint-Cloud

There has been great confusion concerning the authorship of the Château de Saint-Cloud, photographed before its destruction in 1870 during the Franco-Prussian War (Fig. 91).[1] Some writers attribute the entire château to Le Pautre,[2] others assign only the two wings to Antoine[3] and the *corps-de-logis* to Jean Girard.[4] The engraver Perelle gives total credit to Girard;[5] yet other authors name Jules Hardouin-Mansart

1. See the album by Schneider (Estampes, Ve 99b +) and *Prométhée* (1939–40), pp. 292–295.
Two pediments from the château have survived: one is at the Palace of Euxinograd in Bulgaria (G. Darney, *Saint-Cloud* [Paris, 1903], fig. p. 35); a second is on the property of M. le comte de Saint-Léon at Jeurre, near Étampes (A. Marie, "Vestiges du palais," *Les amis de Saint-Cloud* [1955], unpaginated).

2. J. A. Piganiol de la Force, *Nouvelle description de la France*, 2d ed., II (Paris, 1722), ii, p. 688; *idem, Description de Paris, de Marly, de Meudon, de S. Cloud, de Fontainebleau . . .* , new ed., VIII (Paris, 1742), p. 273; P. T. N. Hurtaut and Magny, *Dictionnaire historique de la ville de Paris et de ses environs . . .* , II (Paris, 1779), p. 361; Hautecoeur, II, i, pp. 154–162.

3. J. F. Blondel, *Cours d'architecture*, III (Paris, 1772), p. 444, n. f; A. N. Dezallier d'Argenville, *Voyage pittoresque des environs de Paris*, 4th ed. (Paris, 1779), pp. 41–42; F. Milizia, *Memorie degli architetti antichi e moderni*, 4th ed., II (Bassano, 1785), p. 210; A. N. Dezallier d'Argenville, *Vies des fameux architectes depuis la renaissance des arts . . .* (Paris, 1787), p. 396; J. A. Dulaure, *Nouvelle description des environs de Paris*, 2d ed., I (Paris, 1787), p. 107; L. V. Thiéry,

Guide des amateurs et des étrangers voyageurs dans les maisons royales . . . aux environs de Paris (Paris, 1788), p. 325; G. Poncet de la Grave, *Mémoires intéressans pour servir à l'histoire de France . . .* , III (Paris, 1789), p. 23; J. Vatout, *Palais de Saint-Cloud* (Paris, 1852), p. 210; P. de Saint-Albin and A. Durantin, *Palais de Saint-Cloud, résidence impériale* (Paris, 1864), p. 239; F. Kimball, *Le style Louis XV. Origine et évolution du rococo* (Paris, 1949), p. 26; A. Marie, *Le palais de St-Cloud* (Paris, 1952), p. 14.

4. J. Mariette (inscription on Fig. 86): "Elevations des façades du Château de Saint Cloud, du côté de l'entrée ou de la grande cour. Le grand corps de logis au fond de la cour a été bâti sur les desseins du Sr. Girard et les deux ailes l'ont été sur ceux de Jules Hardouin Mansart." Also: Dezallier d'Argenville, *Voyage pittoresque . . .* , pp. 41–42; Dulaure, *op. cit.*, I, p. 107; Thiéry, *op. cit.*, p. 325; Poncet de la Grave, *op. cit.*, III, p. 23; Vatout, *op. cit.*, p. 210; Saint-Albin and Durantin, *op. cit.*, p. 238; E. Magne, *Le château de Saint-Cloud* (Paris, 1932), pp. 124–125; Marie, *Le palais . . .* , p. 14.

5. "Le Chasteau de St. Clou du costé que l'on arrive, achevé en 1680. appartenant à Monsieur frere unique du Roy. Le sieur Girard en a esté l'Architecte;

as architect of the wings.[6] The loss of the account books of Philippe d'Orléans has prevented a solution of the problem by reference to this source, but sufficient evidence can be gleaned from other quarters to allow a convincing answer to the question of artistic responsibility.

As we have seen, Antoine Le Pautre was appointed architect to Monsieur in 1660, and built for his patron the upper cascade at Saint-Cloud (1664–65). We do not know when Philippe decided to replace the old Maison de Gondi by a more modern château, but by 1671 the left (south) wing of the new structure was complete, built upon the foundations of the original country house.[7] The corresponding wing vis-à-vis to the north was then undertaken on the same design sometime afterwards, and was completed before August 17, 1677; a document bearing that date refers to the two wings as already finished.[8]

During all these years, Le Pautre remained Monsieur's architect-in-chief, and the fact that he still held this position in 1677 is confirmed by the following notice in the minutes of the Royal Academy of Architecture for July 12, 1677:

> M. *Le Pautre* . . . a fait sa plainte qu'ayant donné divers desseins pour Saint Cloud au nommé Girard, masson, le dit Girard s'est si peu soucié de les suivre et de les bien exécuter, qu'au contraire il s'est ingéré de les estropier et gaster dans la plus grande partie; pêchant en mille endroits contre la beauté et la solidité de l'architecture; à laquelle plainte M. *Mansart* s'est joint pour pareil sujet, contre le mesme masson, qui en a usé de mesme à son égard, dont la compagnie leur a donné acte.[9]

We would expect that Jean Girard, the mason here referred to, was instantly replaced, but one month later, on August 17, 1677, we find him still active at Saint-Cloud and referred to as "entrepreneur des Bastimens de Monseigneur." [10] This

---

et Mr. Mignard en a peint la gallerie qui est a main droite, et le Salon attenant. les ouvrages de Peinture qui sont de l'autre costé, sont de Mr Nocret Peintre ordinaire de son Altesse Royale." Also: "Le Chasteau de St. Cloud veu du costé de la grande piece d'eau Faite par le Sr. Girard Architecte."

6. Mariette (see n. 4); Magne, *op. cit.*, pp. 118–124.

7. An engraving by Silvestre dated 1671 (Fig. 77) shows this wing completed.

A comparison of the plan of the Maison de Gondi (Fig. 76) with that of the ground floor of the subsequent château (Fig. 84) reveals that the first thirteen bays of the south wing of the later structure (counting from the east) corresponded almost precisely with the southern rectangular block of the earlier building. The utilization of the foundations of the Maison de Gondi is also indicated in AN, QI 1494, liasse: Domaine de St Cloud, April–May 1759; Vatout, *op. cit.*, pp. 125, 376 n. 1.

Hautecoeur (II, i, p. 161) states that Le Pautre's plans were drawn up at the end of 1670, but since the later, north wing was not finished until 1677, it seems more likely that construction was first undertaken in

the mid- to late 1660's. Kimball (*op. cit.*, p. 26) gives 1660 as the start of construction, but this appears to be too early.

8. Minutier, CXIII 84[bis]: "Devis des ouvrages de maconneries qu'il convient faire pour la construction du grand bastiment que desire faire faire Son Altesse Royalle Monsieur frere unique du Roy en son chasteau de St Clou entre les deux ailles a present construites. . . ."

9. Lemonnier, I, p. 147. Girard apparently was acting at the same time as mason for Hardouin-Mansart, probably at the Château de Clagny (begun 1675). The *Comptes* bears the following entry: "31 janvier 1679–20 janvier 1680: à Le Maistre, Girard, Gabriel et Hardouin, maçons, à compte de leurs ouvrages de maçonnerie au corps de logis principal, à l'aile et à l'orangerie en retour de lad. aile, à Clagny" (Guiffrey, I, col. 1187). If Jean Girard is indeed referred to here, then he retained his post as mason even after Mansart had complained to the Academy in 1677, just as he remained at Saint-Cloud despite Le Pautre's protestations.

10. Minutier, CXIII 84bis.

reference occurs in a detailed contract for the *corps-de-logis* of the château which is accompanied by a proposed plan of the *rez-de-chaussée* (Fig. 92). This plan is unquestionably by Le Pautre; Girard is referred to as *entrepreneur* rather than as architect, and the stair (which will be analyzed later) is of a form which only Le Pautre among French architects would have devised.[11] But this plan of 1677 was not executed, for reasons that remain obscure, as is demonstrated by a comparison of it with the realized scheme, published by Mariette (Figs. 84, 85).[12] We do know, however, that on November 25, 1683 — several years after the death of Le Pautre — Monsieur made a donation to Jean Girard, who was then referred to as "son [Monsieur's] intendant et architecte des bâtiments."[13] Thus, this mason succeeded in remaining in the favor of Philippe d'Orléans even after his superior complained of his ineptitude at the Royal Academy, and advanced to Le Pautre's post after the latter's death.[14]

11. Since Le Pautre had been a member of the Royal Academy of Architecture since its foundation in 1671, he was forbidden to act as *entrepreneur*, and hence is not mentioned in the contract, which was signed by Girard and Joachim Seiglière de Boisfranc, Monsieur's treasurer.

12. Mariette's plates of Saint-Cloud were published in 1738, but there is no record of any significant alterations to the original structures until the time of Mique and Marie-Antoinette.

13. Minutier, CXIII 117.

14. The earliest reference we have concerning Jean Girard dates from 1668 when he was referred to as a master mason in association with Jean Le Pautre, master mason (AN, Z¹ʲ 300). It is not clear whether this Jean Le Pautre was the brother-in-law of Adam Philippon (see Introduction, n. 13) or whether he was that younger brother of Antoine Le Pautre who was born in 1627 and is mentioned in a document dated October 1, 1656 (A. Jal, *Dictionnaire critique de biographie et d'histoire*, 2d ed. [Paris, 1872], p. 774; Jal confuses this Jean with his brother, also a master mason, born in 1622, died in 1648: see Laborde, nouv. acq. franç. 12141, no. 42.356 [June 14, 1648]). Be that as it may, Jean Girard married on September 19, 1671, and the marriage document refers to him as "Jean Girard, architecte"; his wife died shortly thereafter on October 11, 1674, at which time he was termed "architecte entrepreneur de bâtiments de Monsieur, frère unique du Roy" (H. Herluison, *Actes d'état-civil d'artistes français* [Paris and Orléans, 1873], p. 156). On March 14, 1675 he appears as a master mason in connection with the construction of a new "chastelet" in the rue Saint-André-des-Arts in Paris (Guiffrey, I, col. 813). On March 28, 1695 he acknowledged receipt of 600 livres a year from Philippe d'Orléans (A. Lance, *Dictionnaire des architectes français*, I [Paris, 1872], p. 311 n. 1).

Aside from the *corps-de-logis* of the Château de Saint-Cloud, another work which can be attributed to Girard is the stair of the Hôtel de Vic, Paris (A. C. d'Aviler, *Cours d'architecture*, new ed. [Paris, 1738], pl. 63Q: "Plan et elevation de l'escalier de l'hôtel de Vic ruë St. Martin du dessein du Sr. Girard Architecte de Mr. le Duc d'Orléans."). According to Dezallier d'Argenville (*Voyage pittoresque* . . . , p. 54), Girard was the designer of the Bassin des Cygnes (Bassin du Fer-à-Cheval) in front of the park façade of the south wing. This construction still exists (Fig. 88). It would appear that Girard also bears responsibility for the pendant orangery, which extended towards the west (Fig. 90). Fig. 90 also shows the park façade of the *corps-de-logis*, also attributable to Girard, which was later covered by a new construction due to Mique under Marie-Antoinette. Probably also Girard's were the service buildings of the *avant-cour*, one of which still exists as the École normale supérieure d'enseignement primaire. Magne (*op. cit.*, p. 141) gives the date 1678 for these buildings without furnishing evidence.

References also occur in the *Comptes* of payments to a "Girard, maçon," but it is open to question whether Jean Girard is here referred to (Guiffrey, I, cols. 329, 500–501 [Bastille, 1669, 1672]; cols. 472, 639, 819, 890, 949, 988, 1027 [Pépinière du Roule, Paris, 1670–78]; col. 888 [Palais-Royal, 1676]; col. 1187 [Clagny, 1679–80; see above, n. 9]). A "Sr Girard, inspecteur à la pépinière du Roule" is mentioned between 1698 and 1710 (*ibid.*, IV, cols. 412, 421, 552, 680, 796, 911, 1020, 1126, 1233; V, cols. 94, 101, 186, 192, 283, 290, 295, 389, 469, 470).

On the subsequent history of the Château de Saint-Cloud see the bibliography in Magne, *op. cit.*, pp. 201ff. and D. Meyer, "Les appartements royaux du Château de Saint-Cloud sous Louis XVI et Marie-Antoinette, 1785–1792," *GBA*, s. 6, LXVI (1965), pp. 223–232.

These facts perhaps strengthen the traditional attribution of the *corps-de-logis* to Girard, and (as will subsequently be analyzed) there is, indeed, a clear distinction in terms of style between the wings and the main block. But upon closer examination of the former elements, we note that, although each wing consists in plan of fifteen bays (Figs. 84, 85), there is an abrupt change in elevation between the thirteenth and fourteenth bays (counting from the ends of the wings along the court façades towards the *corp-de-logis;* Fig. 87, lower). Furthermore, the style of the last two bays is extremely similar to that of the main block. It is therefore of crucial importance to determine the dates of the last two bays of each wing. The contract for the unexecuted *corps-de-logis* referred to above speaks of "les deux ailes a present construites," [15] and the accompanying plan (Fig. 92) stops short at the beginning of the last wing bays. Hence, it would appear that those bays were completed by August 17, 1677. Certainly, all was ready by October 6, 1678, for on that date Monsieur viewed Mignard's decoration of the long gallery for the first time, and those paintings, devoted to the Four Seasons, occupied all fifteen bays of the *premier étage* of the north wing.[16]

The contract of August 17, 1677 specifically called for the erection of the *corps-de-logis* during 1677 and 1678 but, as noted above, this project was not carried out. On May 9, 1680, however, Louis XIV paid an official visit to the château, and the *Mercure galant* specifically mentions that the royal party passed through the apartments of Monsieur and Madame before reaching the long gallery.[17] These apartments were located on the *premier étage* of the *corps-de-logis*, and hence it would appear that this part of the building was virtually complete by that date. Certainly, the decoration of the *grand salon* of the *premier étage* (the Loves of Mars and Venus, by Mignard) was finished by December 1680, for this fact is noted in the *Mercure galant;*[18] this room was under construction at least as early as June 1679.[19] A royal visit on a grander scale took place during March 15–22, 1681, and the *Mercure galant* this time describes the movement of the court in detail, tracing a progression up the main stair in the left wing, across the *premier étage* of that wing, through the *corps-*

15. See n. 8.

16. *Mercure galant* (October 1678), p. 210: "Il [Monsieur] en visita les Appartements [on October 6], & ne pût que loüer l'exactitude du Sieur Billon, à qui la direction de cette belle Maison a esté donnée. Son Altesse Royale alla en suite dans la Gallerie qu'il n'avoit point encor veüe depuis qu'elle est achevée & meublée." Billon was not an architect but a concierge, who operated the cascade in 1665 when Bernini visited Saint-Cloud (see Chapter 7). Louis XIV officially viewed the gallery during October 10–15, 1678 (*ibid.*, pp. 209ff.). The paintings are described in detail in *ibid.* (June 1680), pp. 92ff. Monsieur himself visited Mignard early in 1677 (*ibid.* [January–March 1677], p. 137), and the decoration was presumably begun that year.

17. *Ibid.* (May 1680), pp. 295–311.

18. *Ibid.* (December 1680), pp. 111–112: "Le

plaisir que vous a donné la Description de la Galerie de S. Cloud, peinte par Monsieur Mignard, me fait juger que c'est vous donner une agreable nouvelle, que de vous apprendre qu'il a enfin achevé de peindre le magnifique Sallon qui fait une des beautez de ce mesme Lieu. Il avoit pris pour sujet les Amours de Mars, & de Venus." A description of the paintings then follows.

19. That the *grand salon* was under construction in June 1679 is proven by the following lines from the journal of Baron de Vuoerdan (le grand Condé) for June 28, 1679: "On travaille à un salon, au bout de la galerie, qui sera plus magnifique encore, et, au sortir du salon, il y a un vestibule d'une pareille magnificence" (M. Sautai, "Une visite à Versailles et à Saint-Cloud en 1679. Le grand Condé à Chantilly," *Les marches de l'est,* IV [1913], pp. 777–778).

de-logis to the *grand salon* and the long gallery of the right wing.[20] Thus, it would appear that the *corps-de-logis* was essentially finished by 1680 or 1681, and this analysis is confirmed by other contemporary sources.[21]

The problem which confronts us is the following: the wings (fifteen bays each) of the château were completed by August 1677 (certainly before October 1678), hence during a time when Le Pautre was still active as an architect.[22] The fourteenth and fifteenth bays of each wing, however, are quite unlike the main body of the wings in style, and are much closer in spirit to the *corps-de-logis*. Granted that the first thirteen bays of each wing were designed by Antoine, was he also responsible for the sudden shift in design between bays thirteen and fourteen? If so, is he then to receive credit for the *corps-de-logis* (Figs. 86, 90, 91)? As we shall see when discussing the Château de Clagny (Chapter 10), Le Pautre in 1674 produced a design which has several elements in common with the problematical elevations at Saint-Cloud: untextured, planar surfaces, straight-headed openings, and bas-relief panels over windows. Hence, given the tendencies within Le Pautre's last period, it is not outside the realm of possibility to assign the last two bays of the wings and the main château block to him. Nevertheless, I reject the attribution of these parts of the building to Le Pautre on several grounds. First, it seems highly unlikely that the same architect would have created so radical a stylistic dichotomy within a building over all the parts of which he had complete control. In particular, the break between the thirteenth and fourteenth bays is exceedingly sharp, and there are a number of solecisms in the continuity and linkage of parts. Although the string course dividing the ground floor from the first floor is continuous between the two sections of the wings, this is not true of the moldings above, where the entablature and balustrade over the main section of the wings end unceremoniously and rather incoherently against the terminal sections. In addition, one would have expected the main body of each wing to have been entirely symmetrical, but upon close examination it is evident that an area of wall and a terminal pilaster have been omitted at the juncture of bays thirteen and fourteen. These features suggest an intruding personality, and this could only have been Jean Girard. This analysis may also provide some grounds for the belief that Le Pautre's bitter complaint to the Academy on July 12, 1677 was provoked by Girard's interference with Le Pautre's project at precisely this point. This state of affairs may seem incredible: how could an *entrepreneur* have succeeded in altering a design so radically? But we have evidence of an equally extraordinary nature in that Girard remained at his post even after having been formally and acridly denounced in the Royal Academy of Architecture.

There is an additional piece of evidence—an undated print by Silvestre (Fig. 89)—which shows the south (park) façade of the château. Here we find that the sec-

20. *Mercure galant*, April 1681, pp. 327ff.

21. See Perelle's inscription, quoted in n. 5; also Combes, *Explication historique, de ce qu'il y a de plus remarquable dans la maison royale de Versailles. et en celle de Monsieur à Saint Cloud* (Paris, 1681), pp. 2–3, where the *corps-de-logis* is spoken of as standing.

22. See Introduction, p. 5. There is no evidence for Magne's assertion (*op. cit.*, pp. 117–118) that Jules Hardouin-Mansart replaced Le Pautre at the end of 1675 or the beginning of 1676. Hautecoeur wrongly states (II, ii, p. 585) that Mansart intervened at Saint-Cloud from 1677 on. For Mansart's actual role see n. 30.

tion of elevation corresponding to bays fourteen and fifteen on the court façade is expanded to three bays, and this accords with Mariette's plan (Fig. 85).[23] But the design of this section as well as the fragment of the *corps-de-logis* which follows is quite different from the building as executed (cf. Figs. 88, 89).[24] In Silvestre's print, the horizontal moldings of the various sections of elevation join smoothly; the buildings are lower in height, contain fewer stories, and many details are present which do not appear in the executed structure. There is, in addition, a more unified quality to the entire expanse. In view of these facts, it is highly likely, I believe, that Silvestre here depicted Le Pautre's intended scheme, of which the engraver apparently had knowledge. The design for the terminal wing bays was drastically altered by Girard, as we have attempted to demonstrate; that for the *corps-de-logis*, accepted on August 17, 1677, was subsequently abandoned. Hence, the *corps-de-logis* itself must also be due to Girard.[25]

With this proposed solution of dating and attribution in mind, let us proceed to a stylistic analysis of the forms themselves.

When Le Pautre turned his attention to the task of creating a new château for Monsieur, a building already existed on the site—the Maison de Gondi (from 1577).[26] The plan of its ground floor is fortunately preserved (Fig. 76). It consisted of a rectangular block, with a rectangular vestibule and chapel appended on the west (the chapel was of quatrefoil plan internally; the external walls were polygonal). To the west, and attached to the southern block to form an L-shaped layout, was a service wing composed of kitchens and a court. The center of the southern range (the *corps-de-logis*) was taken up by a large stair cage which filled the entire width of the building, to the east and west of which were *appartements* composed of square and rectangular rooms.

The elevations of the Maison de Gondi were decidedly old-fashioned by 1665, with their picturesque exterior frescos, accumulation of small details, vertical emphasis, and steep single-sloped roofs.[27] Clearly, Monsieur had no use for this sixteenth century mode, and called upon Le Pautre to design in a style more respresentative of the royal status of the new owner. But, as previously indicated,[28] Monsieur's new southern wing (completed by 1671) was built precisely upon the foundations of the *corps-de-logis* of the Maison de Gondi, and preserved the ground floor arrangement of a central stair cage flanked by *appartements*.[29] Fig. 76 makes clear that the Maison de Gondi was meant to be approached from the south: the visitor, after traversing the garden, mounted a large outdoor stair to an upper terrace upon which the house

23. That there were three bays on the park façade at this point is also indicated in Fig. 88.

24. Old photographs published in *Prométhée* (1939–40), pp. 292–295 indicate that by 1870 these parts of the château had been radically altered from their seventeenth century condition.

25. As is pointed out in the text, Girard's probable interference with the terminal bays of the wings took place while Antoine was still active and nominally in charge of architectural matters at Saint-Cloud. Antoine died on January 3, 1679 (see pp. 5–6). It

would appear that Monsieur advanced Girard to Le Pautre's post in that year, when the *corps-de-logis* was begun (see n. 19).

26. On the Maison de Gondi see Chapter 7, n. 1.

27. See Hautecoeur, ii, i, fig. 158.

28. See n. 7.

29. Fig. 84 shows Mansart's stair, constructed in 1687/88 (see n. 30); Le Pautre's stair occupied the same location.

was placed. In the center of the southern façade was the entrance, which led to the stair cage. Hence, the building was clearly oriented towards the south as a freestanding block, without introductory wings enclosing a *cour d'honneur*. The history of the construction of the Château de Saint-Cloud strongly suggests that Monsieur originally intended his new southern range to constitute, by itself, *the* château, and to be, like its predecessor, a freestanding rectangular unit, oriented, likewise, toward the south. At some subsequent date, a radical change of program occurred: it was decided that the freestanding southern block was to form one wing of a much larger château of characteristic U-shaped plan. This scheme, probably inspired by contemporary developments at Versailles, resulted in an east–west orientation, a change of 90 degrees in the axis of the château so that it now faced the Seine (Fig. 78). Construction of the second wing could be undertaken next since its elevation, at least, was given by the southern unit. The steep hill to the north, however, dictated a drastic reduction in the thickness of the northern wing (Figs. 84, 85).

With reference to the plan, we note that for the first time in his career Le Pautre has completely opened up the entrance side of the courtyard. The concept of an enclosed court is completely abandoned; thereby Le Pautre was again following the example of Versailles, where Le Vau in 1668–69 had pulled down the arcaded screen which closed the *cour de marbre*, thus creating a totally open court, a feature that was in harmony with seventeenth century development. As we have noted, it was in the northern wing, on the main floor, that Antoine placed the long gallery, which terminated in a smaller *salon* placed at right angles to it. Our analysis indicates that Girard must be responsible for the *grand salon* which preceded the gallery, but it is not unlikely that Le Pautre would have proceeded in a similar manner. However, the eccentric placing of the far *salon* in Antoine's scheme did not permit the orderly spatial progression achieved in contemporary French gallery design. This breakdown of the Baroque conception of dramatic but orderly spatial movement is also reflected in the additive treatment of square and rectangular rooms. No curves of any sort appear on the plan, and no greater contrast could be imagined between this undynamic conception of planning and the effects achieved by Le Pautre during the 1650's. As previously noted, Antoine utilized the existing foundations of the Maison de Gondi in the southern wing, and this was an important factor in his choice of room shape. But the foundations did not dictate the total spatial configuration; the architect did enjoy a substantial measure of "freedom," and the conception of this work indicates his stylistic position as he entered his final phase.[30]

Le Pautre conceived of the court façades of his wings in terms different from those of the end and outer façades. In the former, he used a small-scale order of

30. The great staircase of the southern wing was attributed to Hardouin-Mansart by d'Aviler (*Cours d'architecture* [Paris, 1750], pp. 224–225, pl. 63R). He was followed by Dezallier d'Argenville (*Voyage pittoresque . . .*, pp. 42–43), Thiéry (*op. cit.*, pp. 325–326), and Poncet de la Grave (*op. cit.*, III, p. 24). An indication of its date is provided by the Marquis de Dangeau, who wrote on November 28, 1688: "S. M.

[Louis XIV] alla d'abord à Saint-Cloud, qu'on trouva fort embelli par le nouvel escalier que Monsieur a fait faire" (E. Soulié *et al.*, eds., *Journal du Marquis de Dangeau*, II [Paris, 1854], p. 219). We do not know precisely when Mansart became architect to Monsieur (thus supplanting Girard who, nevertheless, continued in the service of Philippe d'Orléans; see n. 14), but this entry would seem to indicate that the stair was

Tuscan pilasters (reminiscent of those used in the early Hôtel de Fontenay-Mareuil) over a more vigorous ground floor of channeled masonry, with niches adding a slight degree of plasticity. The central pavilion was accentuated by an unbroken, triangular pediment and by four full columns on the ground floor. The uniformity and placidity of the design were enhanced by the uninterrupted double-sloped roof and by the balustrade.[31]

Because of Mansart's alterations of the park façades of the wings, Le Pautre's original intentions are best conveyed by the prints of Silvestre (Figs. 77, 89).[32] On the end and outer façades, Antoine used an over-all texture of smoothly channeled masonry, as in the executed design for his Château de Seiglière de Boisfranc at Saint-Ouen (finished by 1672; see Chapter 9) and the subsequent orangery there (1678/79) — a textural treatment favored during the architect's final phase.[33] On the park façade of the south wing, Le Pautre was forced to place the two main stories on a podium because of a sharp declivity, and he treated this as a totally flat, unarticulated wall, punctuated by great arches, which forms a strong textural contrast with the elevations above.[34] Small bas-relief panels appear above the top floor windows.

The long, low massing of these wings stands in strong contrast to Le Pautre's earlier designs of the 1650's, and constitutes a characteristic of his last phase of development, along with the use of over-all channeling. The wings at Saint-Cloud provide evidence of the architect's movement away from his full Baroque style, towards a more placid, calm architectural expression, and this is reflected in the interior

executed in 1688. Furthermore, Nicodemus Tessin the Younger wrote in 1687 that "Cet Escailler sera aggrandy . . ." ("Relation de la visite de Nicodème Tessin à Marly, Versailles, Clagny, Rueil et Saint-Cloud en 1687 [suite et fin]," *Revue de l'histoire de Versailles et de Seine-et-Oise*, XXVIII [1926], p. 296). Hence Mansart's stair can be dated 1687/88. Mansart remodeled Le Pautre's stair (design unknown), for which Antoine may have simply retained the old stair of the Maison de Gondi. See also n. 32 for other work by Mansart at Saint-Cloud.

31. The balustrades on all façades of the wings may be later additions since they do not appear in Fig. 89.

32. Mansart probably built the columnar screen across the first two stories of the park façade of the southern wing (Figs. 84, 87, 88). The screen was first attributed to Mansart by Hautecoeur (II, ii, p. 586). Because the land falls away sharply on the south, this façade had three stories. The screen does not appear in several prints which depict this façade (Figs. 77, 78, 89), and it cannot be linked with Le Pautre, who never used such a conception. But, as noted by Hautecoeur (*ibid.*), Mansart was fond of such columnar screens, as at the Hôtel de Lorge, Paris (before 1680), and at his own house in the rue des Tournelles, Paris (1687).

Turning to the exterior elevations of the wings, we note that all representations of the park façade of the southern wing which do not indicate Mansart's screen depict square-headed windows on the two upper stories (Figs. 77, 78, 89). However, all prints which do depict this screen show round-headed windows on the upper floor (Figs. 87, 88), and old photographs confirm that such windows actually existed. There can be little doubt that these windows were altered by Mansart, just as he had transformed Le Vau's flat-headed windows at Versailles when creating the Galerie des Glaces (begun 1678). All the visual evidence is in agreement concerning the fact that the windows of the *premier étage* of the end façades of the wings were round-headed, but that its *rez-de-chaussée* as well as the stories of the court façades contained flat-headed fenestration.

33. This type of articulation, characteristically used without the orders, appeared earlier in France, as at the Châteaux de Cheverny (Jacques Bougier [or Boyer], finished 1634) and de Fayelles (Jacques Bruant?, ca. 1654?).

34. Le Pautre's design bears a resemblance to the east and south façades of the Louvre (begun 1667 and 1668, respectively, hence precisely contemporary with the south wing at Saint-Cloud): all feature a smooth, flat basement with arched openings, contrasting with the richer treatment above. Were Monsieur and his architect attempting to infuse Saint-Cloud with the royal symbolism embodied in the new Louvre façades? I owe this observation and suggestion to Prof. John Coolidge.

planning, as previously analyzed. This change seems to have set in during the mid- to late 1660's, when the southern wing was begun.[35]

Le Pautre's plan for the *corps-de-logis* (Fig. 92) was accepted on August 17, 1677, but was subsequently abandoned for unknown reasons. Here again, all rooms were rectangular and static,[36] but the plan included one very remarkable feature, a converging staircase. This immediately brings to mind Bernini's Scala Regia in the Vatican (1663–66), nearing completion when Bernini visited Paris in 1665. Unlike the Roman prototype, however, Le Pautre's stair does not extend laterally to occupy the entire width of the cage, but is flanked by corridor spaces. Furthermore, the stair lacks a columnar order [37] and was not planned to be dramatically lit by outdoor lighting, as was Bernini's. Nevertheless, Le Pautre's design is unique in French architecture—a last, eleventh-hour experiment with a form inspired by the Italian High Baroque, but treated in a devitalized manner.

With the Château de Saint-Cloud, Le Pautre entered upon his final phase of development, characterized by the abandonment of the intensive Baroque style of his middle years and the adoption of a number of design elements which resulted in a calmer, less dramatic architectural expression. These included the emphasis on long, low silhouettes, the reduction of sculptural elevational elements and the use, instead, of over-all channeled masonry. Indicative of the architect's altered approach are the open court, the additive manipulation of square and rectangular rooms, and the lack of orderly and dynamic spatial progressions. We shall now see how these features were elaborated upon at Saint-Ouen and Clagny while Saint-Cloud was rising.[38]

---

35. See n. 7.

36. The large oval chamber on the south does not communicate with the rest of the *rez-de-chaussée*, and may be an indication of the upper space of a service area in the *sous-sol*.

37. The Royal Academy of Architecture formally condemned the use of orders in stairs on June 15, 1682 (Lemonnier, II, p. 12).

The rejection of Le Pautre's scheme necessitated the retention of the main stair in the south wing. This scheme echoed Versailles and the Escalier des Ambassadeurs (1671–79). At Saint-Cloud, the journey from the stair to the *pièce de résistance*—Mignard's decorations in the northern wing—was a long and circuitous one.

38. Two prints by Perelle (Hautecoeur, II, i, figs. 160, 162) are very troublesome because they neither agree with one another nor with the other visual evidence here reviewed. Hautecoeur (II, i, pp. 157–159) wrongly attributes these prints to Silvestre, and attempts to interpret them as depictions of a transformation of the Maison de Gondi, presumably during the 1660's. I find his analysis totally unconvincing, and he grossly errs in identifying his fig. 161 as the state of the château at this time, when in reality it shows the southern façade of Le Pautre's wing and Girard's *corps-de-logis*, the latter element finished in 1680/81. I rather tend to regard Perelle's prints as fantasies.

Hautecoeur (II, i, p. 161) also states that Thomas Gobert collaborated with Le Pautre in designing the château, but I have found no evidence for this. Gobert was, however, active at Saint-Cloud: he executed unspecified work there in 1670 (M. Dumolin, *Études de topographie parisienne*, I [Paris, 1929], p. 359) and built the Trianon (before 1681).

9
Château de Seiglière de Boisfranc, Saint-Ouen

Joachim Seiglière de Boisfranc, Monsieur's treasurer, employed his master's architect to design his country residence at Saint-Ouen and his *hôtel* in Paris.[1] The château, attributed to Le Pautre by numerous late seventeenth and eighteenth century writers,[2] was completed by 1672, as is indicated by the inscription on a print by Silvestre (Fig. 94).

Although the structure was destroyed in the early nineteenth century, a fairly clear idea of its exterior can be formed from Figs. 93 and 94. These prints reveal that Le Pautre erected a château of moderate dimensions, arranged in a U-plan, with the garden façade oriented towards the Seine which flowed nearby.

At Saint-Ouen we find several design features which were present at the Château de Saint-Cloud, features which are characteristic of the architect's last period. These include the over-all horizontal channeling of the masonry, the use of a small-scale pilaster order, and an open, or semi-open, courtyard.[3] The château, organized in the

1. For the *hôtel* in Paris see Appendix I.

2. G. Brice, *Description nouvelle de ce qu'il y a de plus remarquable dans la ville de Paris*, 2d ed., I (Paris, 1694), p. 87; F. Le Comte, *Cabinet des singularitez d'architecture, peinture, sculpture, et gravure*, I (Paris, 1699), "Sommaire historique d'architecture et des architectes" (unpaginated); J. A. Piganiol de la Force, *Nouvelle description de la France*, 2d ed., II (Paris, 1722), ii, pp. 698–699; *idem, Description de Paris, de Versailles, de Marly, de Meudon, de S. Cloud, de Fontainebleau . . .* , new ed., VIII (Paris, 1742), p. 287; J. F. Blondel, *Architecture françoise*, II (Paris, 1752), p. 121 n. a; *idem, Cours d'architecture*, III (Paris, 1772), p. 444 n. f; P. T. N. Hurtaut and Magny, *Dictionnaire historique de la ville de Paris et de ses environs . . .* , III (Paris, 1779), p. 693; A. N. Dezallier d'Argenville, *Vies des fameux architectes depuis la renaissance des arts . . .* (Paris, 1787), p. 396.

3. Le Pautre invariably closed the entrance sides of his courtyards with substantial constructions until he designed the Château de Saint-Cloud. In this context the Château de Seiglière de Boisfranc constitutes an intermediate stage in this closed-open development. The tendency during the seventeenth

traditional French pattern of projecting pavilions, strikes a rather cool, restrained mood, additional evidence of Le Pautre's movement away from more dramatic Baroque expression.[4]

A lateral view of the château is provided by Perelle (Fig. 96). This is puzzling because of the difficulty of harmonizing it with Fig. 93. Fig. 96 shows the side of the *corps-de-logis* with its attached lower pavilion; from this extends a lower wing, which seems to be curiously and abruptly interrupted by a small, low fragment which then appears to link up with a long, single story building with central and end pavilions and a double-sloped roof. One might wonder if at some date between Perelle's print (1704) and Rigaud's (1757) there was a remodeling of the wings to effect a smooth unification. We have no evidence of such work, but another and more probable alternative presents itself, namely, that Perelle has misrepresented the length of the wing, and that the long, one story building in his print is not the wing of the château, but the orangery. In an account of a reception held in 1679 for the Spanish ambassador, the *Mercure galant* reported that "l'orangerie . . . fut admirée, tant par la bonne culture & le nombre des Orangers, que par le Bâtiment de la Serre de 32. à 33. toises de long, couvert d'ardoise, considérable par sa grandeur, son bon goust, & mesme par le peu de temps qu'on a employé à le mettre en état d'estre veu d'une si Illustre Compagnie."[5] If we accept this interpretation of Perelle's rendering, then we are considering a building finished by July 1679, and hence begun earlier that year or, more probably, during 1678. Now Le Pautre last attended the Royal Academy of Architecture on November 21, 1678, and died on January 3, 1679 (see pp. 5–6). The biographical facts, therefore, permit an attribution to Antoine, in which case the orangery must be regarded as his last known work. It would have been consistent for Boisfranc to have re-employed Le Pautre to design this sizable addition several years after having completed the château.

The orangery at Saint-Ouen, therefore, with its over-all channeled surfaces, unified roofing, and long, low elevation, takes its place with the Château de Clagny (Chapter 10) as an expression of Le Pautre's final stylistic position.

century towards the progressive opening up of the court in châteaux is discussed in F. Gebelin, *Les châteaux de France* (Paris, 1962), pp. 120ff.

4. A drawing in Stockholm (CC 2205; Fig. 95), a preliminary design for the garden façade, reveals that Antoine first thought of a central pavilion articulated by a colossal order of Tuscan pilasters. This rather academic composition (recalling Louis Le Vau's royal pavilions at Vincennes, 1654–60) is additional evidence of Le Pautre's latest stylistic position, as is the emphasis on a low, horizontal silhouette. The use of the colossal order is very rare in Le Pautre's work; it occurs elsewhere only in the Fourth Design from the *Desseins de plusieurs palais* (Figs. 30–32).

5. *Mercure galant* (July 1679), pp. 342–343. It follows from this interpretation that the lengths of the wings in Fig. 96 are oddly short; nor can the small connecting block be readily explained. But Perelle was not the most reliable of architectural engravers. However, he was the only artist to have depicted a lateral elevation of the château.

Other engravings of the garden façade by Marot, Perelle, and Rigaud differ only in small details from Silvestre's (Fig. 94). (See also an anonymous drawing in Estampes, Va 204.) Marot's engraving cites Le Pautre as the architect.

10
Château de Clagny

Louis XIV decided to construct a building to house the children borne by the royal mistress, Madame de Montespan. The site chosen was Clagny, a suburb of Versailles, which the crown had acquired in 1665.[1] Our earliest knowledge of the King's intentions is furnished by a letter written by Colbert to Louis, dated May 22, 1674, which alludes to this structure. In it, Colbert advised the Monarch that plans of the new building were being sent to him and to Madame de Montespan, along with accompanying *mémoires*.[2] On May 29, the King replied that he had received the plan and *mémoire*, but was reserving judgment until he had spoken with his mistress.[3] On June 11, Colbert again wrote to Louis, acknowledging receipt of the King's approval to proceed with the project.[4] However, payments are recorded in the *Comptes* for the Château de Clagny from May 27, 1674; by the end of that year, the crown had spent more than 127,176 livres.[5]

1. C. Harlay, *Le château de Clagny à Versailles* (Versailles, 1912), p. 10.

2. P. Clément, ed., *Lettres, instructions et mémoires de Colbert*, II (Paris, 1863), i, p. ccxliii: "Il [Colbert's son] présentera aussy à Vostre Majesté le plan de la maison qu'elle veut faire bastir à Clagny; j'en ay fait faire quatre avant que d'avoir pu le remettre en l'estat qu'il est, j'espère que le mémoire que j'y ay joint expliquera clairement à Vostre Majesté ce qu'il contient. Pour la diligence et la solidité, je supplie Vostre Majesté de s'en reposer sur moy. J'envoye à madame de Montespan un mesme plan et memoire."

3. *Ibid.*, p. ccxliv: "Vostre fils m'a montré le mémoire de Versailles et remis entre les mains le plan pour la maison de Clagny. Je ne réponds rien encore

dessus, car je veux sçavoir les pensées de madame de Montespan."

4. *Ibid.*, p. ccxlvi: "J'attends avec impatience la résolution de Vostre Majesté pour la maison de Clagny. Je reçois cette résolution en écrivant cecy, et je feray travailler au bastiment avec diligence."

5. Guiffrey, I, cols. 772–773. Other payments during 1674 are recorded in cols. 740–741, 786, 787. Activity in the gardens of Clagny during 1670–71 is recorded in col. 423.

The letters exchanged between Louis XIV and Colbert as well as the *Comptes* indicate that plans for Clagny were ready in May 1674, and that work began that month. This date is also confirmed by the inscription by Perelle quoted in the text below. This evidence

That this Château de Clagny preceded the well-known edifice of Jules Hardouin-Mansart is indicated by several sources. The engraver Perelle added the following inscription to his prints of Mansart's Clagny in 1678 and 1679:

Clagni est une Maison de delices que le Roy fit bastir pour la premiere fois l'année 1674. a 200. pas de Versailles, sur le chemin de Paris. Le Bastiment n'ayant pas esté trouvé assés commode le Roy en fit faire un plus considerable l'année 1676. . . . Le Sr. Hardouïn Mansart en est l'Architecte. . . .[6]

Perelle's testimony is reinforced by the Duc de Luynes, who furthermore tells us of Madame de Montespan's opinion of the building:

Il [Louis XIV] y avoit fait construire une petite maison pour Mme de Montespan, qui en désiroit une; . . . elle ne plut pas à Mme de Montespan; elle dit au Roi que cela ne pouvoit être bon que pour une fille d'opéra. En conséquence la petite maison fut abattue, et l'on bâtit le château de Clagny.[7]

This first edifice was attributed to Antoine Le Pautre by Desgots, Mariette, and, following the latter, Dezallier d'Argenville. Desgots tells us that Louis XIV "n'étoit pas content" with Le Pautre, and that Le Nôtre suggested to the King that he use Hardouin-Mansart instead.[8] Mariette further adds to our knowledge of the situation:

. . . il [Le Pautre] en fournit des desseins où, suivant les intentions du ministre [Colbert], il s'étoit restreint et n'avoit aucunement donné l'essor à son génie. Aussi Mme de Montespan en fut tout-à-fait mécontente. Le Nautre étoit présent; il avoit envie de servir M. Mansard avec lequel il étoit alors lié d'amitié. Il proposa adroitement à la maîtresse du roi de lui faire faire par un jeune homme de sa connoissance des desseins qui lui plairoient; elle y consentit, et ils furent faits, présentés, agréés, et Le Pautre en eut tant de chagrin qu'il ne put survivre à cette mortification. Clagny fut commencé en 1676. Cette date peut conduire à trouver celle de la mort de Le Pautre.[9]

Le Pautre was dismissed, his château was pulled down, and work on Hardouin-Mansart's Clagny was begun certainly by April 2, 1675, because the *Comptes* explicitly refer to the "nouveau bastiment" from that date on.[10]

is contrary to the date 1672 given in the "Abrégé de la vie d'André Le Nostre," in P. N. Desmolets, *Continuation des mémoires de littérature et d'histoire*, IX (Paris, 1730), p. 460. This life of Le Nôtre is commonly attributed to his nephew, Claude Desgots.

6. Harlay, *op. cit.*, p. 14.

7. L. Dussieux and E. Soulié, eds., *Mémoires du Duc de Luynes sur la cour de Louis XIV (1735–1758)*, IX (Paris, 1862) [1748–49], pp. 255–256.

8. Desmolets, *op. cit.*, p. 460: "En 1672 Louis XIV voulut faire bâtir la belle maison de Clagny: il avoit pour Architecte Antoine le Pautre, dont on n'étoit pas content; le Nostre dit au Roi que si Sa Majesté vouloit du grand & du beau, il falloit qu'elle employât Hardouïn Mansart, neveu de François Mansart, généralement connu par le grand nombre de magnifiques édifices qui lui ont acquis avec justice le titre de *Grand Architecte;* ainsi le Nostre plaça le neveu de cet homme illustre, & fut la premiere cause de la brillante fortune qu'il fit dans la suite."

9. P. de Chennevières and A. de Montaiglon, eds., *Abécédario de P. J. Mariette . . .* ("Archives de l'art français," II), I (Paris, 1851–53), p. 182. Mariette's manuscript must have been known to A. N. Dezallier d'Argenville, who almost literally follows him (*Vies des fameux architectes depuis la renaissance des arts . . .* [Paris, 1787], pp. 399–400). Mariette was thus responsible for the legend that Le Pautre died of chagrin when replaced by Hardouin-Mansart.

10. Guiffrey, I, col. 843: "2 avril–1er juillet [1675]: aux entrepreneurs du nouveau bastiment, tant à compte de leurs ouvrages que des pierres qu'ils fournissent . . . 133,300 [liv.]." The entries for 1674 do not qualify the château of that year as "nouveau."

Our knowledge of Le Pautre's Clagny would necessarily end at this point were it not for the fact that a drawing in Stockholm (Fig. 98) bears the inscription on the verso, "Elevation de la face du Costé du parterre du Chateau de Clagni. Selon la premier panssé."[11] Three other drawings in Stockholm can be linked with this one. Fig. 97 is a close variant of the garden façade depicted in Fig. 98; Fig. 99 shows a section through the central hall of the *corps-de-logis* along with five bays of the court façade of one of the wings; Fig. 100 is a section of one of the rooms.

Could these drawings depict Jules Hardouin-Mansart's "first thought" for Clagny? I think not. Stylistically, Figs. 97 and 98 cannot be related to Mansart's work, and they depict a building which is quite different from two of Mansart's buildings of long and low silhouette which were built about this time: the Château du Val (begun 1675) and the Hôtel de Noailles (mainly by 1679), both at Saint-Germain-en-Laye. Furthermore, the Stockholm drawings show a building of small dimensions, and this harmonizes with the known facts of Le Pautre's structure. Indeed, its modest size was felt to be one of its major faults, as we have seen. Hence it is altogether improbable that Mansart, when called upon to rectify the situation, would have begun by producing another building of reduced dimensions. For these reasons, I believe that the Stockholm drawings depict Le Pautre's destroyed Château de Clagny.

It must frankly be admitted, however, that these drawings would never have been connected with Le Pautre except for the inscription. Even in the light of the architect's late style as revealed at Saint-Cloud and Saint-Ouen, the style of these designs is so uncompromisingly devoid of Baroque features, the tone so reticent and bland, that one would otherwise seek to attribute them to an architect of a younger generation. Yet it is certainly possible to view these designs as the culmination of that evolution in Le Pautre's development away from the Italianate Baroque of his middle years, towards an ultimate vocabulary of sober forms.

The garden façade is organized as a series of five distinct units: a central pavilion of three bays flanked by two blocks of four bays, terminated at each end by pavilions, again of three bays. Each unit is separately roofed: single-sloped roofs are used, but the central unit is emphasized by a dome. Both drawings of this façade show a series of steps at the base of the dome, recalling the Roman Pantheon; in Fig. 98, the dome seems to be a pure hemisphere; in Fig. 97, a four-sided dome is suggested. The first dome is capped by the crown of France, the second by the fleur-de-lis; the central

Hence I believe that Madame de Sévigné's letter to her daughter of July 3, 1675 refers to the second château, then rising: "Vous ne sauriez vous représenter le triomphe où elle [Madame de Montespan] est au milieu de ses ouvriers, qui sont au nombre de douze cents: le palais d'Apollidon et les jardins d'Armide en sont une légère description." See M. Monmerqué, ed., *Lettres de Madame de Sévigné de sa famille et de ses amis*, III (Paris, 1862), p. 504. On August 7 she wrote (*ibid.*, IV, p. 21): "Nous fûmes à Clagny; que vous dirai-je? c'est le palais d'Armide; le bâtiment s'élève à vue d'oeil. . . ." The King visited this new Château de Clagny in July 1675, where he learned of the death of Turenne (P. Visconti, *Mém-* *oires sur la cour de Louis XIV*, J. Lemoine, ed. [Paris, 1908], p. 112). Visconti informs us that the King took lunch at Clagny but this does not necessarily mean that he visited a completed building. In this analysis I therefore agree with Harlay (*op. cit.*, p. 13) in dating Mansart's Clagny from 1675, not 1676.

An entry in the *Comptes* for 1677 should be noted (Guiffrey, I, col. 985): "25 juin [1677]: à luy [Le Franc], pour les ouvriers qui ont travaillé aux démolitions du vieil bastiment . . . 192 [liv.]." It is problematical whether or not this reference concerns Le Pautre's château.

11. Stockholm, Nationalmuseum, THC 2441.

pediment in Fig. 98 is filled with the arms of France. These royal emblems were clearly meant to emphasize the legitimacy of the royal bastards, whose nursery Clagny was intended to be.

Fig. 97, which is the more detailed drawing, indicates through the use of shade that the central and terminal pavilions are slightly in advance of the intermediate blocks. For the organization of the walls, totally flat, planar surfaces are used, framed at the corners of the advancing pavilions by uniform, channeled quoining strips. Tall, simply framed windows topped with flat lintels provide the openings, surmounted by a mezzanine zone filled with square relief panels.[12] The three mezzanine openings in the central pavilion are windows. Differences can be noted between the two versions in the treatment of the major windows (with molded bases in Fig. 98), in the central openings (three doors in Fig. 98, the central one arched; one flat-covered door in Fig. 97, flanked by windows), and in the form of the steps. Furthermore, tall chimney stacks are indicated in Fig. 98, along with finials on the roof crests. A subtle entablature with small water spouts in mask form on the cornice appears in Fig. 97, a detail which is also present in Fig. 99. The cornice in Fig. 98 is unadorned.

Fig. 99 indicates that a courtyard was provided, enclosed by wings, doubtless the same width as the end pavilions of the garden façade. The drawing indicates a system of fenestration corresponding to that façade, but the designer has filled the spaces between the openings with engaged columns, experimenting with orders with and without pedestals. There is a suggestion of a balustrade above the entablature. The drawing also reveals that the *corps-de-logis* is approached at the end of the court by a series of steps, balanced by a like series on the garden side; a pediment similarly covers the central bays of the court façade of the *corps-de-logis*. The central room extends the full height, through ground floor and mezzanine levels, thus forming a *salon à l'italienne*, covered by a domed vault. The central dome is therefore of double-shell construction.[13] This room is apparently circular or oval, with statue-filled niches, relief panels above the doors, and light, decorative motifs.

Our last drawing (Fig. 100), highly finished, is a section of another room, which is covered with a coved ceiling. Indications to the right show that at certain points, the mezzanine formed a distinct floor. This room is very bare, with simple rectilinear moldings relieved by small consoles and swags over the ground floor windows.

Several important facts emerge from the preceding descriptions. First, Le Pautre emphasized a long, low elevation, the horizontality of which was reinforced by the low-pitched roofs. We have already brought attention to this type of silhouette, which first appeared in Antoine's *oeuvre* in the Sixth Design of the *Desseins de plusieurs palais*, and which was subsequently developed at Saint-Cloud and in the orangery at Saint-Ouen (1678/79), which postdates Clagny. The origins of this trend, which was to be so important for later French architecture, have usually been traced to the early works of J. H.-Mansart: the Château du Val at Saint-Germain-en-Laye (begun 1675),[14]

12. The scenes indicated in Fig. 97 are very difficult to distinguish, but they appear to be vaguely classical.

13. The system of construction is very similar to Fig. 23 from the *Desseins de plusieurs palais*.

14. Modern writers invariably repeat the date 1674, but the *Comptes* clearly indicate that construction was begun in September, 1675. See Guiffrey, I, col. 821.

the Château de Clagny (also begun 1675), and the Hôtel de Noailles, also at Saint-Germain (mainly by 1679).[15] But it would now appear that Le Pautre preceded Mansart in this direction, and that Antoine's Clagny may have exercised considerable influence on Mansart's initial creations. Second, there is a marked preference for totally flat, unarticulated and untextured wall surfaces, with only bland, uniform quoining strips at critical angles. As previously indicated, this wall treatment is approached by one plate from the *Desseins de plusieurs palais* (Fig. 35), but in the latter case the smooth, unadorned surfaces are intended to enhance the dramatic impact of the central motif; at Clagny, such surfaces reign supreme.[16] The relief panels add a pronounced classicistic touch. Finally, the interiors strike out in a new direction. A *salon à l'italienne* is indicated (Fig. 99), but the absence of an order is new for Le Pautre. Statue-filled niches appear elsewhere in his *oeuvre* (see Figs. 23, 26, 32), but the severe use of moldings and panels carries the tone of restraint from the exterior even to this reception room. Delicate motifs provide the only relief; the vault is undecorated. This sparing approach is repeated in Fig. 100, where the rigid, geometrical grid is only slightly relieved by frieze consoles and swags. It must be pointed out, however, that the interiors indicated in the *Desseins* are often sparingly decorated in a manner which even approaches the Clagny designs (see, e.g., Fig. 26). However, Le Pautre's earlier approach always resulted in the accentuation of certain powerfully Baroque rooms because these were played off against the simpler ones. At Clagny, the available evidence indicates an almost unvarying sober decorative tone throughout all rooms — a consistent uniformity consonant with the exterior, instead of the Baroque principle of contrast and climax.

Perhaps we can penetrate somewhat further into the meaning of this radical design by recalling Mariette's note that Le Pautre ". . . en fournit des desseins où, suivant les intentions du ministre [Colbert], il s'étoit restreint et n'avoit aucunement donné l'essor à son génie." These designs for Clagny, in comparison with the second château, were on a much more modest scale, involving far fewer expenditures. This fact may reflect the economic restraint characteristic of Colbert, but his fiscal-mindedness does not sufficiently explain the architectural spirit of Le Pautre's conception. Rather, it is possible to see in Mariette's passage a reference to the artistic tastes of Colbert, which the architect attempted to satisfy.

There can be no question that the King's Minister had definite ideas and attitudes concerning the visual arts. Ever since becoming Surintendant des Bâtiments du Roi on January 1, 1664, Colbert pursued — at least in the realm of architecture — a consistent policy against the powerful Baroque movement which had made such deep inroads into French art during the era of Mazarin. He saw in the creation of academies (all of whose policies he ultimately controlled) the most effective means towards the creation of an official art, geared to serve the state.[17] Colbert, through his support of the Perraults and François Blondel, encouraged the development of an art which

---

15. Hautecoeur, II, ii, pp. 530, 592; Blunt, 1957, p. 195.

16. Le Pautre's aesthetic at Clagny is paralleled by a passage in the minutes of the Royal Academy of Architecture, where it is stated that ". . . les choses qui sont toutes liées sont plus nobles et de meilleur goust" (Lemonnier, I, p. 44 [July 31, 1673]).

17. On Colbert's organization of French artistic life see Hautecoeur, II, i, pp. 411ff.

could be codified and submitted to rules, unlike the emotional and often capricious art emanating from Baroque Italy. While Colbert recognized the necessity for young French artists to study the Antique and the approved High Renaissance masters in Rome, his creation of a French Academy there in 1666 probably was also intended to insulate the pensioners from contemporary Roman artistic life.[18] At times in his correspondence and *mémoires* concerning artistic projects, Colbert's personal views emerge, as in a note dealing with Le Vau's Versailles design of 1669: "Les figures rondes qu'il affecte aux vestibules et salons ne sont point du bon goust de l'architecture, particulièrement pour les dehors." [19] When one thinks of such French Baroque compositions like Vaux-le-Vicomte or the Hôtel de Beauvais, one can appreciate how antithetical Colbert's viewpoint was to architects like Le Vau and the middle-period Le Pautre.

Colbert's career as Surintendant was marked by his continual struggle with the more liberal and Baroque tastes of his master, the King. In one case, however, the Minister was free to build in a manner which he saw fit, at his own Château de Sceaux. Construction of the château (destroyed) was begun in 1673 or 1674, precisely the moment when Le Pautre's Clagny was born, and there is a sobriety in the elevational elements common to the two works.[20] But there is one building in the park of Sceaux which has survived intact and which bears a direct relationship to the first Clagny—the Pavillon de l'Aurore (Fig. 101). Alternately attributed to Perrault, Le Brun, or Le Nôtre (or to a collaboration between the last two),[21] the little structure displays the same planar wall surfaces and corner quoining strips of Le Pautre's building. The dome is virtually identical to that in Fig. 98, and the unworked stone blocks over the windows were intended to be carved into relief panels, another feature which links the work with Clagny.

These relationships may corroborate Mariette's indication of the influence exercised by Colbert upon Le Pautre's Clagny. It is tempting to speculate that pressures from the Minister accelerated a trend in Le Pautre's development which had first manifested itself several years before at Saint-Cloud, and that Colbert specifically proposed the Pavillon de l'Aurore as a model for Clagny, at least with reference to the elevational elements. However, we lack a precise date for the pavilion, and considering the present state of our knowledge of Sceaux, further discussions along these lines would be extremely hazardous. In any event, Clagny I is Le Pautre's most uncompro-

18. F. Kimball, *The Creation of the Rococo* (Philadelphia, 1943), p. 14.

19. Clément, ed., *op. cit.*, V, p. 287 (noted in Kimball, *op. cit.*, p. 17).

20. Claude Perrault is usually cited as the designer of Sceaux. See F. de Catheu, "Le château et le parc de Sceaux d'après les plans et gravures des XVIIᵉ et XVIIIᵉ siècles," *GBA*, s. 6, XXI (1939), pp. 85–102; *idem*, "Le décor du château et du parc de Sceaux," *GBA*, s. 6, XXI (1939), pp. 287–304; G. Poisson, *Le château de Sceaux* (Paris, 1951); *idem, Histoire et histoires de Sceaux* (Sceaux, 1959).

21. On this building see G. Brière, "Le pavillon de l'Aurore au château de Sceaux," *Archives de l'art français* (new series), VIII (1916), pp. 193–206; A. Mauban, *L'Architecture française de Jean Mariette* (Paris, 1945), pp. 173–174; J. Dupont, "Le pavillon de l'Aurore à Sceaux," *BSHAF* (1958), pp. 67–72; P. Reuterswärd [book review], *BurlM*, CV (1963), p. 130. The Pavillon de l'Aurore is often dated 1670, but this would seem to be too early.

misingly anti-Baroque pronouncement, and it is surprising that the design was ever accepted by the King and his mistress. Its failure to please was inevitable, and Mansart's successor, through its large scale, complex plan, and rich exterior and interior articulation, constituted a whole more consonant with the splendors of the new Versailles.

11
Conclusion

The decisive influences in Le Pautre's early years seem to have been his (probable) training in the office of Martellange and the patronage of the French Jansenists. The plan of the Chapelle de Port-Royal is a direct adaptation of the conservative plan of Martellange's Jesuit Noviciate; in the plan of the Hôtel de Fontenay-Mareuil, the architect similarly adhered to the French tradition by producing a loose stringing out of rectangular and square spaces, with no coordination into emphatic spatial sequences. Following Martellange, Le Pautre conceived of walls as planar screens with texturally neutral surfaces and fragile articulation. The latter took the form of pilasters, as in the Chapelle and the Hôtel; in the unexecuted designs for Port-Royal, a free-standing columnar portico was planned, but this was a detachable unit, behind which (and without which) the entrance wall remained intact. Nowhere in the early works do we encounter that specifically Baroque conception in which the wall with its orders and decorative details seems to be sculpturally modeled. Along with these main features of plan and elevation, Le Pautre used sober details, small scale ornament, and a limited number of design elements. His point of departure, then, was a conservative French mode practiced by Martellange and esteemed by the newly arisen classicistic coterie formed around Sublet de Noyers. Le Pautre then adapted this restrained and sober style to serve the Jansenists as a fitting expression of their ascetic artistic outlook.

However, the analyses have indicated that even in his initial buildings, Le Pautre occasionally turned to forms which constituted anticipations of his second, Baroque phase. Such were the oval chapels of Port-Royal (perhaps borrowed from Mansart's Visitation) and the oval dome of the Hôtel de Fontenay-Mareuil (apparently adopted from Mansart's Château de Blois). And other features, executed or merely planned, at Port-Royal point in the same direction: the altarpiece, the sculptural decoration, and the choir rail, with its concave-convex interplay.

It will be noted that the stimuli during this period of Antoine's career were specifically French. Although Jean Le Pautre had probably been in Italy during the early 1640's and had perhaps formed his distinctive Italianate Baroque style during that decade, virtually no influence from this artist can be detected until the next phase, when it was of extreme importance.

Antoine's Baroque period was probably inaugurated in 1652/53 with the publication of the *Desseins de plusieurs palais,* but it may have appeared as early as 1650 when he built two *chambres à l'italienne* in the Hôtel de Guéménée in Paris (appearance unknown; see Appendix I). He evidently did not visit Italy in person, but relied for his knowledge of southern architecture on his brother and on engravings and drawings. That Antoine possessed an up-to-date acquaintance with Roman High Baroque art is indicated, specifically, by his two designs for rustic fountains, the Lyons church façade, and the projected converging stair for Saint-Cloud. Le Pautre was also keenly aware of the activities of other French Baroque architects, and, in particular, Le Vau's Château du Raincy seems to have been an especially potent influence.

The dramatic revolution in Le Pautre's architecture in the early 1650's occurred during the ministry of Mazarin, to whom the *Desseins de plusieurs palais* was dedicated. The Italian Cardinal was an enthusiastic supporter of Baroque art; being a powerful individual in a country which was tending toward ever greater political centralization, Mazarin could determine the course of royal and official patronage, and so influence the entire orientation of French art. From the early 1650's until the mid-1660's, Le Pautre produced some of the most intensely Baroque conceptions ever devised by a Frenchman, and it surely can be no coincidence that this phenomenon largely coincided with the era of Mazarin's political leadership.

Le Pautre's new approach to architecture is illustrated by his use of varied spatial units — including circular, oval, octagonal, trefoil, and apsidal-ended plans — which are combined into graduated, dramatic progressions by means of axial coordination, with the *salon à l'italienne* often used as the climactic element. The elevations of his Baroque period are distinguished by a marked emphasis on weight and mass, achieved by rustication, textural differentiation of the floors, large scale, and complex skylines. His walls partake of Baroque plasticity: they are articulated by dense, bold, rich forms, and create broad concave or convex movements of façades, as in the Fourth Design or in the court of the Hôtel de Beauvais; on the façade of the Hôtel, a convex-concave interplay is formed by the balcony and entrance doors.

The most surprising aspect of Le Pautre's development is the appearance, from about 1665, of a final period in which he abandoned his Baroque style. At Saint-Cloud there was a breakdown of the Baroque concept of spatial progression and a return to an additive treatment of traditional square and rectangular rooms. There and at Saint-Ouen, smooth, horizontally channeled masonry was used to create placid, uniform elevations with none of the lively, incidental detail of the preceding phase; at Clagny, totally flat, planar walls were necessarily devoid of any sculptural effect. The emphasis turned to long, low elevations, and a more academic, colder quality permeated the architecture, with a marked reduction of those elements of fantasy and free imagination which had characterized Antoine's Baroque creations.

There had been anticipations of this final style in the preceding phase, particularly in the Sixth Design from the *Desseins de plusieurs palais*. Furthermore, Le Pautre had organized the façade of the Hôtel de Beauvais with vertical strips of channeled rustication instead of the apparatus of the orders (such strips also appear on the Cascade), and this type of surface—devoid of plastic aggressiveness—was utilized at Clagny; at Saint-Cloud and Saint-Ouen, the channeling spread across entire façades.

Le Pautre's last style may superficially recall some aspects of his initial mode, but it is essentially a new form of expression, both within the architect's development and within the history of French architecture. It will be the task of future research to deal with the significance of this style in connection with later French architecture and, specifically, in relation to Jules Hardouin-Mansart.

By drawing attention to the relationships between Le Pautre's Clagny and the Pavillon de l'Aurore at Sceaux, I attempted to corroborate Mariette's note concerning the restraining influence exercised by Colbert upon Le Pautre's ill-fated creation. It is difficult to discount the fact that Colbert became Surintendant des Bâtiments du Roi in 1664 and that Le Pautre entered upon his final period about 1665. 1665—the year of Bernini's visit to Paris—has traditionally been cited as the turning point away from the exuberant art of the era of Mazarin towards a more rationalistic and academicizing idiom, and Le Pautre's career would seem to offer a precise confirmation of this observation. For, given the highly centralized governmental structure that constituted the French seventeenth century state, it followed that the King's Minister wielded great power in all fields, including the arts. We have noted Mazarin's influence in this respect, and Colbert's stewardship of French artistic life is too well known to need detailed elaboration. Colbert demanded that the arts should specifically be geared to celebrate the glory of the King, and that painting, sculpture, and architecture should be reducible to clear rules which could easily be transmitted from master to pupil. Baroque art, with its emotional emphasis and often bizarre and fantastic forms, was not considered appropriate for these purposes, and a rationalistic and classicistic ideal, earlier voiced by Sublet de Noyers and his circle, returned, to be embodied in the new east and south façades of the Louvre.

In the great architectural triumphs of the age of Colbert—the Louvre façades and the garden façades at Versailles—Baroque expression is markedly reduced, and the same may be said of the private residence of Colbert, the Château de Sceaux. A suppression of Baroque design elements is precisely what we have found in Le Pautre's last works, not to mention the correspondence between Clagny and the Pavillon de l'Aurore. Therefore, at this stage of our knowledge the conclusion is unavoidable that the accession to power of Colbert in 1664 seems to have been the most potent single factor in the shaping of Le Pautre's final stylistic phase. To what extent his membership in the Royal Academy of Architecture reinforced the new tendencies, it is impossible to say, but of course the Academy was not a favorable breeding ground for Baroque architectural ideas.

A paucity of biographical material denies us access to Antoine's personality and thought; the historian in this instance cannot supplement the corpus of visual data with a rich store of letters, anecdotes, etc., which would help to illumine the inner recesses of the artist's mind and clarify his artistic intentions. The available evidence does suggest, however, that Le Pautre's stylistic development was vitally influenced by the artistic policies and tastes fostered by Mazarin and Colbert, and this conclusion provides additional confirmation of the oft-noted tendencies towards centralization and absolutism present in many phases of human endeavor during the second half of the seventeenth century in France. But if Mazarin and Colbert established the general directions of artistic development, it was necessarily left to the artists themselves to embody the dreams and aspirations of the era in tangible forms. Le Pautre's architecture is such a realization.

Recorded Commissions for Which No Projects Survive

a | *Hôtel de Guéménée: Interiors*

The Hôtel de Guéménée (6, Place des Vosges) was one of the buildings of the Place Royale. It still stands today as the Musée Victor Hugo, but none of the seventeenth century interiors have survived.

The Place Royale and its surrounding uniform buildings in the brick-and-stone style were begun in 1605. Number 6 was purchased in 1639 by Louis de Rohan, Prince de Guéménée, who in 1617 had married his cousin, Anne de Rohan.[1] Anne was a friend and benefactress of Port-Royal; in 1643 she received permission from the Abbess Marie-Angélique Arnauld and the nuns of Port-Royal de Paris to construct a private residence within the grounds of the convent which she could occupy whenever she wished but which was to be ceded to the convent after her death. The building was finished in 1646, when the sisters acknowledged receipt from Anne of money to pay for the cost of construction.[2] It was therefore natural for the Guéménées to have called upon Le Pautre in 1650, since he must have been known to them because of his activity at Port-Royal during 1646–48.[3]

The decoration and remodeling of the interiors of the Hôtel de Guéménée were attributed to Le Pautre by Sauval,[4] and a document dated 1650 confirms this attribution and supplies a firm date.[5] In it we find the following entry:

1. L. Lambeau in *Procès-verbaux de la commission municipale du vieux Paris* (1902), p. 204.

2. M. Dumolin in *ibid.* (1931), pp. 8, 10.

3. In addition, at the baptism of Antoine's son Claude on July 5, 1649, the godfather was Claude de Lorraine, duc de Chevreuse, brother-in-law to Anne de Rohan (Laborde, nouv. acq. franç. 12141, no. 42.354).

4. H. Sauval, *Histoire et recherches des antiquités de la ville de Paris*, III (Paris, 1724), p. 4.

5. Document published by Lambeau, *op. cit.* (1902), p. 206. It is a *mémoire*, probably drawn up by Louis de Rohan himself, of expenses incurred in maintaining and remodeling the *hôtel*.

Ce que Madame a fait faire dans sa petitte chambre d'hiver en l'an 1650:
    Pour Le Pautre, architecte.................1.150 liv.
    Pour Le Pautre, menuisier................. 250 liv.
    Pour Costel, peintre......................... 500 liv.[6]

Antoine is here clearly distinguished from another Le Pautre who was a *menuisier*. This could have been his uncle, Jean (still active in 1655), or perhaps his father, Adrien (still active in 1646). "Costel" refers to the painter Jean Cotelle (1607–76), cited by Sauval as a collaborator in the decoration.[7]

Sauval's description provides our only clue to Le Pautre's work:

Cet Hotel est accommodé de vastes & très-commodes appartmens par le Pautre, & principalement du plus grand alcove de Paris, tout doré & peint par Cotelle, accompagné d'une cheminée fort galante & éclairée de grandes croisées qui regardent sur le plus grand jardin de la Place Royale. Il se décharge aussi dans deux petites chambres à l'Italienne qui conduisent dans le jardin.[8]

Interesting in this description is the mention of "chambres à l'Italienne." We have already discussed the significance of this form as a hallmark of Antoine's Baroque phase, and it is therefore quite possible that the architect's second style first appeared in 1650 at the Hôtel de Guéménée. If this was indeed the case, then Antoine's stylistic metamorphosis occurred between 1648 (date of completion of the Chapelle de Port-Royal) and 1650. Let us hasten to note again, however, that Le Pautre was in Paris in 1649 for the baptism of his son Claude,[9] and hence it would not appear that his change in style was prompted by a personal visit to Italy during these years.

b | *Hôtel de Beauvais (Rue de Grenelle)*

Catherine Bellier, for whom Le Pautre constructed the Hôtel de Beauvais in the rue Saint-Antoine, purchased in 1661 two adjacent houses in the Faubourg Saint-Germain.[10] The buildings were thrown together, restored and redecorated, and their newly acquired beauty was extolled by Loret in *La muze historique* on the occasion of a visit by the King, the Queen-Mother, and Monsieur in 1663.[11]

Because of Le Pautre's connection with Madame de Beauvais, Dumolin has reasonably assumed that the work executed from 1661–63 was by that architect,[12] and this hypothesis is considerably strengthened by the fact that André de Bétoulat,

6. *Ibid.*
7. Sauval, *op. cit.*, III, p. 4. Cotelle and Adrien Le Pautre or his brother Jean had worked for the Guéménées when they initially acquired the *hôtel* in 1639 (Lambeau, *op. cit.* [1902], p. 206). According to A. de Champeaux (*L'art décoratif dans le vieux Paris* [Paris, 1898], p. 169), Louis Testelin (1615–55) provided "les camaïeux d'outre-mer sur fond doré représentant des sujets de la Fable."
8. Sauval, *op. cit.*, III, p. 4.
9. See n. 3.
10. J. Cousin, *L'hôtel de Beauvais (rue Saint-Antoine)* (Paris, 1864), pp. 39–40, 66ff.; M. Dumolin, "Les Petites-Cordelières," *Bulletin de la société d'histoire et d'archéologie des VIIe et XVe arrondissements de Paris*, XXXIV (1933–34), p. 394.

The *hôtel* was located in the rue de Grenelle, opposite the opening of the rue des Saints-Pères (Fig. 102). Cousin found no positive evidence to substantiate the belief that Madame de Beauvais purchased the house for her favorite son, the Baron de Beauvais, but he believes, nevertheless, that this was probably the case. See Cousin, *op. cit.*, p. 66 n. 1 and Dumolin, "Les Petites-Cordelières," p. 394.
11. J. Loret, *La muze historique*, C. L. Livet, ed., IV (Paris, 1878), pp. 119–120 (November 3, 1663). See also Cousin, *op. cit.*, pp. 67–68.
12. M. Dumolin, "Notes sur quelques architectes du XVIIe siècle," *BSHAF* (1930), pp. 16–17; *idem, Études de topographie parisienne*, II (Paris, 1930), p. 375, where the terminal date 1664 is given; *idem*, "Les Petites-Cordelières," p. 394.

one of Catherine's lovers, used Le Pautre precisely during these years in constructing his *hôtel* nearby (see below, section c).

The *hôtel* was destroyed shortly after 1763;[13] it is indicated on the Plan Turgot of 1740 (Fig. 102) where one can note its extensive gardens which reached to the rue de la Chaise. However, Loret's vague verses, the conventionalized rendering of the Plan Turgot, and the absence of further evidence prevent any closer comprehension of the nature of the work executed.

c | *Hôtel de Bétoulat (de la Vauguyon)*

André de Bétoulat de la Petitierre, Seigneur de Fromenteau, had a twofold means of coming into contact with Le Pautre: he was First Chamberlain to Monsieur and he was a lover of Catherine Bellier.[14] Documents reveal that Le Pautre was building a house for Bétoulat in 1661 in the Faubourg Saint-Germain, not far from the *hôtel* which the architect was remodeling at the same time for Catherine.[15]

d | *Maison Le Pautre (Rue de Grenelle)*

A document in the Minutier Central in Paris, dated March 6, 1666, informs us that Le Pautre had built a house for himself and his wife "de neuf" on a site acquired on December 1, 1662.[16]

e | *Design for the Louvre*

A letter written in 1704 by G. J. Adelcrantz to Nicodemus Tessin the Younger mentions a design for the Louvre by Le Pautre.[17] The design has not yet been located.

f | *Château de Lieux (de Vauréal)*

In 1667 Le Pautre served as architect to Antoine Guérapin de Vauréal, a nobleman who owned an estate at Lieux (Vauréal), near Pontoise.[18] There is no visual evidence,

---

13. Cousin, *op. cit.*, p. 72. In 1686 the *hôtel* was bought by the Order of Sainte-Claire de la Nativité (Petites Cordelières), which took possession in 1687. For this and the subsequent history of the building see *ibid.*, pp. 71–72; C. Lefeuve, *Les anciennes maisons de Paris*, 5th ed., IV (Paris and Leipzig, 1875), pp. 83–84; Dumolin, "Les Petites-Cordelières," *passim;* M. Félibien, *Histoire de la ville de Paris*, V (Paris, 1725), pp. 232–233. The building should not be confused with the extant Petit Hôtel de Beauvais (20, rue de Grenelle), built by Pierre Capa (Dumolin, "Les Petites-Cordelières," pp. 394–395).

14. Dumolin, *Études* . . . , I, pp. 378–379; *idem,* "Notes . . . ," p. 17.

15. Dumolin, *Études* . . . , I, p. 379. Dumolin variously dates the *hôtel* 1660 (*ibid.,* I, p. 378), 1661–64 (*ibid.,* II, p. 375), and 1661 ("Notes . . . ," p. 17). The *hôtel* was formerly on the site of 102, rue de Grenelle. Dumolin speculates that Madame de Beauvais prob-

ably paid for the work (*Études* . . . , I, p. 379). For the later history of the building see *ibid.,* I, pp. 379ff.

16. Minutier, XVI 497.

17. Stockholm, Riksarkivet, Tessinsaml., II, E 5711. The relevant passage reads: "De desseiner som Le Mercier, Houdin, Le Potre, Cottart, Marott och Perrault giordt, läre allesammans wara uti H:r Håfmarskalkens händer . . ." ("The drawings that Le Mercier, Houdin, Le Potre, Cottart, Marott and Perrault have made are all said to be in Your Excellency's hands . . ."). G. J. Adelcrantz (*né* Törnqvist) was a pupil of Tessin and later architect to the city of Stockholm. His letter, written in Paris, reached Tessin in Stockholm, but I have not succeeded in locating Le Pautre's Louvre project in the Stockholm collections.

18. AN, Z[ij] 301 (September 21, 1668); M. Bourgoin, *Vauréal, village du Vexin français* (Pontoise, n.d.), pp. 16–17; Dumolin, *Études* . . . , II, p. 375.

or written descriptions of Le Pautre's work; a new château erected between 1731 and 1733 by the architect Claude Leclerc effaced all of the older structures.[19]

g | *Château de Versailles: Design*

It is highly significant that Colbert, when faced with the two most important royal undertakings of his term of office—the east façade of the Louvre and the enlargement of Versailles—decided not to accept outright the designs of the First Architect, Louis Le Vau, but called instead for ideas from several architects.

In the case of Versailles, Kimball has advanced the best analysis of the sequence of events.[20] His argument proves that the old château of Louis XIII was being enlarged from October 1668 to June 1669, presumably according to plans furnished by Le Vau. Colbert, however, voiced dissatisfaction and called for an architectural competition during the Summer of 1669. Plans were submitted by Louis Le Vau, Claude Perrault, Antoine Le Pautre, Jacques Gabriel, Thomas Gobert, and Charles de Vigarani. Le Vau's plan was chosen, revised, and construction begun, but in the Fall of 1669 Colbert halted this design, and Le Vau submitted at that time his final plan (the "envelope") which was then carried out to completion.

In a letter dated June 25, 1669, Charles Perrault reported to Colbert on the state of readiness of the six competitive designs, mentioning that "M. Le Pautre m'a mandé qu'il ne pourroit porter le sien avant samedy au matin."[21] When the plans were submitted, Colbert set down his notes concerning the various schemes;[22] unfortunately, his notes for Le Pautre's and Gobert's plans have not survived, nor is Le Pautre's design known to us.

h | *Hôtel de Lauzun, Saint-Germain-en-Laye*

Antonin Nompar de Caumont, Marquis de Puyguilhem, Duc de Lauzun (1633–1723), the flamboyant courtier and soldier, was imprisoned in 1671 by Louis XIV, who thereby prevented the marriage of Lauzun and Mlle de Montpensier. On December 10, 1673, while Lauzun was in prison at Pignerolles, Louvois, then Minister of War, wrote a letter to Saint-Mars, governor of Pignerolles, in which a reference is made to Lauzun's *hôtel* in Saint-Germain, which had been built by Le Pautre.[23] We do not know precisely when this *hôtel* was designed or when construction was begun; perhaps it was built ca. 1669, for Guy Patin noted in that year: "Le roi s'en va passer l'été tout entier à Saint-Germain, où l'on fait bâtir quantité de belles maisons, afin que la cour, qui est fort grosse, y puisse commodément loger."[24]

Louis XIV used the Château de Saint-Germain-en-Laye as a residence from 1661–82; because the nature of the château did not permit its extension with wings, the members of the Court, Lauzun included, were forced to built private *hôtels* in the town.

---

19. Bourgoin, *op. cit.*, p. 15.

20. F. Kimball, "The Genesis of the Château Neuf at Versailles, 1668–1671—I The Initial Projects of Le Vau," *GBA*, s. 6, XXXV (1949), pp. 353–372.

21. P. Clément, ed., *Lettres, instructions et mémoires de Colbert*, V (Paris, 1868), p. 284 n. 1.

22. *Ibid.*, V, pp. 284–288.

23. J. Delort, *Histoire de la détention des philosophes et des gens de lettres à la Bastille et à* Vincennes . . . , I (Paris, 1829), pp. 225–226. The letter was reprinted by A. de Montaiglon in *Archives de l'art français* (2d series), II (1862), pp. 377–378.

Lauzun's *hôtel* at Saint-Germain is mentioned in other letters of Louvois to Saint-Mars (Delort, *op. cit.*, I, pp. 223–225).

24. G. Patin, *Lettres de Guy Patin*, J. H. Reveillé-Parise, ed., III (Paris, 1846), p. 691 (March 19, 1669).

The Hôtel de Lauzun still exists at 1, Place Maurice Berteaux (Fig. 103). However, it was radically remodeled at the end of the eighteenth century,[25] and very little remains on the exterior which suggests the hand of Le Pautre. Nevertheless, the walls are covered with over-all, horizontal channeling, which we found at the Château de Saint-Cloud and at the Château de Seiglière de Boisfranc at Saint-Ouen. On the interior one of the rooms is said to preserve its original proportions; it is a large, square chamber with a high cove and square, flat central panel (undecorated) at the summit. We have no records of the original appearance of the building.[26]

i | *Hôtel du Lude, Versailles*

The Hôtel du Lude was built by Le Pautre for Henri de Daillon, Comte du Lude in 1670–71.[27] The Comte du Lude was one of Louis XIV's outstanding soldiers; in 1669 he was awarded the post of "grand maître de l'artillerie." The building formerly stood at 6, rue des Réservoirs.[28]

j | *Hôtel de Soissons: Interiors*

The Hôtel de Soissons was built for Catherine de' Medici in 1572 by Jean Bullant.[29] Le Pautre's connection with it exactly a century later is indicated by an entry in an account book of Marie d'Orléans, Duchesse de Nemours, who occupied the large building jointly with her half sister, Marie de Bourbon: [30]

> Au Sieur Le Pautre architecte Quatre cent quarante livres pour les desseins quil a faits, & conduite desdites Batimens. . . .[31]

Sauval informs us of the spaciousness of the *hôtel* and its numerous apartments, second only to the Palais-Royal.[32] It was in the apartment of Marie d'Orléans that Le Pautre was engaged. The building was destroyed in the eighteenth century.

k | *Palais-Royal: Interiors*

Philippe de France, Duc d'Orléans, upon his marriage to Henriette d'Angleterre in 1661, was authorized by his brother, Louis XIV, to reside in the Palais-Royal.[33]

25. C. Montjean, *Les hôtels historiques de Saint-Germain-en-Laye* (Saint-Germain-en-Laye, 1932), p. 21.

26. It is sometimes called the Hôtel de la Grande Mademoiselle.

27. The dates of construction are indicated in AN, Z⁰ 313 (October 17, 1671), in which mention is made of "l'hostel que led. sieur Le Paultre y a basty de neuf." The original contract, dated April 22, 1670, is preserved (Minutier, LXXIII 486).

28. The contract cited in n. 27 does not aid us in visualizing the building; mention is made of a stable and "un demi pavillon et une aisle en queue au bout du demy pavillon." According to J. A. Le Roi (*Histoire de Versailles . . .* , I [Versailles, 1868], p. 32), the *hôtel* was entirely reconstructed ca. 1787 by Arnaudin, but was still standing in this condition in 1868. The building is sometimes misleadingly referred to as the Hôtel des Gardes.

29. Blunt, 1957, p. 77.

30. Turin, Archivio di Stato, 1° Savoie-Carignan, cat. 102, §3, no. 85 (1672). I am indebted to Prof. Henry A. Millon for this reference.

31. *Ibid.*, fol. 84r. The entry appears in a chapter of the account book (fols. 83r–87r) entitled: "Depense Pour Les Batimens & reparations que Madame a fait faire en son [appartement] de l'hotel de Soissons."

32. Sauval, *op. cit.*, II, p. 216.

33. See V. Champier and G. R. Sandoz, *Le Palais-Royal d'après des documents inédits (1629–1900)*, I (Paris, 1900), pp. 149ff.

Philippe carried out architectural work in the urban residence; evidence of Le Pautre's activity there during 1675–1677 is furnished by entries in the *Comptes*.[34]

During these years, Le Pautre, as architect to Monsieur, was building the northern wing of the Château de Saint-Cloud. The Chevalier de Lorraine, in whose apartment Le Pautre worked, was the favorite of the homosexual Philippe.

l | Hôtel Mestayer

The minutes of a meeting of the Royal Academy of Architecture (February 1, 1677) contain a passage in which reference is made to designs furnished by Le Pautre for a *hôtel* for a certain Mestayer, "premier valet de chambre de Monsieur."[35]

m | Hôtel de Seiglière de Boisfranc

The Hôtel de Seiglière de Boisfranc stood in the rue Saint-Augustin. It was built for Joachim Seiglière de Boisfranc, the treasurer of Monsieur, who also engaged Le Pautre to build his country house at Saint-Ouen. The *hôtel* was attributed to Le Pautre by Brice and by subsequent writers,[36] but its precise date is not known. It was destroyed at an unspecified date, and a shadow of its appearance is conveyed only by the Plan Turgot of 1740 (Fig. 104), supplemented by a brief description by Brice:

> La Maison de M. de Bois-Franc . . . est une des plus achevées que l'on puisse voir. La face du côté de la cour est d'une tres-grande regularité, ornée dans le fond d'une maniere de portique, dont les colonnes sont Ioniques, avec des Vases au dessus, entourés de Festons & d'autres ornemens; ce qui arrête en entrant agreablement la veüe. Autour de la cour il y a des Busts d'Empereurs, placez entre les Arcades qui soûtiennent le bâtiment. L'Escalier est tres-grand, avec une Balustrade de bois peint en marbre blanc, travaillée avec beaucoup de dessein. Les bas-reliefs qui sont sur les portes des appartemens, quoy qu'ils ne soient que de plâtre, ne laissent pas de donner beaucoup d'ornement. Il y a aussi dans cette maison un Cabinet de Livres tres-bien choisis. En sortant il ne faut pas negliger de remarquer la grande porte, qui est tres-bien ménagée sur un plan fort bizare.[37]

This passage indicates several features which are paralleled elsewhere in the *oeuvre* of Le Pautre. The use of busts to decorate a courtyard is found on the wings of Boisfranc's château at Saint-Ouen (Fig. 93), and this may have been a design element

---

34. Guiffrey, I, cols. 746, 817, 946.

35. Lemonnier, I, p. 130.

36. G. Brice, *Description nouvelle de ce qu'il y a de plus remarquable dans la ville de Paris*, I (Paris, 1684), pp. 72–73; F. Le Comte, *Cabinet des singularitez d'architecture, peinture, sculpture, et gravure*, I (Paris, 1699), "Sommaire historique d'architecture et des architectes" (unpaginated); J. A. Piganiol de la Force, *Description de Paris, de Versailles, de Marly, de Meudon, de S. Cloud, de Fontainebleau . . .* , new ed., II (Paris, 1742), pp. 575–576; J. F. Blondel, *Cours d'architecture*, III (Paris, 1772), p. 444 n. f; A. N. Dezallier d'Argenville, *Vies des fameux architectes depuis la renaissance des arts . . .* (Paris, 1787), p. 396;

L. V. Thiéry, *Guide des amateurs et des étrangers voyageurs à Paris*, I (Paris, 1787), p. 176. Blondel, Dezallier, and Thiéry refer to the building by its later name, the Hôtel de Gesvres. This has led Dumolin to erroneously believe that two separate *hôtels* were here referred to ("Notes . . . ," p. 17). Adding to the confusion often met with in the literature is the fact that Le Pautre's Hôtel de Fontenay-Mareuil was also later known as the Hôtel de Gesvres. The correct succession of owners of the building under discussion is given by Lefeuve, *op. cit.*, III, p. 248.

37. Brice, *op. cit.*, I, pp. 72–73. All the later writers paraphrase Brice.

specifically favored by this patron. In addition, the use of relief sculpture in plaster recalls the staircase of the Hôtel de Beauvais. However, the entrance portal, the plan of which Brice terms "fort bizare," appears on the Plan Turgot in conventionalized form, and it is clear that the map-maker did not attempt to indicate its peculiarities. But this is the extent of our information concerning this *hôtel*.

n | *Maison Leblon*

A document of 1682, drawn up several years after the death of Le Pautre, alludes to a house built by Antoine for "la veuve Leblon."[38]

---

38. AN, Z^{1j} 355 (April 7, 1682).

APPENDIX **II**

Doubtful or Rejected Attributions

a | *Château du Vaudreuil*

I have expressed elsewhere my reasons for casting doubt upon this structure as an authentic work by Le Pautre.[1] I would like to reply here to M. Baudot, who has contested my attribution and dating of two pavilions still standing at the site.[2]

According to Baudot, the two pavilions in question are the remnants of the Château de l'Orangerie, built before 1762 under the Portails by an unknown architect.[3] The new château of du Boullay (again according to Baudot) was entirely destroyed shortly after its commencement in 1821.

I cannot accept Baudot's argument. In the first place, the pavilions in question are absolutely identical to the style of architecture of du Boullay's project.[4] It seems rather improbable that this architect would have so closely modeled his design upon a pre-existing structure. Furthermore, Blancheton supplies the following detail concerning the Château de l'Orangerie:

> Déja, à cette époque [before the French Revolution], l'état de vétusté du vieux château [Girardin's] le rendait irréparable; aussi M. de Conflans [proprietor from 1776 to 1818] occupait-il ce qu'on appelle le château de l'Orangerie, construit par le président Portail, à une petite distance de l'ancien, mais dans une situation moins riante. C'est encore celui-là qu'habite aujourd'hui Mme la Marquise de Coigny, lorsqu'elle vient visiter sa belle propriété.[5]

1. R. W. Berger, "A Note on the Château du Vaudreuil," *GBA*, s. 6, LXVII (1966), pp. 91–98.

2. M. Baudot, "Note complémentaire sur le Château du Vaudreuil," *ibid.*, p. 98; n.b. fig. 5 (attributed by me to du Boullay, ca. 1821).

3. 1759 is the date given by J. Fossey and J. Longnon, *La haute Normandie* (Paris, n.d.), p. 482.

4. A. A. Blancheton, *Vues pittoresques des châteaux de France*, II (Paris, 1831), pl. facing p. 125.

5. *Ibid.*, pp. 125–126.

If the pavilions under discussion are vesitges of the Château de l'Orangerie, why would Blancheton have stated that that structure was located "à une petite distance de l'ancien [Girardin's château], *mais dans une situation moins riante*" [my italics] since these pavilions are only a few yards from the remnants of the seventeenth century château? It seems to me that Blancheton's indication implies a more distant site, probably on the other side of the moat which surrounded Girardin's buildings.

The surviving pavilions are not indicated in the lithograph published by Blancheton,[6] but they may have been intended as isolated structures preceding the main block which, I suggest, was intended to stand at the far end of the *terre-plein*.

Baudot has cited documents indicating that du Boullay's château (never finished) was destroyed in the first half of the nineteenth century. This information is undoubtedly correct, but my point is that such destruction was not necessarily total; small pavilions could have been left standing even though the château was thought of as "demolished."[7]

b | *Fontaine Saint-Victor*

The Fontaine Saint-Victor in Paris derived its name from the fact that it was placed at the base of one of the medieval towers of the Abbaye de Saint-Victor, the Tour d'Alexandre.[8] The site of the fountain is marked by the present Fontaine Cuvier (corner, rue Linné and rue Cuvier), erected between 1840 and 1846 after designs by Vigoureux.[9]

The appearance of the Fontaine Saint-Victor is known to us principally by the engravings published by Blondel and Duval and Moisy.[10] Despite a number of discrepancies, these engravings correspond closely and permit us to form a good idea of the original object.

The date of the fountain is uncertain. Blondel stated that it was erected in 1687;[11] Duval and Moisy dated it 1671.[12] But it was Blondel who started the tradition of attributing the fountain either to Le Pautre or to Bernini (!) when he wrote that some critics assigned the work to the Frenchman, others to the Italian who, they claimed, designed it during his Parisian sojourn.[13] Recently, however, the keen eye of Georges Poisson has noted that the Fontaine Saint-Victor was literally modeled

---

6. *Ibid.*, pl. facing p. 125.

7. In my article cited in n. 1, I wrongly stated (p. 96 n. 8) that one of the Le Pautres, undoubtedly Jean, worked for Fouquet at Vaux-le-Vicomte. In reality, the work was executed for Fouquet's Château de Saint-Mandé. Fouquet probably made contact with the Le Pautres via Pierre Beauvais and Catherine Bellier, from whom he bought property in Saint-Mandé ca. 1657 (U. Robert, *Notes historiques sur Saint-Mandé* [Saint-Mandé, 1889], p. 58). But even before this, Fouquet had been the owner of the site where the Hôtel de Beauvais was later erected, acquired by Catherine Bellier in 1654 (see Chapter 5, n. 4).

8. A drawing which depicts the fountain and its tower is in Estampes, Réserve, Ve 53F, fol. 45. The fountain was sometimes called the Fontaine d'Alexandre or Fontaine de la Pitié.

9. G. Poisson, *Fontaines de Paris* (Paris, 1957), p. 56. Poisson states that the Fontaine Saint-Victor was destroyed during the French Revolution, but J. G. Legrand and C. Landon report that the fountain and the Tour d'Alexandre were still standing in 1818 (*Description de Paris et de ses édifices*, 2d ed., II [Paris, 1818], p. 169). Furthermore, in 1828, C. A. A. P. Duval and A. Moisy stated that the fountain, although mutilated, was still extant (*Les fontaines de Paris*, new ed. [Paris, 1828], p. 80). Hence the fountain was demolished at some date between 1828 and 1840.

10. J. F. Blondel, *Architecture françoise*, II (Paris, 1752), pl. 219; Duval and Moisy, *op. cit.*, pl. 36.

11. Blondel, *op. cit.*, II, pp. 95 96.

12. Duval and Moisy, *op. cit.*, p. 79.

13. Blondel, *op. cit.*, II, pp. 95–96.

after a fountain in Gaeta, recorded in a print by Israel Silvestre, dated 1648.[14] The authorship and date of the Italian fountain are not known, and the monument no longer exists.

Several factors militate against attributing this work to Le Pautre. If we accept Blondel's date (1687) as more accurate than the one supplied by Duval and Moisy, then it is evident that the fountain was built after the death of Antoine in 1679. But even if the date 1671 is correct, it would have been out of character for an architect of Le Pautre's inventiveness and imagination to have resorted to naked plagiarism.

c | *Fontaine Saint-Louis*

The Fontaine Saint-Louis stood until 1845 in Paris, when it was replaced by the present Fontaine de Joyeuse (41, rue de Turenne).[15] Concerning the date of construction, Brice wrote in the first edition of his Paris guide (1684) that "on y a bâti une Fontaine depuis quelques années," [16] and Le Maire in his guide of 1685 stated that it was built in 1674.[17] The fountain was first attributed to Le Pautre by Legrand and Landon in 1818,[18] probably on the basis of a passage in the *Architecture françoise* of Blondel, in which that writer alluded to fountains by Le Pautre in the Quartier du Temple of Paris.[19] Although the Fontaine Saint-Louis formerly stood well within the district known as the Marais, Blondel could conceivably have thought of it as part of the more northerly Quartier du Temple since its location was not far from the northern end of the Marais.

The fountain is known to us through a print published by Duval and Moisy.[20] The rigid and cold architectural composition with its meager and undramatic spout of water hardly suggests the name of Le Pautre at all. The two Tritons riding upon dolphins constitute a motif common to the classical and Renaissance-Baroque traditions; its appearance in Fig. 73 or in the prints of Jean Le Pautre provides no basis for attributing the work to either brother. Finally, the urn which rests between the Tritons, despite its spiral base, lacks the plasticity and dense fantasy with which the Le Pautres habitually infused this type of object. Because of these features and the late date of the attribution, we may confidently exclude this work from Antoine's *oeuvre.*

14. Poisson, *op. cit.,* p. 56. The Silvestre print is in Estampes, Ed. 45b, fol. 61 (top).

15. See the article by L. Tesson in *Procès-verbaux de la commission municipale du vieux Paris* (1917), p. 7. The fountain was also called Fontaine Royale and Fontaine de Joyeuse.

16. G. Brice, *Description nouvelle de ce qu'il y a de plus remarquable dans la ville de Paris,* I (Paris, 1684), p. 153.

17. C. Le Maire, *Paris ancien et nouveau,* III (Paris, 1685), p. 429.

18. Legrand and Landon, *op. cit.,* II, p. 169.

19. Blondel, *op. cit.,* II, p. 96.

20. Duval and Moisy, *op. cit.,* pl. 23.

Illustrations

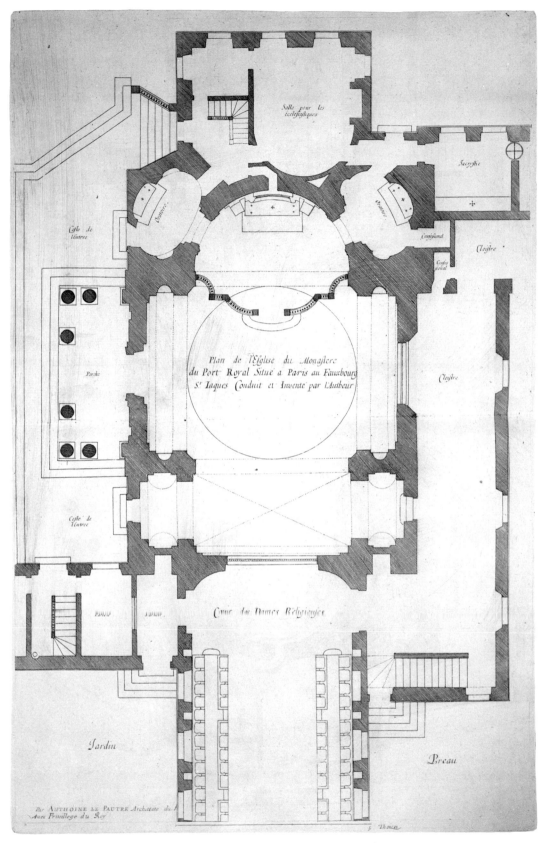

Salle pour les ecclesiastiques

Sacrystie

Oratoire

Cofté de l'entrée

Oratoire

Confesional

Cloystre

Confesional

Porche

Plan de l'Eglise du Monastere du Port Royal Situé a Paris au Fauxbourg St Iaques Conduit et Inventé par l'Autheur

Cloystre

Cofté de l'entrée

Parloir

Parloir

Cœur des Dames Religieuses

Jardin

Preau

Par ANTHOINE LE PAUTRE Architecte du R...
Auec Priuilege du Roy

Thouca

1. Chapelle de Port-Royal. Plan. From *Desseins de plusieurs palais*

ESLEVATION DV PORTAILLE DE L'ESGLISE DV PORT-ROYAL
VEVE EN PERSPECTIVE DV COSTÉ DE L'ENTRÉE.

Par ANTHOINE LE PAVTRE Architecte du Roy.
Auec Priuillege.

2. Chapelle de Port-Royal. Façade. From *Desseins de plusieurs palais*

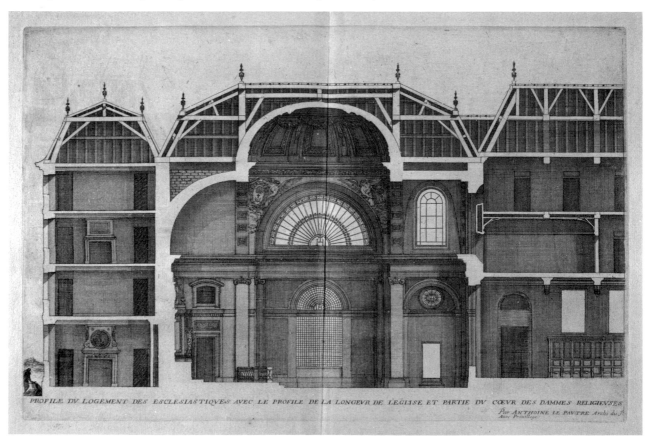

PROFILE DV LOGEMENT DES ESCLESIASTIQVES AVEC LE PROFILE DE LA LONGEVR DE L'EGLISE ET PARTIE DV CŒVR DES DAMMES RELIGIEVSES

Par ANTHOINE LE PAVTRE Archi du R
Auec Priuillege.

3. Chapelle de Port-Royal. Section. From *Desseins de plusieurs palais*

FASCE DV DEDANS DE LESGLISE DV COSTE DE L'HOSTEL VEVE DV CŒVR DES DAMMES RELIGIEVSES ENSEMBLE VNNE PARTIE DE LEVRS CLOESTRE. Par Anthine le Pautre Archi

4. Chapelle de Port-Royal. Section and cloister. From *Desseins de plusieurs palais*

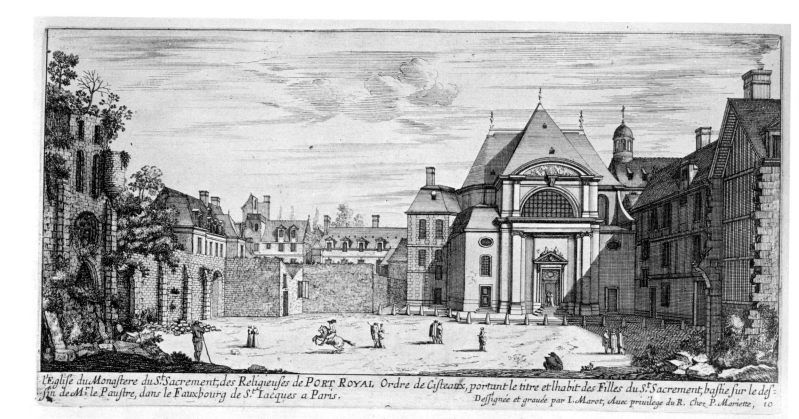

l'Eglise du Monastere du St Sacrement, des Religieuses de PORT ROYAL Ordre de Cisteaux, portant le titre et l'habit des Filles du St Sacrement, bastie sur le dessin de Mr le Pautre, dans le Fauxbourg de St Iacques a Paris.

Dessignée et grauée par I. Marot, Auec priuilege du R. Chez P. Mariette, 10

5. Chapelle de Port-Royal. Façade. Engraving by J. Marot

OPPOSITE: 6. Chapelle de Port-Royal. Façade

7. Chapelle de Port-Royal. Interior

8. Chapelle de Port-Royal. Interior

9. Chapelle de Port-Royal. Interior decoration

10. Chapelle de Port-Royal. Cloister

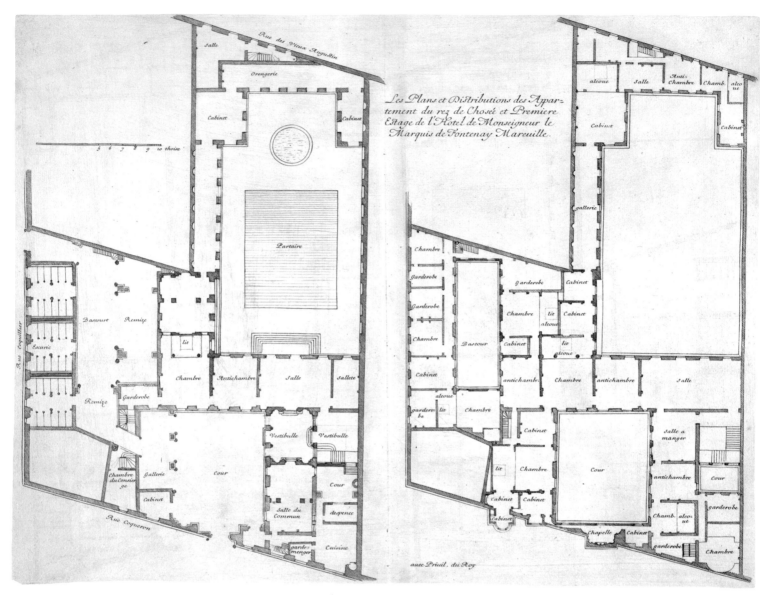

11. Hôtel de Fontenay-Mareuil. Plan of ground floor (left) and first floor (right). From *Desseins de plusieurs palais*

12. Hôtel de Fontenay-Mareuil. Plan of ground floor.
Estampes, Va 230

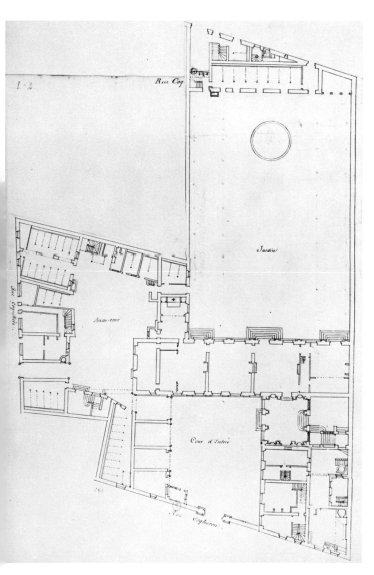

13. Hôtel de Fontenay-Mareuil. Plan of first floor.
Estampes, Va 230

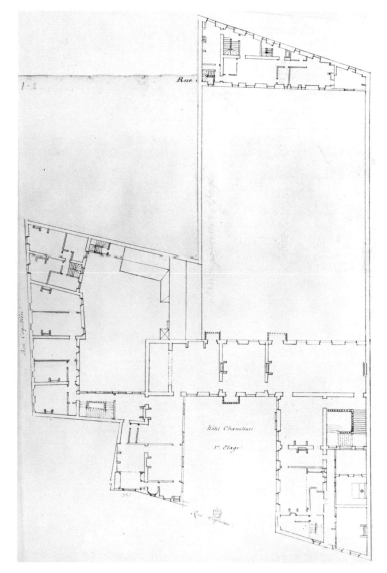

14. Hôtel de Fontenay-Mareuil. Court. From *Desseins de plusieurs palais*

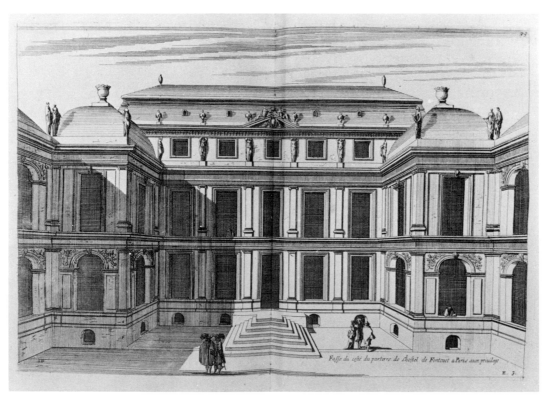

15. Hôtel de Fontenay-Mareuil. Court. From *Desseins de plusieurs palais*

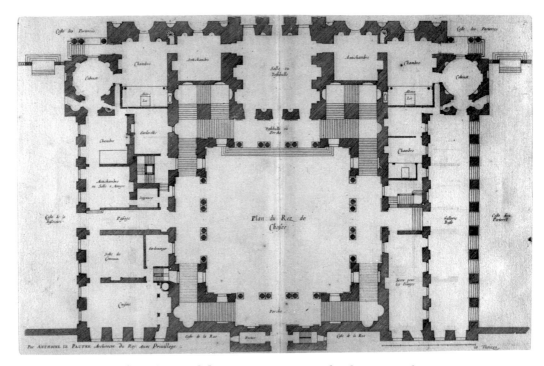

16. First Design. Plan of ground floor. From *Desseins de plusieurs palais*

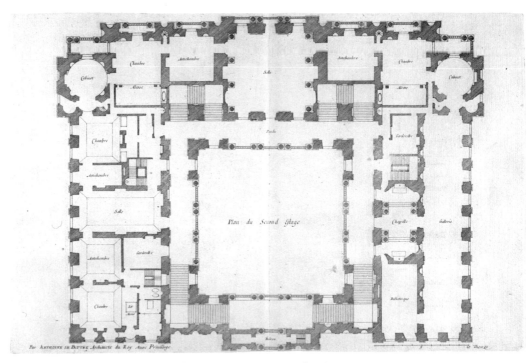

17. First Design. Plan of first floor. From *Desseins de plusieurs palais*

18. First Design. Bird's-eye view. From *Desseins de plusieurs palais*

19. First Design. Garden façade. From *Desseins de plusieurs palais*

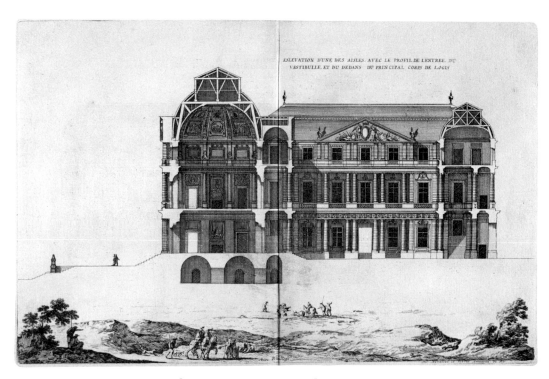

20. First Design. Section and court. From *Desseins de plusieurs palais*

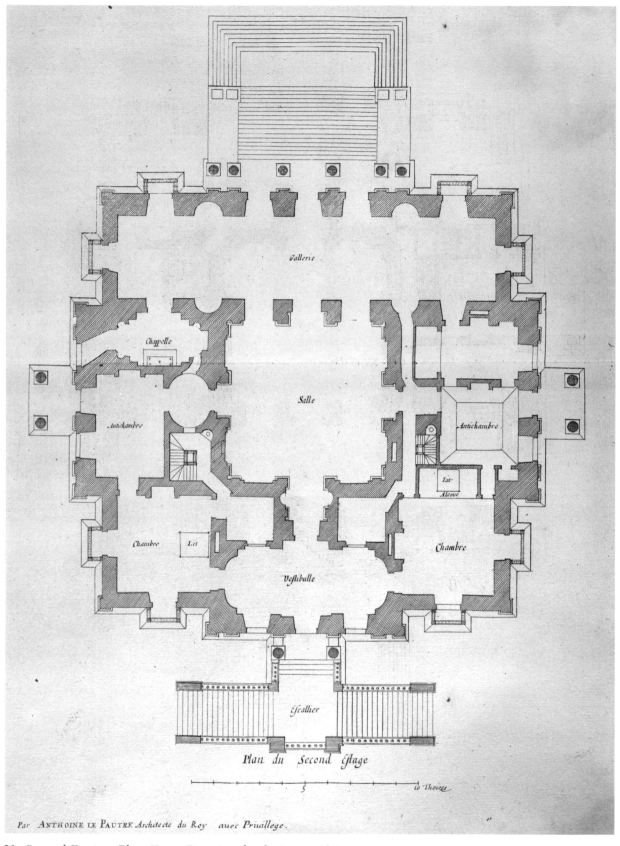

Gallerie

Chappelle

Salle

Antichambre

Antichambre

Lit
Alcove

Chambre

Lit

Chambre

Vestibulle

Escallier

Plan du Second estage

5   10 Thoizes

Par ANTHOINE LE PAUTRE Architecte du Roy   auec Priuillege.

21. Second Design. Plan. From *Desseins de plusieurs palais*

FACE ET ESLEVATION EN PERSPECTIVE AVEC TOUTES SES DEPANDANCES

Par ANTHOINE LE PAUTRE Architecte du Roy. auec. Priuillege.

22. Second Design. View. From *Desseins de plusieurs palais*

PROFIL DU DEDANS DU VESTIBULLE DU SALLON ET DE LA GALLERIE &c.

Auec Priuillege.

23. Second Design. Section. From *Desseins de plusieurs palais*

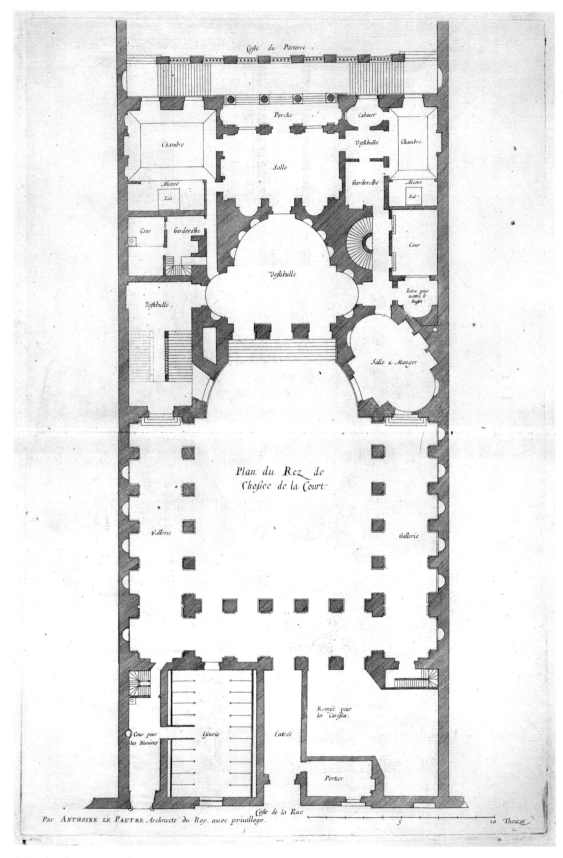

Ceste du Parterre

Porche   Cabinet

Chambre   Vestibulle   Chambre

Salle   Garderobe

Alcove   Alcove

Lit   Lit

Cour   Garderobe   Cour

Vestibulle   Lieu pour mettre le Buffet

Vestibulle

Salle a Manger

Plan du Rez de Chossee de la Court

Gallerie   Gallerie

Remise pour les Carosses

Cour pour les Fumiers   Escurie   Entrée

Portier

Ceste de la Rue

Par ANTHOINE LE PAUTRE, Architecte du Roy. auec priuillege.   5   10 Thoises

24. Third Design. Plan of ground floor. From *Desseins de plusieurs palais*

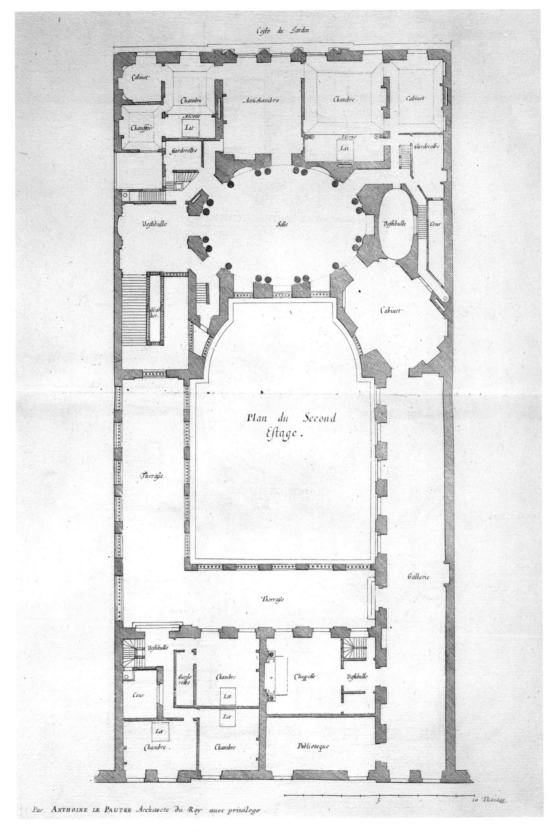

Coste du Jardin

Cabinet

Chambre

Antichambre

Chambre

Cabinet

Chauffoir

Alcove
Lat

Alcove
Lat

Garderobbe

Garderobbe

Vestibulle

Salle

Vestibulle

Cour

Escallier

Cabinet

Plan du Second
Estage.

Therasse

Gallerie

Therrasse

Vestibulle

Garderobbe

Chambre

Chappelle

Vestibulle

Cour

Lat

Lat

Lat

Lat

Chambre

Chambre

Bibliotheque

5   10 Thoizes

Par ANTHOINE LE PAUTRE Architecte du Roy auec priuilege

25. Third Design. Plan of first floor. From *Desseins de plusieurs palais*

26. Third Design. Section and court. From *Desseins de plusieurs palais*

27. Third Design. Garden façade. From *Desseins de plusieurs palais*

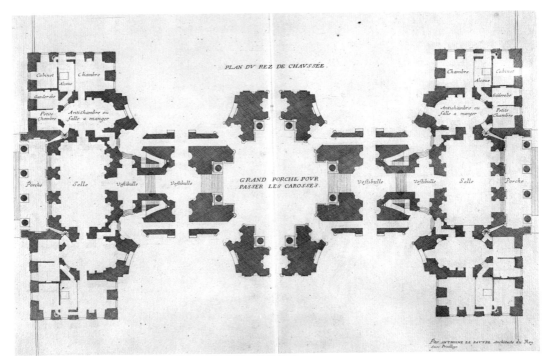

28. Fourth Design. Plan of ground floor. From *Desseins de plusieurs palais*

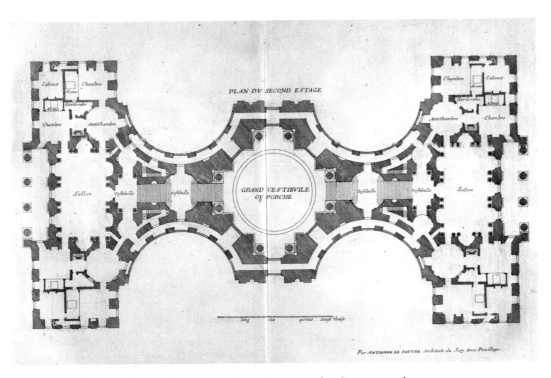

29. Fourth Design. Plan of first floor. From *Desseins de plusieurs palais*

30. Fourth Design. Bird's-eye view. From *Desseins de plusieurs palais*

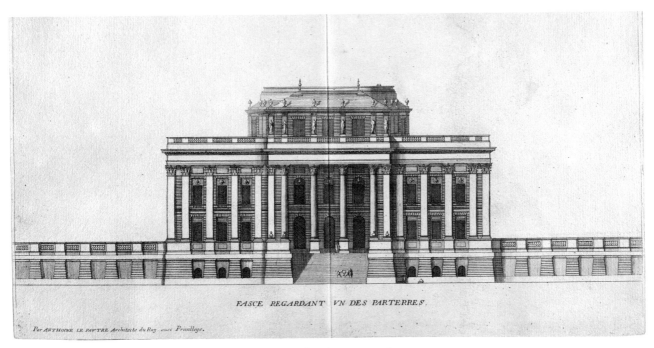

FASCE REGARDANT VN DES PARTERRES.

Par ANTHOINE LE PAVTRE Architecte du Roy. auec Priuillege.

31. Fourth Design. Lateral façade. From *Desseins de plusieurs palais*

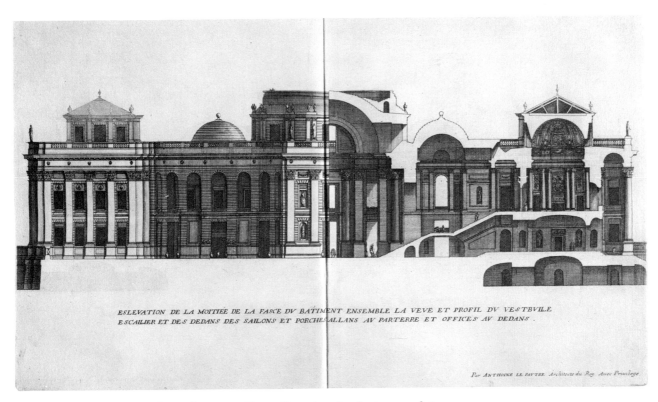

ESLEVATION DE LA MOITIÉE DE LA FASCE DV BATIMENT ENSEMBLE LA VEVE ET PROFIL DV VESTBVILE
ESCAILIER ET DES DEDANS DES SAILONS ET PORCHES ALLANS AV PARTERRE ET OFFICES AV DEDANS.

Par ANTHOINE LE PAVTRE Architecte du Roy. Auec Priuilege

32. Fourth Design. Façade and section. From *Desseins de plusieurs palais*

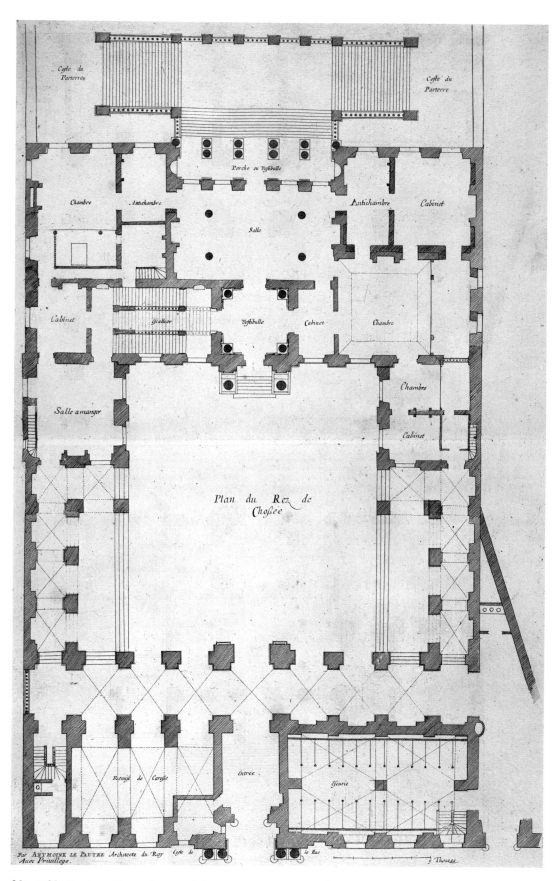

Coste du
Parterre

Coste du
Parterre

Porche ou Vestibule

Chambre   Antichambre   Antichambre   Cabinet

Salle

Cabinet   Escallier   Vestibule   Cabinet   Chambre

Cabinet

Chambre

Salle a manger

Cabinet

Plan du Rez de
Chossee

Remise de Carosse   entree   Escurie

Par ANTHOINE LE PAUTRE Architecte du Roy   Coste de   la Rue
Auec Priuillege.   5 Thourez

33. Fifth Design. Plan of ground floor. From *Desseins de plusieurs palais*

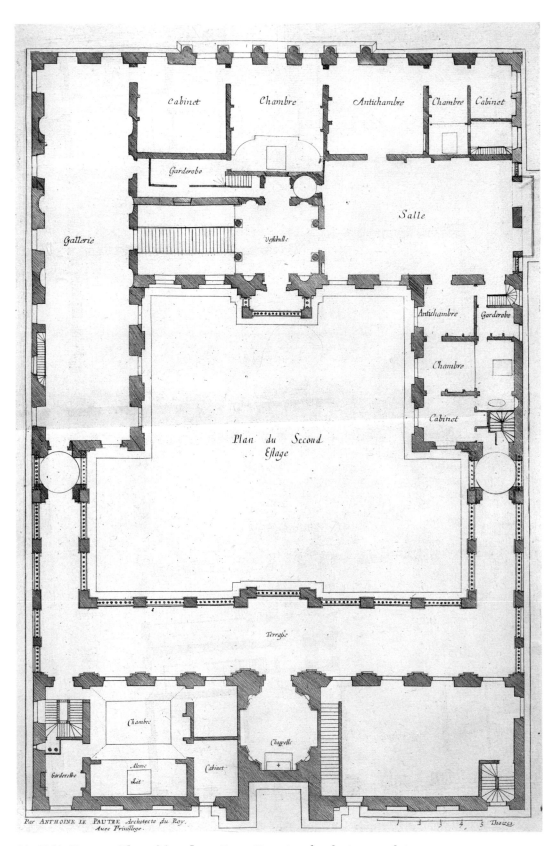

Cabinet

Chambre

Antichambre

Chambre Cabinet

Garderobe

Salle

Gallerie

Vestibulle

Antichambre

Garderobe

Chambre

Plan du Second
Estage

Cabinet

Terrasse

Chambre

Chappelle

Garderobe

Alcove
Lit

Cabinet

Par ANTHOINE LE PAUTRE Architecte du Roy.
Auec Priuillege.

1 2 3 4 5 Thoizes

34. Fifth Design. Plan of first floor. From *Desseins de plusieurs palais*

35. Fifth Design. Street façade. From *Desseins de plusieurs palais*

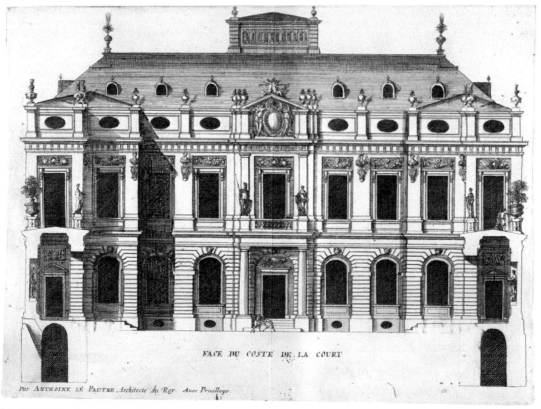

36. Fifth Design. Court façade. From *Desseins de plusieurs palais*

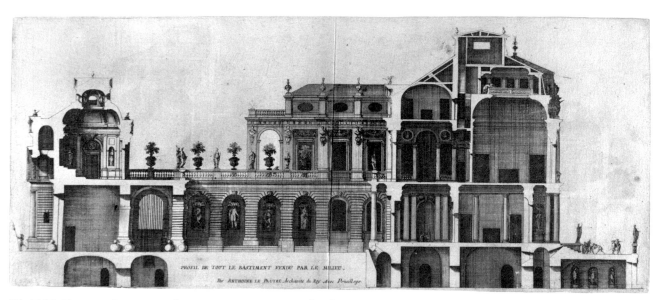

PROFIL DE TOUT LE BASTIMENT FENDU PAR LE MILIEU.

Par ANTHOINE LE PAUTRE Architecte du Roy Avec Privilège.

37. Fifth Design. Section and court. From *Desseins de plusieurs palais*

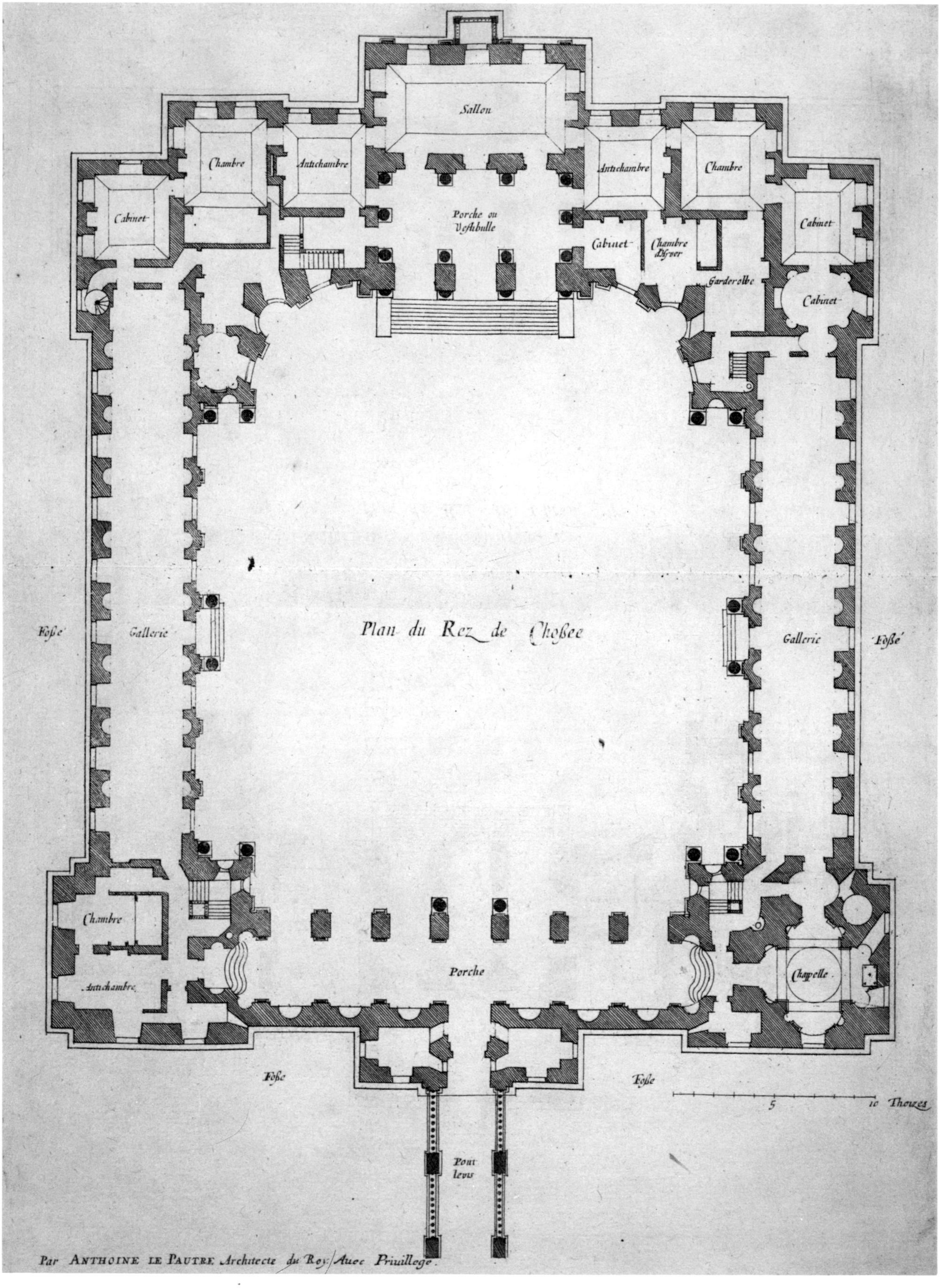

Sallon
Chambre
Antichambre
Cabinet
Antichambre
Chambre
Cabinet
Porche ou Vestibulle
Cabinet
Chambre d'Hyver
Garderobbe
Cabinet
Fossé
Gallerie
Plan du Rez de Chossee
Gallerie
Fossé
Chambre
Antichambre
Porche
Chappelle
Fosse
Fosse
5
10 Thoizes
Pont levis
Par ANTHOINE LE PAUTRE Architecte du Roy Auec Priuillege

38. Sixth Design. Plan. From *Desseins de plusieurs palais*

ESLEVATION GENERALLE EN PERSPECTIVE VEUE DU COSTE DE L'AVANT-COURT AVEC UNE PARTIE DE SES IARDINAGES

Par ANTHOINE LE PAUTRE Architecte du Roy

Auec Priuillege.

39. Sixth Design. View. From *Desseins de plusieurs palais*

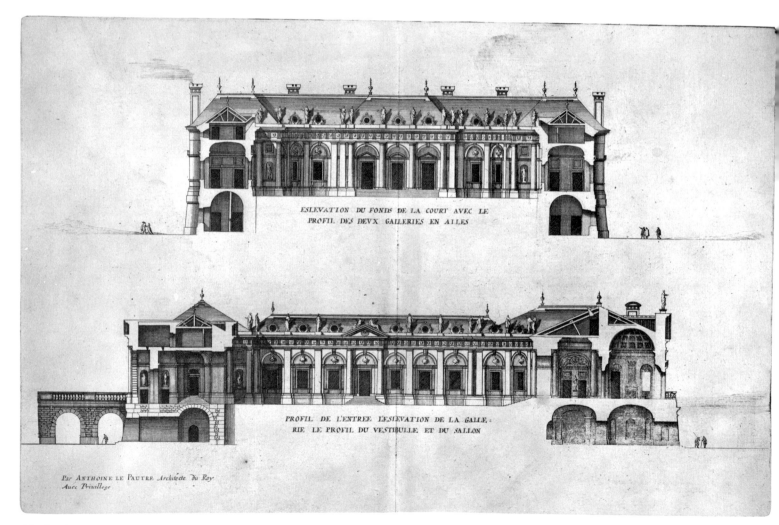

ESLEVATION DU FONDS DE LA COURT AVEC LE
PROFIL DES DEVX GALLERIES EN AILES

PROFIL DE L'ENTREE L'ESLEVATION DE LA GALLE:
RIE LE PROFIL DU VESTIBULLE ET DU SALLON

Par ANTHOINE LE PAUTRE Architecte du Roy.
Auec Priuillege.

40. Sixth Design. Section and court. From *Desseins de plusieurs palais*

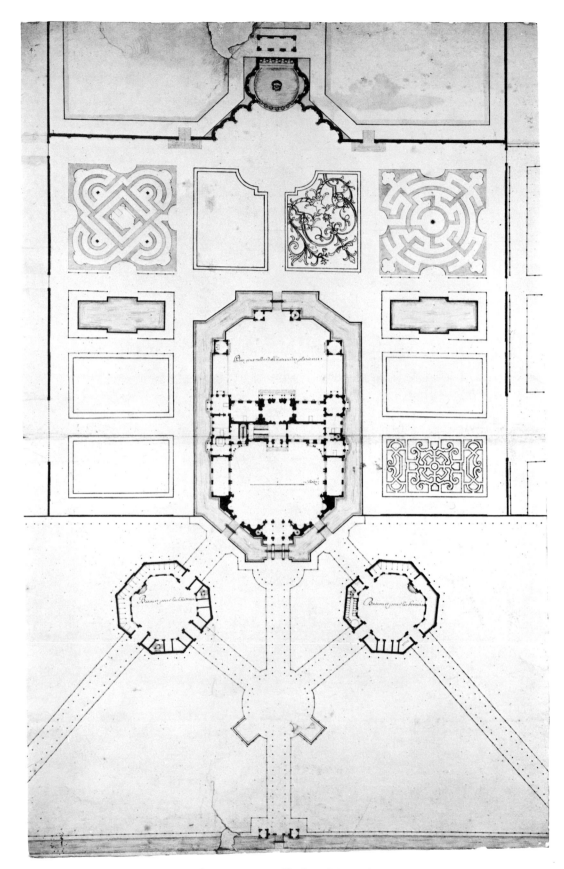

41. Plan of a château. Nationalmuseum, Stockholm, CC 2109

42. Saint-Laurent. Choir. Print by Malliet, 1709

OPPOSITE: 43. Saint-Laurent. Choir

44. Saint-Laurent. Choir

45. Saint-Laurent. Choir

46. Ceiling design. From *Desseins de plusieurs palais*

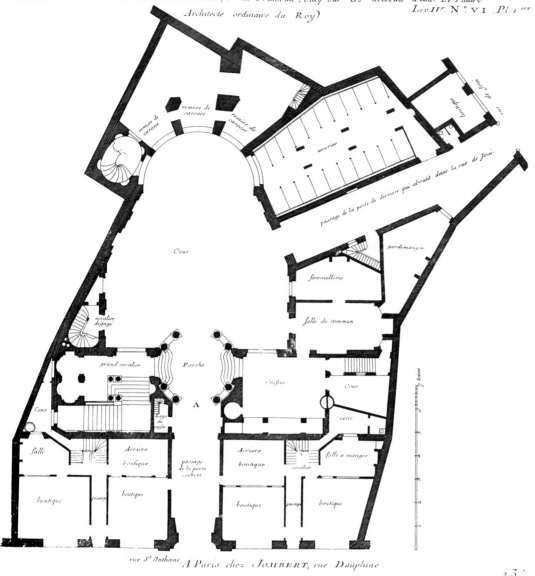

47. Hôtel de Beauvais. Plan of ground floor. Print by J. Marot.
From Blondel, *Architecture françoise*, 1752

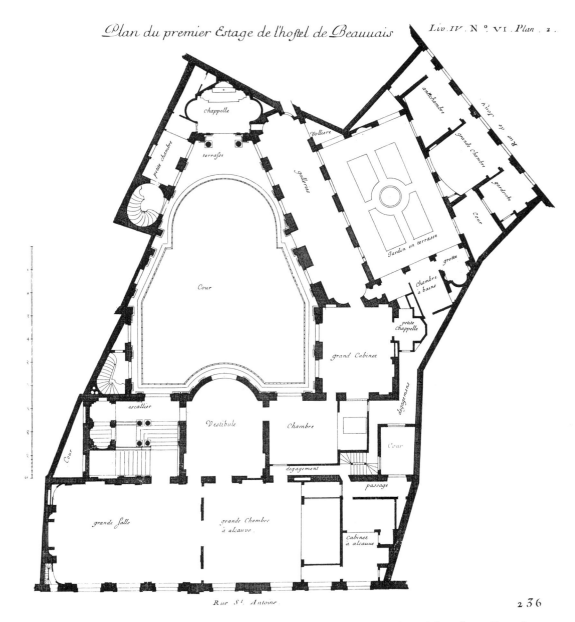

chappelle

terrasse

petite Chambre

Volliere

gallerie

antichambre

Grande Chambre

R.ue de Jouy

Garderobe

Cour

Cour

Jardin en terrasse

grotte

Chambre à bains

petite Chappelle

grand Cabinet

degagemens

escallier

Vestibule

Chambre

Cour

degagement

passage

grande Salle

grande Chambre à alcouve

Cabinet à alcouve

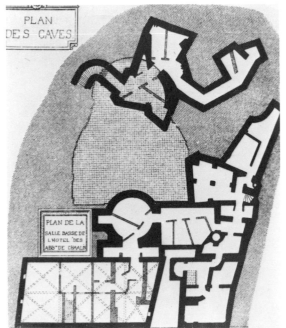

ABOVE: 48. Hôtel de Beauvais. Plan of first floor. Print by J. Marot. From Blondel, *Architecture françoise*, 1752

LEFT: 49. Hôtel de Beauvais. Plan of medieval foundations. By M. Du Seigneur. From *La construction moderne*, 1886

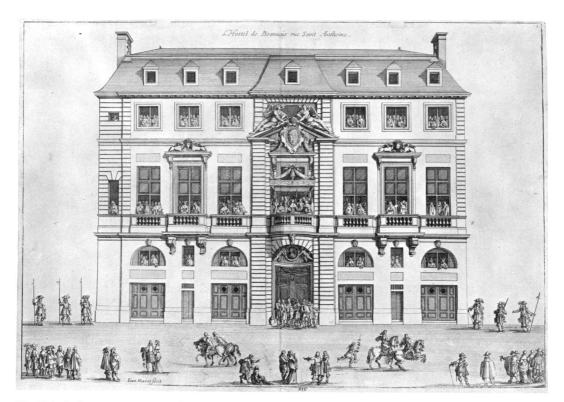

50. Hôtel de Beauvais. Façade. From Marot, *Histoire de la triomphante entrée du roy et de*

51. Hôtel de Beauvais. Preparatory façade design. Nationalmuseum, Stockholm, THC 6513

OPPOSITE: 52. Hôtel de Beauvais. Façade

OPPOSITE: 53. Hôtel de Beauvais. Entrance

BELOW: 54. Hôtel de Beauvais. Court from entrance passage

57. Hôtel de Beauvais. Vestibule

58. Hôtel de Beauvais. Vestibule and court. Reconstruction by M. Du Seigneur.
From *La construction moderne*, 1886

59. Hôtel de Beauvais. Section and court. Reconstruction by M. Du Seigneur (interior decoration imaginary). From *La construction moderne*, 1886

60. Hôtel de Beauvais. Vestibule

OPPOSITE: 61. Hôtel de Beauvais. Stair cage

63. Hôtel de Beauvais. Stair cage

64. Hôtel de Beauvais. Balustrade

VUE DE LA PLACE DE CONSORT,
dite la Place des Dominiquains.

65. Church of the Jacobins, Lyons. View of church and Place Confort.
Engraving after F. D. Née. Estampes, Va 176, vol. ix

66. Church of the Jacobins, Lyons. Façade. Lithograph. Estampes, Va 176, vol. ix

67. Anonymous: S. Nicola da Tolentino. Rome. Façade

68. Cascade, Saint-Cloud. Drawing by A. Perelle. Cabinet des Dessins, Musée du Louvre, Paris, Inv. 34.210

69. Cascade, Saint-Cloud

70. Cascade, Saint-Cloud

OPPOSITE: 71. Cascade, Saint-Cloud

72. Cascade, Saint-Cloud

73. Cascade, Saint-Cloud

74. Fountain design. From *Desseins de plusieurs palais*

75. Fountain design. From *Desseins de plusieurs palais*

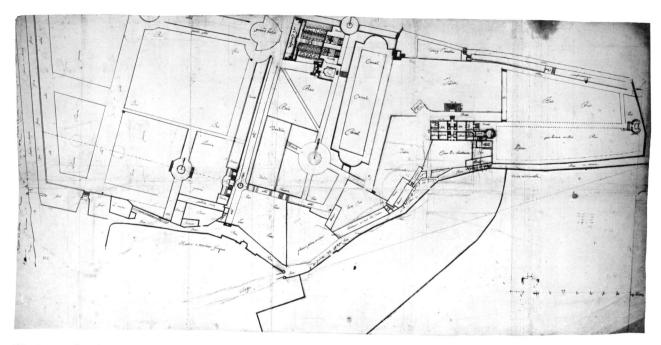

76. Saint-Cloud. Plan with cascade and Maison de Gondi. Estampes, Va 448a

77. Saint-Cloud. View. Engraving by I. Silvestre, 1671

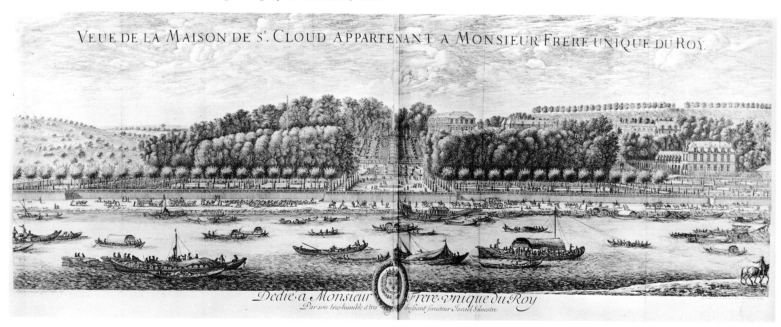

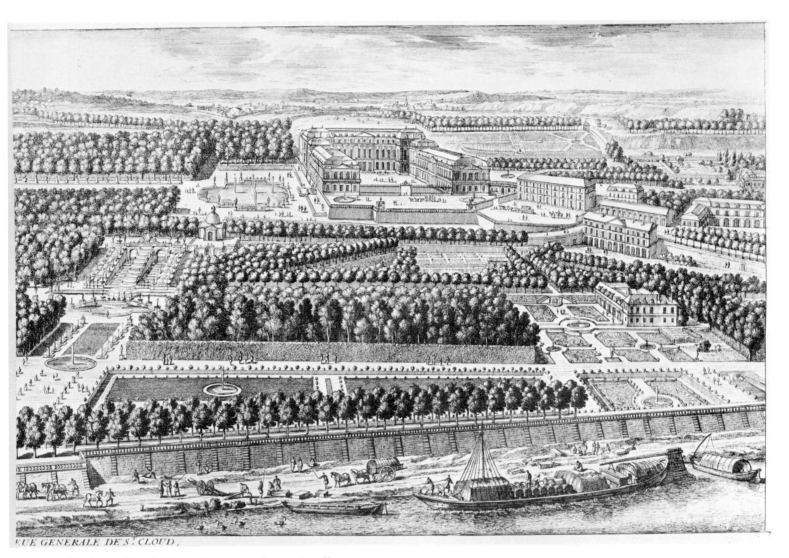

EUE GENERALE DE S? CLOUD,

78. Saint-Cloud. View. Engraving by A. Perelle

79. Saint-Cloud. View. Painting by Allegrain. Château de Versailles

Veüe et Perspectiue de la Cascade du Jardin de l'Illustrissime Archeuesque de Paris a sainct Cloud.

53

Israel ex.

80. Anonymous: Gondi cascade, Saint-Cloud. Etching by I. Silvestre

81. Gianlorenzo Bernini: Cascade of Water Organ, Villa d'Este, Tivoli. Engraving by G. F. Venturini

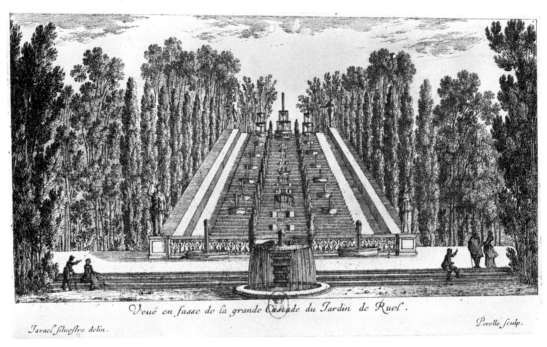

Veuë en fasse de la grande Cascade du Jardin de Ruel.

Israel filuestre delin. *Perelle sculp.*

82. Jacques Lemercier and Jean Thiriot: Cascade, Rueil. Engraving by A. Perelle after I. Silvestre

83. Pirro Ligorio and Curzio Maccarone: Fountain of Rome, Villa d'Este, Tivoli. Engraving by G. F. Venturini

84. Château de Saint-Cloud. Plan of ground floor. From Mariette, *L'architecture françoise*, 1738

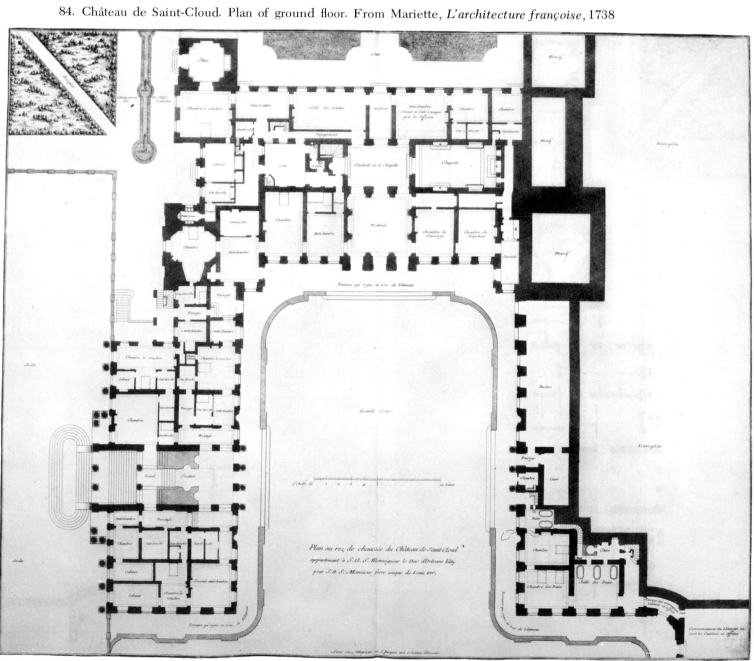

85. Château de Saint-Cloud. Plan of first floor. From Mariette, *L'architecture françoise*, 1738

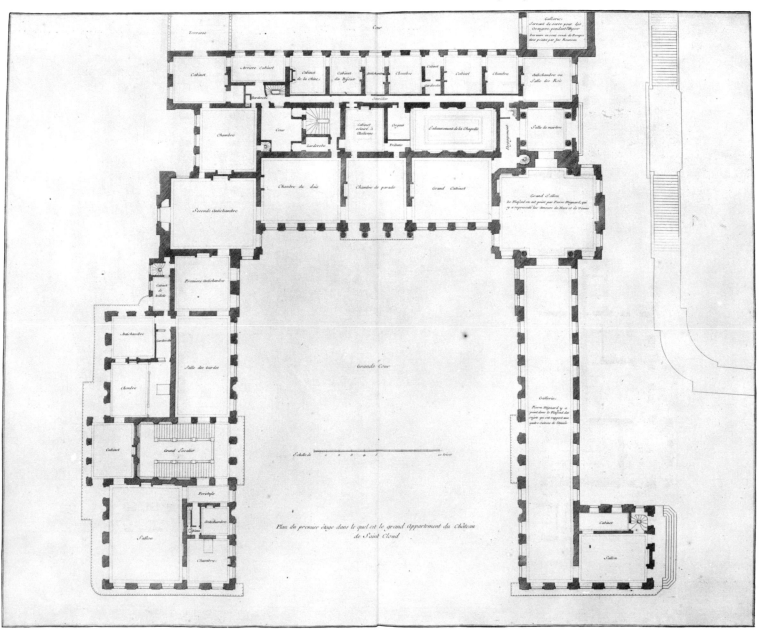

Plan du premier étage dans le quel est le grand Appartement du Château
de Saint Cloud

86. Château de Saint-Cloud. *Corps-de-logis* and ends of wings. From Mariette, *L'architecture françoise*, 1738

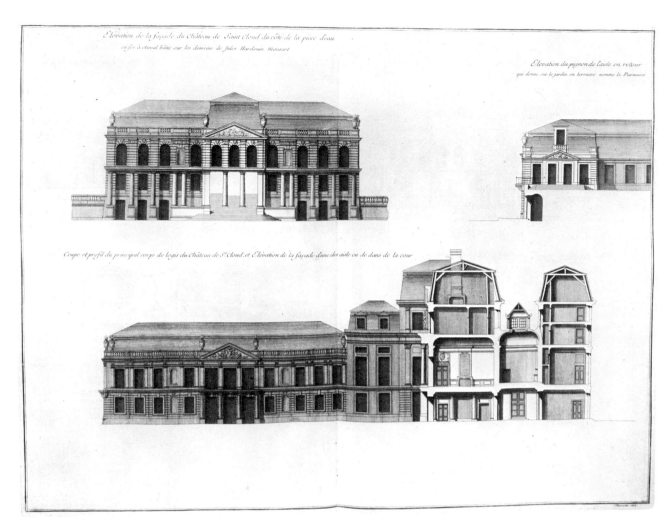

Élévation de la façade du Château de Saint Cloud du côté de la pièce d'eau
en fer à cheval bâtie sur les desseins de Jules Hardouin Mansart

Élévation du pignon de l'aile en retour
qui donne sur le jardin en terrasse nommé le Parnasse

Coupe et profil du principal corps de logis du Château de St Cloud et Élévation de la façade d'une des ailes en de dans de la cour

87. Château de Saint-Cloud. Garden façade of south wing (above, left) and court façade of south wing and section of *corps-de-logis* (below). From Mariette, *L'architecture françoise*, 1738

VEUE D'UNE DES AISLES DU CHATEAU DE St. CLOUD DU COTÉ DU FER A CHEVAL OU DU CHEMIN DE VERSAILLE.

88. Château de Saint-Cloud. Garden façade of south wing and flank of *corps-de-logis*.
Engraving by J. Rigaud, 1730

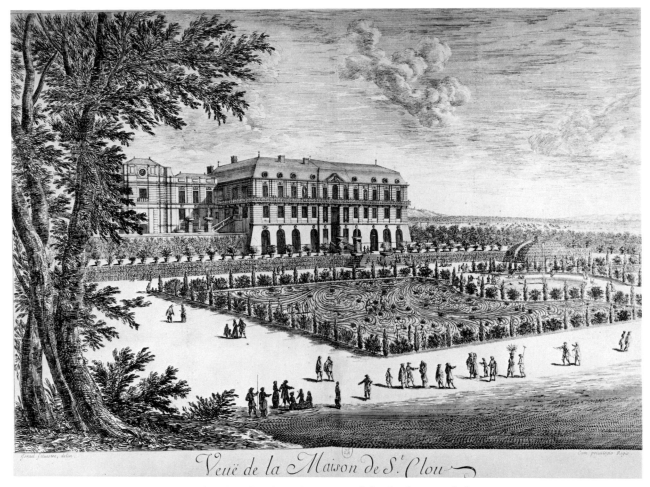

Veüe de la Maison de St. Clou

89. Château de Saint-Cloud. Garden façade of south wing and flank of *corps-de-logis*.
Engraving by I. Silvestre

VEUE DU CHATEAU DE S.^T CLOUD. DU COSTÉ DE L'ORANGERIE.
1730.

90. Château de Saint-Cloud. Garden façade of *corps-de-logis*. Engraving by J. Rigaud, 1730

91. Château de Saint-Cloud. *Corps-de-logis*

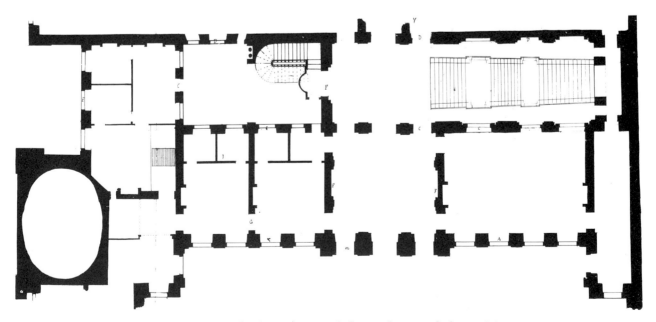

92. Château de Saint-Cloud. Proposed plan of ground floor of *corps-de-logis*. Minutier,
CXIII 84bis

93. Château de Seiglière de Boisfranc, Saint-Ouen. Court. Engraving by J. Rigaud

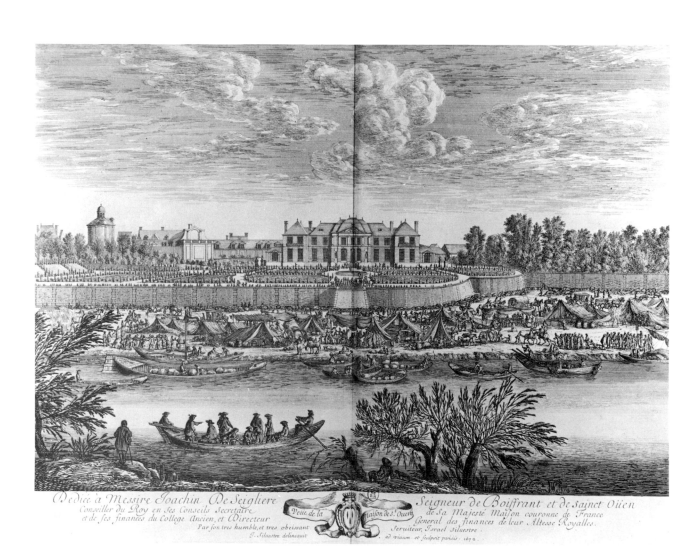

94. Château de Seiglière de Boisfranc, Saint-Ouen. Garden façade. Engraving by I. Silvestre, 1672

95. Château de Seiglière de Boisfranc, Saint-Ouen. Preparatory design of garden façade.
Nationalmuseum, Stockholm, CC 2205

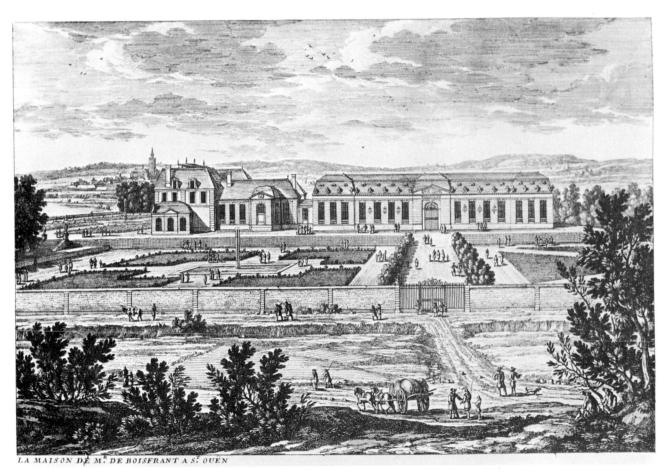

LA MAISON DE M^R. DE BOISFRANT A S^T. OUEN

96. Château de Seiglière de Boisfranc, Saint-Ouen. Château and orangery.
Engraving by A. Perelle

97. Château de Clagny. Garden façade. Nationalmuseum, Stockholm, CC 2136

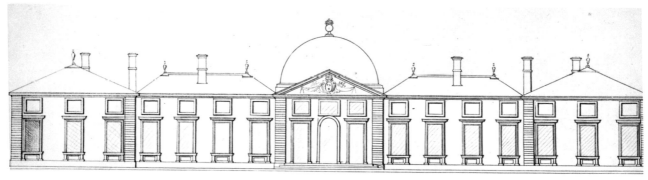

98. Château de Clagny. Garden façade. Nationalmuseum, Stockholm, THC 2441

99. Château de Clagny. Section and court elevation. Nationalmuseum, Stockholm, CC 107

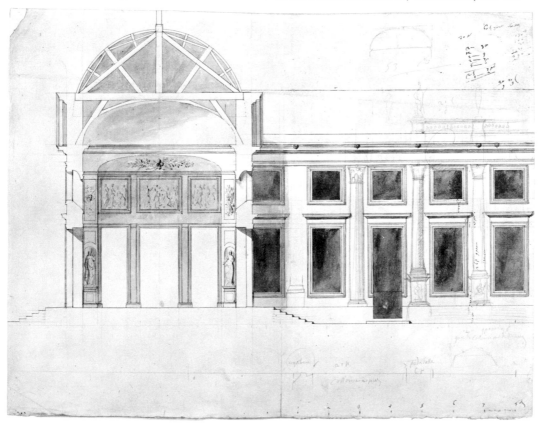

100. Château de Clagny. Section. Nationalmuseum, Stockholm, CC 83

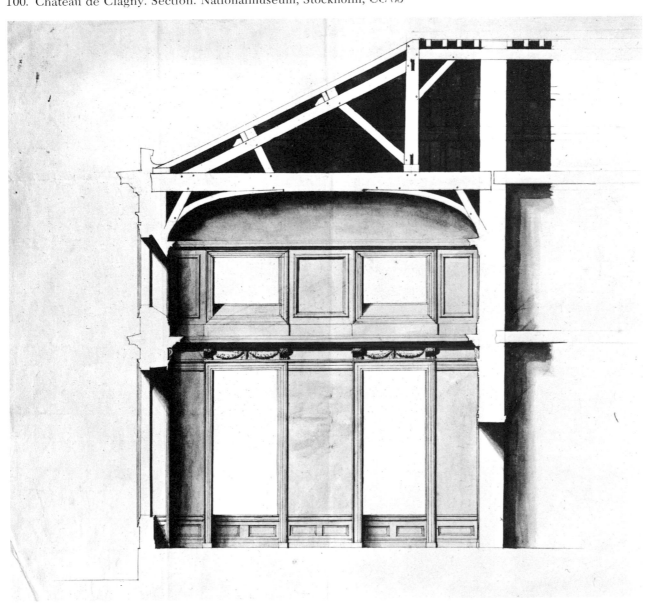

101. Claude Perrault, Charles Le Brun, or André Le Nôtre (?): Pavillon de l'Aurore, Sceaux

102. Hôtel de Beauvais (Rue de Grenelle). From the Plan Turgot, 1740 (marked "Cordelieres")

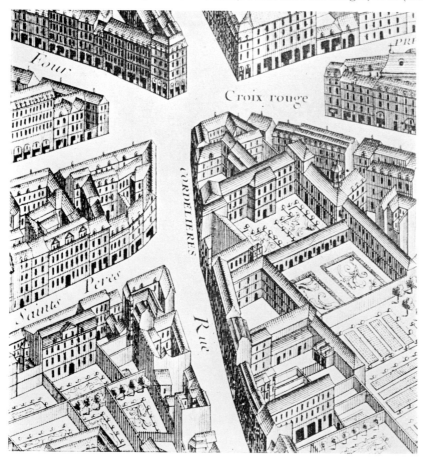

103. Hôtel de Lauzun, Saint-Germain-en-Laye. Façade

104. Hôtel de Seiglière de Boisfranc. From the Plan Turgot, 1740 (marked "H de Gesvres")

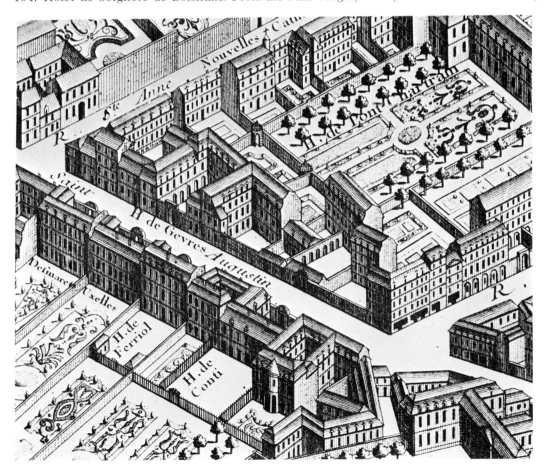

Index